CW00431944

TEXTBOOK

Criminology

CONSULTANT EDITOR: LORD TEMPLEMAN
EDITOR: MICHAEL DOHERTY
BA Law, MA Criminology
Senior Lecturer in Law, University of Glamorgan

OLD BAILEY PRESS

OLD BAILEY PRESS
200 Greyhound Road, London W14 9RY

1st edition 1997

© Old Bailey Press Ltd 1997

Previous editions published under The HLT Group Ltd.

ISBN 1 85836 224 5

British Library Cataloguing-in-Publication.
A CIP Catalogue record for this book is available from the British Library.

Acknowledgement

The publishers and author would like to thank the Incorporated Council of Law Reporting for England and Wales for kind permission to reproduce extracts from the Weekly Law Reports, and Butterworths for their kind permission to reproduce extracts from the All England Law Reports.

Printed and bound in Great Britain

Contents

Preface

Old Bailey Press textbooks are written specifically for students. Whatever their course, they will find our books clear and concise, providing comprehensive and up-to-date coverage. Written by specialists in their field, our textbooks are reviewed and updated on a regular basis.

The *Criminology* textbook provides a comprehensive coverage of the subject area, encompassing the principal topics which feature in the syllabus of almost every course in criminology. All students reading criminology as part of an undergraduate course will find it an invaluable aid to their studies.

The contents of this edition reflect the law as at January 1997.

Acknowledgements

The author and publishers wish to express their thanks to the following publishers for allowing the publication of extracts from materials in which they hold copyright:

The Controller of Her Majesty's Stationery Office
The Free Press
The University of California Press
The University of Chicago Press

For the purposes of academic comment, short quotations have been included from a variety of other sources. Information from some publications has been reconstructed to form tables which are different from those contained in the original works. The cumulative contribution of these small extracts is gratefully acknowledged. Care has been taken to avoid any infringement of the rights of other copyright owners. Original sources are indicated in the text.

Table of Cases

Tables and Diagrams

PART ONE:
OBJECTIVES AND METHODS
OF CRIMINOLOGY

1

The Nature and Scope of Criminology

1.1 Introduction

1.2 The early history of criminology

1.3 The scope and objects of criminology

1.4 Is criminology a science?

1.5 Conclusion

1.1 Introduction

Crime, and the way society deals with crime, are subjects which interest almost everyone. No matter where you go, the chances are that every now and then you will be involved in, or overhear, a conversation connected with crime. Comments such as: 'I blame it on the parents'; 'Prisons are far too soft'; and 'No wonder they smash things up, there's nothing else to do', are typical snippets from discussions in pubs or supermarket queues. Crime is a standard source for the media both as a news item and as a subject of entertainment. If you happen to visit a video rental shop, try to imagine that the shelves have been stripped of every video with some relationship to crime. Unless the shop is a very unusual one, you'll find that it would be almost empty.

The point of these examples is to show that we all have thoughts about crime. Criminology is a field of study which goes beyond simply thinking about crime. Hall Williams describes it as the 'scientific' study of crime (1982:1), but I hesitate to use that term because, as we shall see, it is often given a special meaning. Young (1981) suggests academic theorisation about crime is not entirely separate from lay discussions of the subject, but that it reproduces those discussions in a more systematic form.

Criminology is essentially a multi-disciplinary subject. Theorists and researchers who have made valuable contributions in this field include specialists in psychology, sociology, medicine, law, geography and architecture. Although no one discipline is dominant, it is fair to say that since the 1930s, particularly in the United States, sociologists have tended to shout more loudly and more often than their counterparts in other disciplines. As Hall Williams (1982) points out, the usual (and sensible) approach is to work within one's own discipline. Later in this book it will be suggested, on a number of occasions, that criminology would benefit if cross-disciplinary research were conducted more often.

To say that criminology involves the study of crime is a little vague. What is meant by 'crime'? That question has arisen continually, and has been answered in many different ways during the 100 years or so in which criminology has stood out as a separate field of study. Unless we define crime, we can't define criminology. Section 1.3 below will examine the scope of criminology, and will include several examples of definitions put forward for 'crime'. For the time being, it is worth considering the comment by Quinney and Wildeman that '... there are several concepts of crime. Each concept serves the interests of those who treasure it' (1977:8).

Controversy about the meaning of crime usually surrounds the fact that if only those types of behaviour which are proscribed by the criminal law are included, many other forms are ignored. In a sense, legal definitions are arbitrary, and do not help us to identify conduct which is inherently criminal or deviant when compared with other ways of behaving. This leads on to another problem area, namely, the proper scope of criminology. A large amount of criminological work has involved searching for the causes of crime. However, the origins of criminal laws, the process of law enforcement, and the effects of social reaction to crime or deviance are among a variety of topics which are now recognised as suitable areas for criminological research. The arguments will be explored in greater depth at section 1.3.

1.2 The early history of criminology

This section provides a brief description of the early history of criminology and the ideas from which it grew. Its purpose is to provide a background to the more detailed coverage of the major criminological theories presented in Part Two. The following three topics will be dealt with: the Classical School, positivism, and contemporary developments.

The Classical School

The central themes of the Classical School are not really part of criminology. Its major concern was with reform of the criminal law and, in particular, of the way criminals were punished. It is preferable to see these ideas as belonging to an 'administrative and legal criminology' (Vold and Bernard, 1986:25), or better still as a school of 'criminal justice philosophy' (Hall Williams, 1982:9). Writers who could be identified with the classical approach did not attempt to explain why some individuals committed crime, which was viewed as the result of something akin to rationalistic hedonism. The Classical School was largely inspired by the notion that society was governed by a social contract. This emphasised the importance of free will, so that criminal behaviour (like other forms of behaviour) was the result of a rational choice. Society had the right to punish offenders, and it was considered that doing so would have a deterrent effect.

The writer most often associated with the Classical School is Beccaria, whose essay *Dei delitti e delle pene* was published in 1764. An English translation entitled *An Essay on Crimes and Punishments* appeared in 1767. Beccaria was highly critical of the courts in Italy which were seen as imposing arbitrary punishments on offenders. This situation was not greatly dissimilar from the uneven, frequently cruel ways in which sentences were handed out by English courts during the eighteenth century. An excellent account is provided by Hay (1977). Some of the main ideas included in Beccaria's essay are as follows:

1. In order to escape chaos, each member of society must sacrifice part of his liberty to form the sovereignty of his nation.
2. To prevent individuals from infringing the liberty of others by breaking the law, it was necessary to introduce punishments for such breaches.
3. The despotic spirit (for present purposes, the propensity to offend) was in everyone.
4. Punishments were to be decided by the legislature, not by the courts.
5. To preserve consistency and certainty of punishment, judges could only impose punishment set by the law.
6. The seriousness of a crime was connected to the harm it caused society, not to the intention of the offender.
7. Punishment must be in proportion to the crime. It would be set on a scale, with the most severe penalties corresponding to offences which caused the most harm to society. The most serious crimes were those which threatened the stability of society.
8. Punishment which followed more promptly after a crime would be more just and more effective.
9. Punishment had to be certain to be effective.
10. Laws and punishments had to be well publicised so that people were aware of them.
11. As punishment was imposed for the purpose of deterrence, capital punishment should be abolished.
12. Prevention was better than punishment.
13. Activities which were not expressly prohibited were permissible.

Beccaria's ideas are clearly prescriptive rather than explanatory, and many of the principles set out by him were incorporated into the French criminal law code of 1791.

In Britain, Bentham adopted some of the ideas from the classical approach to punishment. He regarded our own system of punishments as illogical and called for the introduction of a more precise and wholly enforced criminal code. Some of Bentham's views are set out in his *Introduction to the Principles of Morals and Legislation*, published in 1780.

Although many of Beccaria's principles were intended to prevent the imposition of unjust sentences, the lack of flexibility itself led to injustice. For example, juveniles received the same sentences as adults, first offenders were punished in the same way as recidivists, and no allowances were made for mental handicap. Gradually, changes were introduced in the French code to allow the criminal courts to make allowances for a small range of extenuating circumstances. The motivating force behind these changes is usually referred to as neo-classicism. There was no change from the basic principle that human behaviour is the result of a rational choice, and that certainty of punishment can provide an effective deterrent.

Positivism

The origins of modern criminology are usually traced to the work of the 'Italian School' in the latter part of the nineteenth century. Two of the central features of the positivist approach are that it tries to find the causes of criminal behaviour, and that it adopts scientific methods to do so.

It has been argued that attempts to explain crime in a scientific way had been adopted long before the Italian School began to publicise its work. For example, Lindesmith and Levin (1937) highlight work done by Guerry and by Quetelet during the 1830s, in which crime rates were systematically compared against social factors. Their contributions will be explained in more detail in Chapter 10.

Notwithstanding such arguments, the greatest amount of attention has undoubtedly been paid to the work of Cesare Lombroso and his fellow members of the Italian School. Lombroso's ideas are examined more fully in Chapter 3. In his earlier writings, Lombroso concentrated on finding a biological explanation for the behaviour of individual criminals. He hit on the idea of there being a category of born criminals who were throwbacks to a less fully evolved form of human being. One of his pupils, Ferri, was instrumental in spreading the word of positivist criminology, by means of books and lecture tours. Ferri also insisted that criminal anthropology must focus on 'the antisocial individual in his tendencies and in his activity' (1917:79). The use here of the term 'antisocial' illustrates another feature of the positivist approach, namely, the need to identify relevant behaviour by means of a non-legal definition. Ferri and Garofalo both recognised the importance of environmental factors in influencing human behaviour. Lombroso also gave increased importance to non-biological factors in his later publications. A number of developments had occurred which might explain why the ideas of the Italian School were able to attract such attention. First of all, the natural sciences had themselves developed. It was not surprising that social scientists should attempt to emulate developments elsewhere, and that they should assume that the use of measurements, observations and experimentation could provide explanations of human behaviour. From a classical viewpoint, such an assumption would have been ridiculous because the existence of free will in humans made them fundamentally different from the inanimate subjects of research in the natural sciences. However, the intellectual atmosphere in the latter part of the nineteenth century was such that the importance of free will in controlling human conduct could be played down. Darwin's theory of evolution had been influential in bringing about this change of attitude. It was now considered that the behaviour of individuals was largely determined by biological and cultural factors outside their control. Rather than the level of crime being determined by the rational decisions of different human beings, Ferri suggested that there was a law of criminal saturation whereby 'in a given social environment with definite individual and physical conditions, a fixed number of (crimes), no more and no less, can be committed' (1917:20–9).

The emphasis on criminal behaviour being related to characteristics of individuals, rather than to social factors, may partly account for the popularity of the early ideas of the Italian School. Such a view made it possible to regard criminals as belonging to a separate, dangerous class. Politicians and law-abiding citizens could thus absolve themselves of any blame for the behaviour of this race apart (Lindesmith and Levin, 1937:670; Radzinowicz, 1966:38).

The ideas underlying the positivist approach obviously supported different types of response than were suggested by the Classical School. As free will was largely irrelevant, so were attempts at deterrence. Crime rates could only be altered by techniques which affected the criminal disposition of individuals, or the social conditions which led to crime. Garofalo (1914) was doubtful about the possibility of rehabilitating criminals and, drawing a parallel with Darwin's theory of evolutionary adaptation, he suggested society could adopt different means to eliminate individuals whose criminal behaviour showed they had not adapted to a civilised way of life. Criminals who were shown to be incapable of such adaptation could be put to death. Individuals who were fit only to lead a primitive tribal lifestyle might be transported or given long terms of imprisonment. Some offenders with a potential to adapt to a more civilised way of life could be placed for shorter terms in agricultural colonies. One effect of elimination would be to reduce the number of criminals who produced offspring. Unlike Garofalo, Ferri saw no value in the death penalty. As an ardent socialist, he proposed a number of social reforms to reduce crime.

As with any basic treatment of a topic, it has been necessary to provide exaggerated accounts of both the classical approach and positivism. Careful examination of writings from both 'camps' shows that supporters of one side sometimes held views which would have fitted more comfortably into the other. For example, Beccaria considered that robbery was often the effect of misery and despair. Bentham accepted that prison could act as a school for wickedness. There we have two leading supporters of the classical approach recognising the effects of environmental influences. Garofalo, in spite of his positivist standing, believed that a side-effect of the elimination of some criminals would be to deter others.

As Mannheim (1960) points out, positivism really has many meanings and several different branches. Legal, sociological and philosophical branches of positivism all have features in common, but they are not identical. A writer may be a positivist in one sense but not in another. Mannheim suggests the term positivism has become a slogan which is sometimes used by critics to cast in the face of an opponent as an alternative to reasoned criticism.

Contemporary developments

When you come to read Chapters 3 to 6, you will see that strong grains of positivism are evident in many of the major theories of crime causation. Social factors are often given greater prominence than individual characteristics, but there is frequently a heavy emphasis on the use of scientific methods. Furthermore, some of the major theories concentrate on behaviour which their supporters regard as antisocial or deviant, rather than activities labelled as criminal by the law. The use of scientific procedures is a regular feature of research conducted in mainstream criminology. Numerous examples can be found among the publications of the Home Office Research and Statistical Unit (formerly the Research and Planning Unit), as well as in the work of academics.

The theories described in Chapter 7 represent a reaction to positivism's denial of free will, in that they emphasise the meaning which deviance has to the individual who takes part in it. The ideas discussed in Chapter 8 go even further by looking at the notion that the criminal law is itself the formal cause of crime, since ultimately it is the law which determines who will or will not be regarded as criminal. For the writers mentioned in both of those chapters, a positivist approach is misguided because of its focus on individual criminals. Criminologists would be more gainfully employed by examining the sources of criminal law and the process of law enforcement.

Not all of the recent developments in criminology represent such a major departure from the traditional approach. During the 1970s, there was renewed interest in deterrence. A useful review is provided by Gibb (1975). Wilson (1975) argues that criminological research into the motivation of offenders has provided little in terms of realistic options for policy makers. Wilson favours a return to deterrence instead of attempts to treat offenders.

There have also been attempts to give greater recognition to free will in the causation of crime. Becker (1968) describes the way individuals choose whether or not to offend in terms of an economic model. Cornish and Clarke (1986, 1986a, 1987) provide a modern example of the decision-making process of potential offenders. Their version of rational choice theory is examined in Chapter 10.

1.3 The scope and objects of criminology

Determining the scope of criminology requires us to address a number of related issues. First, it was said earlier that to define criminology we must define crime. Secondly, having defined crime we need to ask whether criminologists should simply look for causes of crime, or whether they can go beyond that to examine connected matters such as the processes of law making and law enforcement. Thirdly, in relation to explaining crime, we need to ask what is meant by explanation. Finally (in the present book), it is necessary to ask whether criminologists are entitled only to state their findings or if they can make practical suggestions. These issues will be dealt with under the following headings:

1. Definitions of crime.
2. The content of criminology.
3. The nature of explanation.
4. The role of the criminologist.

Definitions of crime

The life of the criminologist would be made easier if he were able to accept, without question, the notion that crime includes only those acts which are made punishable by the criminal law. However, as was suggested earlier, the criminal law is not a naturally occurring phenomenon. It is man-made and, more importantly, its content is influenced by powerful interest groups within society. Although some forms of behaviour, such as murder, rape, assault and theft, will be almost universally regarded as crimes in modern societies, the criminal law covers a much broader range of activities and cannot be regarded as an objective method of identifying the types of conduct which criminologists should study. Apart from anything else, variations in laws mean that international or cross-cultural comparisons of criminological findings are made very difficult.

The early positivists recognised the arbitrary nature of legal definitions. Ferri (1917) remarked on the way in which people with similar personality traits but from different social backgrounds might behave in ways which were equally antisocial or immoral. However, the behaviour of one might be proscribed by the criminal law while the conduct of the other was not. For example, a lower class individual might commit robbery, while his middle class counterpart might indulge in the reprehensible but lawful practice of usury. Garofalo (1914) tried to counter this problem by developing a concept of 'natural crime'. Recognising that it was impossible to identify activities which would be legally regarded as criminal in all societies at all times, Garofalo instead defined crime as comprising those acts which offended against the two altruistic sentiments of probity and pity which he considered were constantly and universally held. In effect, the positivists were identifying antisocial conduct as the proper subject matter of criminological study.

The potential for value judgements to influence the practical application of such a definition is obvious. Small wonder, then, that in 1933 Michael and Adler asserted strongly that '*The most precise and least ambiguous definition of crime is that which defines it as behavior which is prohibited by the criminal code*' (1933:2).

Ironically, the Italian School rejected a legal definition of crime because it was unscientific, but Michael and Adler supported a legal definition because they considered it to be the safest starting point from which to develop a scientific criminology.

The debate continued and, within a few years, Sellin argued that uncritical reliance on a legal definition of crime 'violates a fundamental criterion of science' (1938:23). Sellin felt that a scientist studying human conduct must define his own terms, independently of the limits imposed by the criminal law. He wanted to discover universal categories of conduct norms which would apply anywhere irrespective of any boundaries.

Tappan was highly critical of criminologists who studied types of behaviour which fell outside the criminal law, or who accepted that people who had not been convicted by a court could be criminals for the purpose of their research. He regarded vague definitions of crime as 'a blight upon ... a system of sociology that strives to be objective' (1947:99).

Some criminologists have studied only convicted offenders. Given the low detection rates for some crimes, it is highly debatable whether such criminals are typical. The results of such research are, therefore, of questionable validity. As you will see in later chapters, some criminologists have ignored critics like Michael and Adler, and Tappan, and have examined forms of conduct described as deviance or delinquency.

In recent times, some writers have argued for the inclusion of an even greater range of behaviours. For example, Schwendinger and Schwendinger (1970) have argued that activities which breach human rights should be regarded as crimes. They see racism and sexism as forms of conduct which should be subject to criminal sanctions and as proper topics for criminological research. In view of society's past performance in preventing existing forms of criminal behaviour, Bottomley (1979) observes that it is questionable what purpose would be served by making such activities crimes.

As yet, there is no universally accepted definition of what should or should not be accepted as crime for the purposes of studying criminal behaviour. Bottomley makes the further suggestion that no such definition can ever be attained. Even a legal definition of crime includes a wide range of activities which have little in common apart from the fact that they are proscribed by law. The adoption of a broader definition based on such a concept as social harm does not necessarily create any more meaningful connections between the types of behaviour which are covered.

The content of criminology

Notwithstanding difficulties about defining crime, one of the central features of criminology is bound to be an interest in explaining criminal behaviour. Understandably, criminologists continue to try to explain why some individuals commit crime and others do not, as well as examining variations in rates or types of crime between different areas or different countries, and during different periods. Only a few years ago, Mannheim argued that the analysis of law and of society's attitude to crime and punishment might be subjects for study by sociologists of law rather than by criminologists (1960:33). However, it now seems to be beyond argument that criminology must include an examination of the processes by which some types of behaviour attract criminal status. Furthermore, the functioning of all aspects of the criminal justice system is a legitimate area for criminological inquiry (Bottomley, 1979:viii).

The nature of explanation

It is possible to spend a vast amount of time embroiled in arguments about the precise meaning of 'explanation', and about distinctions between 'causes' and 'causation'. However, it is not necessary to do this here and only a few basic points will be made.

Walker (1974) discusses a long-running feud among sociologists who fit into the positivist approach to criminology. This is the battle between supporters of multiple factor theories who try to explain crime as the result of different factors acting together, and their opponents who attempt to construct a unitary theory to explain crime. Walker describes the search for a single explanation of crime as a quest to find 'the criminologist's stone' (1974:47). At the end of the nineteenth century, Durkheim (1950) was arguing that for each effect there could be only one cause. In relation to his work on suicide, Durkheim accepted that suicide could result from different causes, and said that this was possible because there were different types of suicide. Some criminologists have produced typologies of criminal behaviour, and suggested that the causes of one type of crime might be different from the causes of another (eg Clinard and Quinney, 1973; Gibbons, 1975). However, some supporters of unitary theory have tried to provide a global theory which purports to explain any form of criminal behaviour. Lombroso's theory of the born criminal, and some of the other explanations discussed in Chapter 3 are examples of attempts to provide a biological version of a unitary theory of crime. During the twentieth century, sociologists took on the challenge of providing a general theory of crime. Sutherland's theory of differential association (discussed in Chapter 6) is one such example. Interestingly, Bottomley (1979) describes Merton's theory of anomie (also covered in Chapter 6) as another general theory, but Walker (1974) identifies Merton as having questioned the feasibility of developing a single theory of crime. The source of this disparity may lie in the fact that some theories try to explain crime in terms of a single factor (eg biological inferiority; social learning) while others embrace several factors within a single theory (but without becoming so diversified as to qualify as a multi-factor theory). As you will see later, an external observer could fit Merton's theory into the latter category, although Merton apparently did not.

The usual response to the failure of unitary theories of crime has been to attempt to explain crime by means of multi-factor theories. Such theories are not new. Burt, in *The Young Delinquent*, claimed that crime stemmed from a multiplicity of sources, and that 'The nature of these factors, and of their varying combinations, differs greatly from one individual to another' (1944:600). Burt found over 170 factors which were related to delinquency, from which nine or ten would generally act together to push an individual child towards crime. It should be noted that Burt did not claim that every child subjected to the same factors would become a criminal.

A well-known English example of a multi-factor approach to the explanation of delinquency is the longitudinal study of 400 London schoolboys by West and Farrington (1969, 1973, 1977). A very wide range of individual and social factors was considered, and statistical analysis of these enabled West and Farrington to identify those boys who were more likely to become delinquent. They admitted that a 'statistical correlation does not imply a direct casual link' (1973:191) but, having modestly accepted that all they were able to show was the potential for predicting delinquency, West and Farrington went on to claim that their study 'suggests that delinquency arises from a complex interaction between the individual home atmosphere, the personal qualities of the boy and the circumstances in which the family live ... a multi-causal theoretical approach seems necessary' (1973:201). It is not clear, then, whether the authors were offering a method of explaining crime, or one for predicting it.

The multi-factor approach has been subjected to heavy criticism. Matza (1964) argues that when a host of factors are included, it is unrealistic to regard them all as factors. He says some of them should be viewed as contingencies instead. A factor has an effect on everyone who comes into contact with it, although its influence varies. A contingency is something which may or may not matter, depending on the existence of other conditions which can properly be regarded as factors. Taking this point a little further, Matza suggests that the multi-factor approach might be a way of ignoring findings which suggest that some factors out of a large number are not related to crime. These are valid points. When criminologists try to link criminal behaviour to different combinations of factors drawn from a very large number, it is possible that some of those factors are totally irrelevant, but that the overall picture has become so confused that it is impossible to exclude them.

In order to claim to be scientific, a theory ought to be capable of being disproved. Wilkins suggests that multi-factor theories are unscientific because they are constructed in such a way that they cannot be proved wrong. He adds that an explanation framed in terms of multiple causes does not deserve to be called a 'theory', but should instead be seen as 'an anti-theory which proposes that no theory can be formed regarding crime' (1964:37).

The brief descriptions above of the work of Burt, and of West and Farrington, indicate one of the difficulties which affects many criminological studies. This is the tendency for researchers to attempt to explain crime whilst at the same time searching for ways of predicting it and of preventing it.

Bottomley (1979) suggests that research which seeks to predict crime rates or to predict criminal behaviour at an individual level is valid in its own right. Simon (1971) has subjected prediction studies in criminology to heavy criticism.

Furthermore, there is a potential for injustice if tests to predict the future behaviour of individuals are used as the basis of sentencing decisions. This risk has been most heavily criticised in relation to the treatment of so-called dangerous offenders. Although the government is now promoting less frequent use of imprisonment in relation to less serious offenders, the use of imprisonment in order to protect the public from hardened offenders is still considered to be valid (Home Office, 1990). Although an offender who persistently commits property offences might be regarded as a hardened criminal, the term 'dangerous' is more likely to refer to someone who commits, or is likely to commit, offences of a violent or sexual nature. Offenders who are considered to fit into such a category are likely to receive longer sentences and to have less chance of being released early on parole. Morris (1974) and Bottomley (1979) both suggest that tests to predict the likelihood of future dangerous behaviour are so prone to error that they could lead to the unjust detention of people who are not dangerous. The United States Supreme Court seems to have agreed with this view in *Baxstrom* v *Herald* (383 US 107). In that case, decided in 1966, the court ordered that 967 patients held in state hospitals for the criminally insane must be transferred to ordinary mental hospitals. All of these people had been considered dangerous at the time of being sentenced, but proper procedures were not followed in relation to the way they were committed. A follow-up study discovered that in the next five years, only 26 of the patients were returned to hospitals for the criminally insane. Half of the total were released into the community, and 83 per cent of those were not arrested again (Steadman, 1972). The case is a good illustration of the risk of over-predicting future dangerousness.

Even if prediction studies can provide information of value for anticipating crime, the data obtained will not necessarily have any explanatory value. A different but related point is made by Hall Williams when he suggests that 'There is no necessary connection between criminological knowledge and the measures applied by society in dealing with offenders or protecting its members from crime' (1982:6). He is not proposing that crime prevention practitioners or those responsible for treating offenders should totally ignore existing findings in choosing the actions they should take. Hall Williams draws an interesting analogy with the world of medicine where doctors are able to prescribe treatments which are known to work for some illnesses even though the causes have not been discovered. Such a view seems to accord with the pragmatic approach to crime currently favoured by the Home Office (see Chapter 10). In any event, surely the evaluation of preventive measures is a valid area for criminological research?

The role of the criminologist

Having already described the range of topics which can fit under the umbrella of criminology, it would be easy to identify the task of criminologists as being to study those different topics. However, we are not concerned here with describing the areas with which a criminologist's work should be concerned. Our focus of interest is the criminologist's role, that is, his purpose in concentrating on certain areas, and the uses to which his findings are put.

From our earlier discussions it is clear that the boundaries of criminological research go way beyond attempts to explain criminal behaviour. The present concern, though, is with assessing a criminologist's motives when he studies the conduct of individual criminals, or the origins of the criminal law, or the way police deal with offenders, or any other topic. From a perspective in which criminology must be scientific, criminologists would be expected to set aside value judgements and to approach their studies in a purely objective manner. Similarly, they would be confined to presenting their findings to policy makers and allowing the latter to draw up their own action plans. Hall Williams (1982) claims that when criminologists make recommendations, they are more influenced by their own political or social philosophy, than by their studies. Bottomley (1979) also suggests that personal values occupy a central role in criminology, and both writers argue that the subject would benefit if criminologists openly acknowledged their own views. As will be seen in Chapter 8, a similar suggestion is made by some radical criminologists (eg Greenberg, 1981). This seems to be a very valid point. It is true that criminologists with a strong desire to suppress certain types of behaviour or to change particular laws might be tempted to present their findings in a slanted way, but at least if they show their colours, onlookers are able to form their own opinions. It would be a great shame if certain topics were excluded from being studied because they were politically contentious or because they were exceptionally emotive. Indeed, if such an approach were adopted in relation to crime and the treatment of offenders, there would be very little left to study.

Furthermore, in the case of a subject as important as crime, it is difficult to accept that researchers or theorists should not also be entitled to take part in the practical implementation of change. According to Mannheim, it can be 'difficult and invidious to distinguish between the scientific and the technological side of criminology' (1965:20). There are good reasons for suggesting that applied criminology is just as valid a subject as theoretical criminology.

1.4 Is criminology a science?

The notion that value judgements will eventually creep into criminological work might be one reason to argue that the subject cannot be fully scientific. However, it must be possible to level the same argument at psychology, sociology, jurisprudence and even the natural sciences.

The cross-disciplinary nature of criminology has also attracted criticism. As criminologists are drawn from the different disciplines, Sellin has called them 'Kings without a country' (1950). Frey labelled the subject as a clearing house for the other disciplines. Mannheim, who cites both of those criticisms, argues that the growth of teaching and research in criminology means that such comments are no longer valid

(1965:18–19). Criminology, he says, has produced research which benefits other branches of the social sciences, rather than feeding from them in parasitic fashion.

Like some of the questions posed earlier in this chapter, such as 'What is crime?' or 'What should criminology include?', there is no definite answer to the question of 'Is criminology a science?', the answer depends on who you ask. You are invited to ask yourself the question again, when you have read the rest of this book.

1.5 Conclusion

In reviewing this chapter, it seems that a fairly bleak picture has been painted of the past performance of criminology. It has not yet provided an answer to the question of why certain people commit crime. Nor have criminologists defined their terms of reference or set any clear targets for the future development of their subject. These findings should not cause you to lose heart. When you come to read Part Two you will discover that many valiant attempts have been made to explain crime and that a fair proportion of these are quite persuasive. You will also see that some of the new perspectives on criminology throw a different light on earlier work, and provide valuable suggestions as to the direction in which criminology could travel.

2

Sources of Data

2.1 Introduction

Criminology contains a fair number of armchair theories, as well as some theories which are supported by exhaustive research. Even an armchair theorist has to rely on some form of background information to spark off his ideas. The sources of data which are used by criminologists fall into two categories: primary and secondary. Social scientists interpret those terms in a different way from historians. For a social scientist, a primary source includes data he has collected himself. A variety of research methods might have been used, such as interviews, questionnaires and observation. Secondary sources contain data collected by others, which the social scientist draws on for his own purposes. As secondary sources have been produced by someone else's research, they will include any biases built into the original work. The secondary user may well be unaware of those biases. Obviously, many criminologists are interested in various ways of measuring crime. A useful starting point is the official statistics, and the rest of this chapter will concentrate on the way they are produced, their strengths and weaknesses, techniques for testing their validity, and ways of supplementing them.

2.2 Official statistics

The Home Office and various other government departments produce a mass of statistics each year, and many of these are of potential value to criminologists and other social scientists. The *Criminal Statistics* are an obvious example, but others include *Prison Statistics* and *Social Trends*. If you have never done so before, you would be well advised to spend some time thumbing through the most recent volume of *Criminal Statistics* that you can obtain, especially if you are one of the many people who try to steer clear of tables and percentages. You will find that they are easier to understand than you might have expected.

Before we look at officially recorded crime in more detail, just consider a parallel example which illustrates the kinds of issue to be addressed by anyone using statistics. There is an old joke which runs along the lines of:

> 'I read in the paper that 10 per cent of accidents are caused by drunk drivers ... it's the sober ones who cause the other 90 per cent that we need to watch out for!'

If its contents are broken down, several questions are raised:

- Is the newspaper noted for its objective reporting?
- What source did the newspaper use?
- How reliable was the original research?
- What is meant by accidents? Is the definition used a legal one, or one chosen by the researchers?
- If the source was official statistics, how many accidents were never reported?
- What does 'caused by' mean? Has causation been established in court or by the researcher's judgment?
- What is a 'drunk driver'? Are only convicted motorists included?
- How valid is it to assume that 90 per cent of accidents must be caused by sober drivers? Aren't there other factors to be taken into account for sober or drunk drivers, such as tiredness, weather conditions and mechanical failures?

Accidents are not directly relevant here, but the same sort of questions must be asked in relation to crime statistics. This should be made clear by an examination of the way in which criminal statistics are produced.

2.3 The production of crime statistics

The statistics which purport to show the number of crimes committed are produced by means of a multi-staged process summarised in the flow chart (Fig 1):

Fig 1: *Flow chart illustrating the production of official crime statistics*

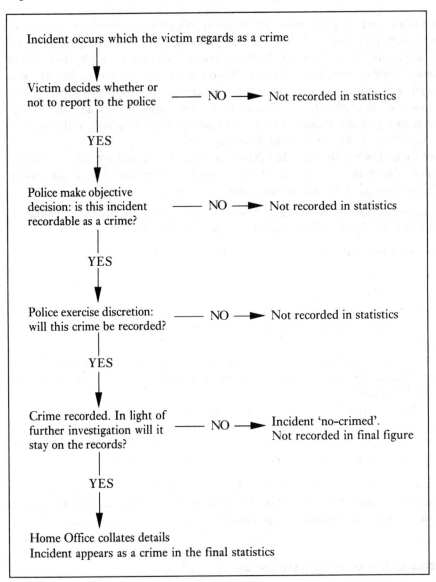

Incident occurs which the victim regards as a crime

Victim decides whether or
not to report to the police   —— NO ——▶ Not recorded in statistics

YES

Police make objective
decision: is this incident   —— NO ——▶ Not recorded in statistics
recordable as a crime?

YES

Police exercise discretion: —— NO ——▶ Not recorded in statistics
will this crime be recorded?

YES

Crime recorded. In light of   Incident 'no-crimed'.
further investigation will it —— NO ——▶   Not recorded in final figure
stay on the records?

YES

Home Office collates details
Incident appears as a crime in the final statistics

It is clear that the process by which criminal statistics are constructed has several filters built into it, so that an incident which could be recorded as a crime might instead be filtered out at any stage. The operation of these filters, especially in the early stages, helps to produce the so called 'dark figure' of unrecorded crime. There is no doubt that recorded crime only accounts for a proportion of the crimes which actually occur. Some would say that recorded crime is only the tip of the iceberg, but even if that is so, the proportions of ice above and below the water line (and therefore the size of the 'dark figure') vary between different crimes and different areas. In any event, official crime statistics can be deceptive if studied on their own.

Using residential burglary as an example, the official figures suggest that occurrences of this crime almost doubled from 262,131 in 1977 to 504,702 in 1986 (Home Office, 1988: Table 2.10). At first sight, the enormous rise appears alarming, but the bare figures are misleading. Elliott and Mayhew (1988) discuss data available for 1972, 1973, 1979, 1980 and 1985 from the General Household Survey, and for 1981 and 1983 from the British Crime Survey (surveys will be discussed later in this chapter). They use survey estimates of the numbers of residential burglaries involving loss of property which actually occurred, to present the table below:

Table 1A: *Burglaries with loss, England and Wales*

(Survey estimates)	Percentage reported	Ratio of offences committed to offences recorded	Ratio of offences reported to offences recorded
1972 GHS	78	2:2	1:7
1973 GHS	80	2:3	1:8
1979 GHS	76	1:9	1:4
1980 GHS	83	1:8	1:5
1981 BCS	88	1:4	1:3
1983 BCS	89	1:3	1:1
1985 GHS	88	1:4	1:2
1986 GHS	90	1.2	1.12
1987 BCS	94	1.1	1.06
1991 BCS	94	1.2	1.20

GHS = *General Household Survey*
BCS = *British Crime Survey*
(Source: Criminal Statistics England and Wales 1992)

Table 1B: *Residential burglaries involving loss, 1972–1991*

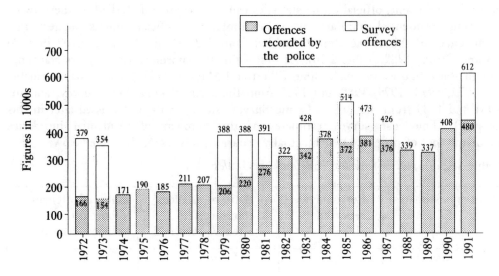

Notes:

1. Figures for survey burglaries are derived from the GHS for 1972, '73, '79, '80, '85 and '86, and from the BCS for '81, '83, '87 and '91. The BCS figures have been calculated to be comparable with GHS figures.

2. Offences recorded by the police are burglaries involving loss (ie burglaries in a dwelling minus nil-value cases).

3. GHS respondents were asked about their experiences during the last 12 months, a period which usually began before the relevant year shown in the figure.

(Source: BCS 1992, Home Office Research Study 132)

The table supports the notion that fluctuations in crime can be exaggerated by changes in the reporting practices of victims and police procedure for recording crimes. The second British Crime Survey estimated the true increase in domestic burglaries between 1972 and 1983 at about 20 per cent (Hough and Mayhew, 1985:51). That is a substantial rise, but is considerably less than official figures would have suggested, since they would have yielded an estimate of close to 100 per cent.

The findings of surveys, particularly in relation to the under-recording of crime, will be dealt with below under '2.8 Supplementing the official statistics'. Discussion of possible reasons for victims not reporting crimes will be deferred until then. With the exception of the stage involving the victim's decision whether to report a crime, it is proposed to run briefly through the different steps in the process, shown in Fig 1, by which criminal statistics are produced.

In the flow chart it is assumed that a crime must have a victim. In fact, the law prohibits a number of activities, such as prostitution and some forms of drug abuse, which are generally referred to as 'victimless crimes'. For such offences to come to official notice they would need to be reported by witnesses or discovered by the police. As we will see below, even then, few such offences are included in criminal statistics.

Assuming that a victim reports an incident to the police or that they discover it by some other means, the police first have to consider whether it amounts to a crime. For example, circumstances which a victim regards as an offence might not amount to a breach of the criminal law. In that case the police would quite rightly not record the incident as a crime. If the circumstances do reveal an offence, the police then have to assess whether it is recordable as a crime. Crimes which are recordable are known as 'notifiable offences'. The meaning of this term and the offences covered are described in the appendices to the annual statistics published by the Home Office. Broadly speaking, it includes indictable offences. For this reason, most victimless crimes are not recordable.

Having reached a decision, on objective grounds, that an incident could be recorded as a crime, the police might then exercise discretion as to whether or not to record it officially. For example, they could suggest to the victim of an alleged assault that police involvement is inappropriate. If he does not press his complaint, it might not be recorded. In another instance, if money is stolen from a house in circumstances where there are no obvious signs of unlawful entry, practice could vary as to whether the offence is recorded as a burglary or as a theft in a dwelling (Bottomley and Coleman, 1981).

In addition to deciding which offences are notifiable, the Home Office has produced counting rules. The most recent set was implemented in 1980. They outline the recording procedure to be adopted when a number of offences are committed against one victim by the same offender, or against numerous victims in the course of a single incident. Generally speaking, in such cases only one offence will be counted. The counting rules are intended to achieve consistency between police forces, but it would not be surprising to find some variations since it will not always be clear whether the same offender was involved or whether all the offences were part of the same incident.

After the crime has been recorded, it is possible that before the police forward the relevant paperwork to the Home Office, the offence will be written off by a process called 'no-criming'. Further investigation might show that no offence has been committed. A simple example would occur when someone reports property as stolen, but later discovers that it has been mislaid. A routine example concerns bicycles. Theft of a bicycle is a notifiable offence, but the unauthorised taking of one is not. Therefore, if a person reports that his bicycle has been stolen, a crime report must be completed and the incident will be recorded as a crime. If soon afterwards the bicycle is found abandoned but intact, the report will be no-crimed because it is assumed the taker had no intention of stealing the bicycle.

Police forces in England and Wales inform the Home Office of the notifiable offences recorded in their areas, and the figures are then collated. By this stage, the classification rules have already influenced the nature of the data. The influence of the Home Office obviously continues through the manner in which the statistics are presented.

Recent trends

The number of notifiable offences which were recorded by the police in England and Wales during 1995 was 5.1 million. The figure was 4 per cent lower than those for 1994. The figures represent the third consecutive fall in the annual figures.

A statistical overview of the criminal justice system for 1995 shows that the majority of crimes were property offences involving burglary, theft, fraud and forgery, criminal damage and arson. These offences represent 4.7 million or 93 per cent of all crime. Between the years 1994 and 1995 decreases occurred for property offences, with 754 homicides recorded during 1995.

The 'Criminal Statistics for England and Wales relating to Crime and Criminal Proceedings in 1995' were presented to Parliament in November 1996 (Cm 3421) Home Office (1996a). The publication states that 'the statistics of recorded crime do not necessarily portray the full picture of crime experienced by society at large'.

'Trends in Crime: Findings from the 1994 British Crime Survey' (Research Findings No 14 Home Office Research and Statistics Department) estimates that of all offences committed, only about half are reported to the police and fewer than a third are recorded.

Of the notifiable offences recorded by the police, the Home Office survey states that 'the impact of attrition effects will be felt at other levels in the criminal justice system'. It continues by saying that changes in the numbers of persons who are to be prosecuted and found guilty may not reflect changes in the numbers of crimes actually being committed, or the number of criminals not in custody.

2.4 Clear-up rates

Official statistics include details of how many crimes are cleared up, and of people proceeded against. Once again, the official figures can only give a partial picture of the true situation. The Home Office has prescribed the occasions when a crime can be regarded as cleared up. The most common covers circumstances when a person has been proceeded against for an offence (even if he is not subsequently convicted) or has been cautioned. A crime is cleared up if a person has admitted it and a court has taken it into consideration. It is also possible to endorse an offence as cleared up if a person admits it but no useful purpose would be served by prosecuting him. The police practice of writing off crimes admitted by people in custody for other offences falls into that category. That practice has attracted considerable controversy, in particular through claims that prisoners are persuaded to help the police to boost their clear-up rates by admitting crimes they know nothing about, in the knowledge that they will not be prosecuted. In 1989, a detective was dismissed and 34 more policemen faced disciplinary action, three years after a colleague had made allegations of that nature (*The Times*, 20 September 1989). Home Office guidelines on police interviews with sentenced prisoners were redrafted in 1987. A study of burglary in Chapeltown, Leeds, showed that 90 per cent of detections were achieved by means of prison write-offs (Burrows, 1986). During 1992 several police forces, including Humberside and Northumbria, announced that they would no longer actively seek prison write-offs and would concentrate their efforts on primary detections. They accepted this would inevitably lead to reduced clear-up rates but considered a more accurate picture will be provided of the effectiveness of police investigative techniques. Ironically, some other forces regard prison visits as increasingly important, not simply to bolster detection rates, but also to gather intelligence to use in proactive investigation (*Police Review*, 11 February 1994:16).

Box (1981) argues that the way the police investigate crime contributes to the over-representation of disadvantaged people among those prosecuted for crime. The police are said to concentrate on offenders from the least powerful sections of the community because of a variety of factors, including their own ideological conceptions about crime and criminals, and the knowledge that such people cannot threaten a police officer's career prospects.

Matza (1969) argues that the police adopt a system of methodic suspicion, particularly in relation to theft and burglary. This means that when they investigate these offences, the police focus their enquiries on people with a previous criminal background or who resemble police stereotypes of criminals. The net result of the claims of both Box and Matza is that police practices let outwardly respectable people off the hook and cause the underprivileged and powerless to make up an undue proportion of detected offenders in official data.

Both writers largely ignore the existence of legal constraints on police practices. Matza produces no supporting evidence and Bottomley and Coleman describe his account as 'pure conjecture' (1981:103). Box cites a number of American studies which suggest that official statistics 'over emphasise the contribution of lower class individuals and/or negroes' (1981:182–3).

Much of the research used to justify claims of police stereotyping of different groups is concerned with the way police deal with people with whom they come into contact in the course of proactive policing. These findings are not necessarily relevant to the reactive investigation of a crime which has already occurred. Bottomley and Coleman (1981) have pointed out the need to distinguish between the police identifying certain people as suspicious, and police officers coming to suspect people as a result of their investigations into reported crimes. The same authors suggest that findings from studies of proactive policing have been transferred uncritically to other areas of police work. Sanders (1977) discovered that the response of CID officers to crime was essentially reactive.

The prospect of police practices making a major contribution to biases in official data is not that great when one considers how little crime is discovered by the police. Seventy-eight per cent of the detected cases in a study by Zander had been brought to police attention by victims or other non-police sources. Several more writers have pointed to the very low proportion of recorded crime which is discovered by police on patrol (Bottomley and Coleman, 1981; Mawby, 1979; Steer, 1980).

Furthermore, many offences require little or no detective work on the part of the police. Chatterton (1976) suggests that in nearly half of the cases where police made arrests for crime, the public had provided them with a suspect. Steer (1980) found a sample where in more than 70 per cent of detected cases there was little or no doubt as to the identity of the offender. Mawby (1979) made similar findings and also found that in only six out of 136 cases the police had directed their enquiries at suspects with existing reputations. Findings such as these question suggestions that the police operate a system of methodic suspicion. However, Bottomley and Coleman (1981) found that in cases where the police had no information to follow up, they were more willing to speculate about the identity of a suspect. They preferred to regard such suspicion as incidental rather than methodic. In any event, speculation does not necessarily lead to action.

Another weakness of the methodic suspicion argument is that it fails to recognise that suspicion on its own does not allow a crime to be written off. Almost without exception, a crime can only be written off if the police have sufficient evidence to charge someone, even if he is not ultimately charged.

Even though the capacity of the police to produce significant biases in crime statistics appears to be more limited than Box or Matza would suggest, there are other routes by which such biases could enter. For example, research has indicated that members of the public and employers are more willing to report crimes committed by members of socially deprived or minority groups (eg Cohen and Stark, 1974).

The number of offences which are described as 'clear-ups' fell in 1995 to 1,277,000. This was a clear up rate of 26 per cent which was the same as the previous year. A great deal of variation exists within the clear-up rate depending on the type of offence committed. It should be noted that when dealing with the most serious category of crime, rates are much higher with 77 per cent of violent crime being cleared up.

2.5 Advantages of using official statistics

The discussion so far seems to imply that official crime statistics are fatally flawed. However, a moment's thought shows that such statistics have several points in their favour, that is:

1. *There are lots of them.* Statistics in relation to a host of matters of interest to social researchers are routinely collected by the government.
2. *There is usually free access to them.* The same information is usually published on either an annual or an *ad hoc* basis.

3. *Ethical problems have been ironed out.* A social scientist who wishes to produce his own primary source of data, has to choose which methods to adopt. Almost any method can involve ethical problems. At the collection stage, these are most acute in the case of observational research, especially when the researcher keeps his identity and motives secret. Even research using questionnaires or interviews requires the researcher to weigh up ethical issues. Will he be open about the true purpose of the research? How much of an opportunity will he give to his subjects to comment on the final report before it is published? If the research is being sponsored, will the researcher be able to remain independent? Anyone using official statistics as a secondary source is unlikely to have to consider these ethical difficulties.

   If this subject area interests you, you might like to see the excellent *Social Research Ethics* (1982), edited by Martin Bulmer.
4. *Someone else has done the spade work.* The government has already sifted and analysed the raw data, before presenting it in a fairly sophisticated but easy to consult manner.
5. *Official data provides a useful starting point.* During the early part of the twentieth century, Bowley (1915, 1928) was one of the strongest critics of governmental statistics, recognising that official data was imperfect and not produced for sociological purposes, but he was still prepared to use them to show the magnitude, nature and locality of a problem. His comments were made before some of the more recent attempts to discredit official statistics, but Baldwin and Bottoms (1976) were prepared to use official crime data as a starting point in their detailed study of crime in Sheffield.

2.6 Safeguards when using official statistics

Walker (1971) suggested that criminologists can draw on official figures to make useful inferences about crime and the penal system, provided they use common sense and follow certain guidelines. The following safeguards ought to be adopted if official statistics are used:

Recognise definitional problems

In the construction of official statistics, the contributors (police) and the compilers (Home Office) adopt formal definitions. A researcher using the data needs to be aware of these definitions and to be careful not to assume that they coincide with definitions used by victims or other people. The media and victims of crime often use the term 'robbery' to describe a burglary. The slang expression 'mugging' can embrace crimes which might technically be regarded as either robbery or theft from the person. To complicate matters further, even officials might vary in their use of definitions. As was suggested earlier, one police officer might record a sneak-in theft as a burglary, while another could describe it as a theft in a dwelling.

Recognise bias in the process of data collection

A feature of official statistics is that they are a product of an administrative or organisational activity (Halsey, 1972) so they are not really suited to being plundered by social scientists. It is essential to realise that any secondary source can suffer from biases built in at the collection stage. Researchers might ask questions or interpret answers in a way which proves the point they wish to make. This can happen inadvertently as well as deliberately. It is possible to look for tell-tale signs of bias. Most statistical reports which differentiate between the sexes will always show males first. Although there has been a recent trend towards allowing the respondent to decide who is head of a household, it was traditionally the norm, in the official surveys which assessed the social status of subjects, to focus on the husband's occupation. You will have your own ideas about whether this amounts to sexism, and if so whether that matters. It certainly seems indicative of fixed ideas on the part of the compilers. You can gain a useful insight by simply studying the headings used and the methods of presentation.

Be crime specific

Aggregate data of any kind is likely to be more misleading than data examined in a specific context. Even if a researcher is interested in general crime rates in an area, it would be beneficial to separate different crimes at first.

Be problem orientated

This means little more than that researchers must know what they are examining the statistics for. A directed examination allows extraneous factors to be ruled out. Similarly, if the researcher is interested in particular factors, and these played no part in the compilation of the statistics, the limited value of the statistics can be quickly recognised.

Recent criticisms of statistical data

Writing in the New Law Journal (19 April 1996), Dr Gary Slapper of Staffordshire University saw through what were then the current batch of official figures in his article 'Criminal statistics and white lies'. Here, Slapper described Home Secretary Michael Howard as coyly pretending to suggest that thanks to 'an identifiable Conservative philosophy on crime' strategy, 'crime has recently been falling', whereas Slapper says there are good reasons to believe it has not.

Slapper presents the then most recent figures from the Home Office, 'Notifiable

Offences, 3/96', as showing that the 5.1 million offences represented a 2.4 per cent fall in England and Wales, an apparent fall for the third year running.

Dr Slapper baldly states that 'the official Criminal Statistics ... do not disclose the true levels of crime. They register crime reported to and recorded by the police, and most of such reportings are insurance–driven'. He goes on to describe the Home Office's British Crime Survey as periodically measuring the 'true' level of crime because detailed questionnaires are completed with '10,000 randomly chosen people' who are asked about how they have been victimised even if the offences had not been reported. He says the BCS 'estimates that the real level of crime is about four times the recorded level ... about 20 million annual offences' with 'twice as many domestic burglaries as those reported, and three times as many thefts from vehicles'.

Slapper concludes his own survey of crime by writing that 'to a great extent, the error made by Michael Howard is trying to tackle the results of offending, rather than recognise and debate its social causes' suggesting that this approach is shared by many other leading politicians. He poses the question that when, in 1997, the 160th birthday of British crime statistics arrives, 'is it too vain a hope that the law and order debate will by then be better informed about the real nature of the problem?'

2.7 What do the official statistics mean?

Wheeler (1967) describes crime recording as a three-way interaction between citizens, police and offenders. Having examined the production of crime statistics under '2.3 The production of crime statistics' (above), it is obvious that the legislature also has an input, by defining certain actions as criminal. In addition, the executive influences the final figures by issuing guidelines to the police on which offences are notifiable, on counting procedures, and on legitimate methods for recording crimes as cleared up.

From a viewpoint such as Wheeler's, the activities of the different parties are an inherent feature of the production of crime statistics, rather than an external source of error and unreliability. This position is sometimes referred to as the 'institutionalist' perspective. Wheeler argues that it is necessary to study each of the contributing parties before any sense can be made of criminal statistics.

Wilkins (1965) also suggests that criminal statistics are the end processes of interaction and decision making. Wilkins suggests that when members of the public decide whether or not to report a crime, they are deciding whether or not the incident is one the police should do something about. In a sense they are producing a democratic definition of crime. Coleman and Bottomley (1976) argue that official statistics begin their life as products of the actions and definitions of members of the public. Later, they are subject to official processing. In that sense they are a product of both community attitudes and professional practices.

In many other accounts, the public role in influencing criminal statistics is seen as passive, rather than active. This seems unfortunate given the fact that any subsequent action by the police and others is inevitably affected by whether or not a crime is reported. The 1988 British Crime Survey indicates that in relation to personal or household offences, 94 per cent were reported by victims or their families or friends. The police had been at the scene of such crimes, when they occurred, in only 3 per cent of cases (Home Office, 1989e:26).

Kitsuse and Cicourel (1963) are among those who concentrate on the roles of officials in influencing the production of statistics. According to them, crime rates measure organisational processes rather than the occurrence of certain forms of behaviour. Douglas (1971) says official statistics are primarily determined by the political goals of officials.

No matter how wide one chooses to go, there is considerable strength in the argument of Box (1981) that official data are social products, in the sense that they are produced by interactions between a number of different parties. Adopting such a point of view, criminal statistics are an assessment of the effects of those interactions and not a foolproof measurement of how much crime actually occurs. For this reason, the production of criminal statistics is worthy of study in its own right (Black, 1970; Bottomley and Coleman, 1981).

It is also important to consider other misinterpretations of crime figures. From the information discussed in this chapter it should be clear that officially recorded clear up rates are, at best, a weak indicator of police effectiveness. As we have seen, only a small percentage of detections are based on exhaustive detective work. Many reported crimes are pre-detected. Furthermore, the value of detections achieved by prison write-offs is highly questionable.

It has also been seen that official figures can create a misleading image of horrific rises in certain types of crime. The images created can be seized on by the media, or by politicians, and further exaggerated. For example, in Hall's analysis of 'mugging', he suggests that at times of crisis, moral panics are able to arise. He argues that during the late 1970s, British capitalism was at the centre of such a crisis and that attention was deflected from this by convincing people of the need for law and order. Public acceptance of the need for law and order is said to allow governments to assume more power (Hall *et al*, 1978).

Young, and Cohen have shown how press reaction to social problems or types of behaviour can lead to 'deviancy amplification'. For example, Young (1971) argues that by focusing attention on drug abuse, the press forced addicts to go underground and separate themselves from the rest of society. If drug abuse is a response to problems, any activity which worsens those problems is bound to be counter-productive. Cohen's *Folk Devils and Moral Panics* shows how the attitudes of the press and the public to fights between mods and rockers during the 1960s created a picture of violence and mayhem which was out of proportion with the true state of affairs. These examples are not specifically linked to criminal statistics, but they are indicative of the potential for misinterpreting information about crime. Chapter 7 will take a closer look at the relevance of social reaction to crime.

2.8 Supplementing the official statistics

As was mentioned earlier, official statistics do not give a true picture of the extent of crime, largely because of the 'dark figure' of unrecorded crime. It is also argued that convicted offenders are not necessarily representative of criminals generally. Therefore, any findings derived from official data about offenders cannot be treated as totally accurate. In order to fill in the gaps left by official methods, researchers generally carry out either a victim survey or a self-report survey. These are explained below.

Victim surveys

Sparks *et al* (1977) comment that the dark figure of crime is like the weather – criminologists had talked about it for 100 years, but had done little about trying to measure it. During the last 25 years or so, that criticism has become less valid. In 1967, the President's Crime Commission interviewed members of 10,000 households in the United States about the incidence of crimes affecting them during the previous year. Of those who reported being the victim of an incident which matched the legal definition of a crime, only half had reported it to the police. The police only attended half of those reports, and recorded just a proportion of the incidents attended. Since 1972, the US National Crime Survey has continued to carry out similar research. Skogan (1976) has carried out extensive research into the reporting of crime in the United States.

In Britain, officially sponsored research of a more general nature has sometimes included questions about victimisation. From time to time, since 1972, the General Household Survey has included questions about residential burglaries.

In 1972, Sparks carried out a victim survey in three areas of London (Sparks *et al*, 1977). Using the survey data, recorded crime rates were compared with those estimated to be the true level. When the three areas were taken together, the ratio of survey-estimated crime (all types of crime) to recorded crime was 11:1. Ratios varied between areas, as did the contributions of under-reporting by victims and of differential recording by the police. In Hackney, victims were fairly willing to report crimes, but the police usually recorded offences which were reported. In Kensington, rates for both reporting and recording were higher. In the last area, the proportion of offences subsequently no-crimed was smaller.

In Britain, the most extensive victim surveys have been sponsored by the Home Office. The British Crime Survey (BCS) has estimated crime levels and studied other types of information for the years 1981, 1983, 1987, 1991, 1993 and 1995. The surveys are carried out in the year after the one being studied, and carry the later dates in their titles.

It is worth taking a brief look at the 1996 BCS to see what it covers and how it can add to our knowledge about crime and related matters, Home Office (1996). Using the Postcode Address File as their starting point, BCS researchers identified a core sample of households. After various stages a final sample was produced. A booster sample of ethnic minority respondents was also identified. Further selections were then made at random, until eventually the researchers set out to interview one person aged 16 or over at each address. Nearly 16,500 adults were interviewed.

The questionnaire used for the survey was made up of five parts. Every interviewee completed a Main Questionnaire which, *inter alia*, assessed whether a member of that household had been a victim of crime during 1995. If there was a positive response, a Victim Form was completed for each offence, up to a maximum of six per household. Details from this form were used to classify the incident. Each respondent also completed a Follow-Up Questionnaire. Two versions of this questionnaire were used: one dealt with matters such as the attention of respondents to crime prevention, the other assessed respondents' attitudes to the police. Every interviewee provided personal details by completing a Demographic Questionnaire. The above description is only a very truncated summary of the procedures adopted during the 1996 BCS. A more detailed account is provided in Appendix B to the report.

For present purposes we are interested in BCS assessments of crime levels, and of how much crime is not reported, as well as explanations offered by victims for not reporting crime. Because of the way it is conducted, the BCS can only estimate the levels of household or personal crime. It does not include crimes for which the victims are organisations or businesses. Nor does it include corporate crime. Victimless crimes are obviously not covered.

In producing the BCS, a legalistic definition of crime is adopted. However, the BCS is less likely than the police to disregard offences on such grounds as triviality (Home Office, 1993c:4). It is acknowledged in the BCS that the behaviour of respondents may affect the accuracy of its findings. For instance, respondents may overlook a relevant incident, or believe that it occurred outside the period being studied. They might accidentally report an incident which happened before the period being surveyed began. Respondents may be reluctant to disclose some incidents. Some interviewees may even invent incidents. It is claimed that the result of such factors is to provide a low estimate of incidents actually occurring (Home Office, 1993c:6). Once again, a more detailed discussion of methodological problems, including sampling error, can be found in the report itself.

Using data from the survey sample, BCS researchers estimated the levels of different crimes in England and Wales as a whole, using formulae linked to estimates of the number of households and the number of persons aged 16 or over. The survey revealed almost three times as many domestic burglaries as the official statistics. Also found were almost four times as many woundings, seven times as many acts of vandalism and eight times as many robberies. The 1996 BCS thus confirmed the findings of earlier surveys that all types of offence are under-recorded, but that proportions vary between crimes. This is illustrated in Table 2 below.

Only thefts of motor vehicles and burglaries where loss occurred can be said to have a high reporting rate. The need to report a crime in order to claim on insurance may be a motivating factor. Vandalism is very much under-reported. Respondents were asked about their reasons for not reporting crimes to the police. In the 1996 survey four per cent said that they thought that the matter was not serious enough to be reported to the police. Twenty-nine per cent failed to report the matter because they felt that the police would be unable to do much about it. Reasons, such as fear or dislike of the police, were rarely put forward. The 1984 BCS had asked victims why they *did* report offences. The main reasons given were, firstly, the personal advantages that might result (eg recovery of property, claiming against insurance) and, secondly, a feeling of social obligation. Reporting of offences has increased since the earlier British Crime Surveys. This might be partly explained by more widespread use of insurance cover, increased home ownership, and greater access to telephones (Forrester *et al*, 1988; Home Office, 1993c:18).

Table 2: *Percentages of notifiable offences occurring in England and Wales in 1995, according to BCS estimates, which were reported by victims and recorded by the police*

Offence	Percentage reported	Percentage recorded
Vandalism	29	47
Burglary	73	63
attempt only or no loss	52	33
with loss	84	72
Theft from a motor vehicle	50	52
Theft of motor vehicles	97	83
Robbery	46	27

(Source of data: *British Crime Survey 1996*, Figure 2–3. Only selected offences are shown here, so totals are omitted as they would be misleading.)

The 1994 report suggests one explanation for the under-recording of crime is that the police do not accept some victims' descriptions of events and therefore do not record their complaints as crimes. It also mentions that some incidents classified by the BCS in one category may have been placed in a different category by the police (Home Office, 1993:16).

Victim surveys can be seen to be a valuable means of putting apparent changes in crime into perspective, and for creating a more accurate picture of crime rates than official statistics provide. Victim surveys are now used quite often at a local level, as part of broader examinations of patterns of crime and official responses to it (eg Farrington and Dowds, 1985; Baldwin and Bottoms, 1976; Forrester *et al*, 1988). It is not uncommon for the police to carry out a victim survey before implementing a Neighbourhood Watch scheme.

Recently, in 'Rights of Victims in the Criminal Justice System: Rhetoric or Reality?' [1995] Crim LR 843, Helen Fenwick examines the Victim's Charter and what she describes as 'associated government instruments'. Fenwick's view is that an impression is conveyed that victims of crime have rights to certain services within the criminal justice process. The article also considers how far such instruments reveal any real commitment to the notion of 'victims' rights', and whether proposals for the direction in which reforms should go is the correct one.

Fenwick concludes that 'the current scheme conveys an appearance of a commitment to victims' rights which is seriously misleading', and she ends her article by describing the 'Victim's Charter' as 'internally inconsistent'.

Self-report studies

The purpose of self-report studies is to obtain more information about the characteristics of offenders. Many theories suggest that crime is more prevalent among the working class. However, if only a proportion of offenders ever come to light, any generalisation of data obtained in relation to them may well be unreliable.

Self-report studies can be used in a variety of ways. If the aim is to assess how widespread criminal behaviour is, the likely approach will be to question a sample of people about their involvement in crime. If the sample is taken at random it is likely to include some people with convictions and others without them. A researcher might deliberately pick a group whose members are traditionally under-represented in the known criminal population. Another variation is to ask convicted offenders about their behaviour since they were sentenced, as a means of checking official reconviction rates. Self-report studies can give some information about the dark figure of crime, but their capacity for doing so is limited by the difficulty of comparing admitted offences against police records.

Porterfield (1946) found that a sample of students, with no previous convictions, admitted offences as serious as those of known offenders. He said the gap in official figures was due either to lenience by law enforcement agencies towards middle and upper class youths, or to the fact that lower class youths committed more offences and were therefore more likely to be caught. Gold (1966) found that lower status boys offended more frequently and admitted more serious offences.

Erickson and Empey (1963) compared youths from different socio-economic backgrounds and found that the majority of youths in one group was neither more nor less delinquent than the majority in another. West and Farrington (1977) suggest that to a considerable extent official figures and self-report studies both pick out the same 'bad boys'.

Even this short discussion shows that whilst self-report studies are illuminative, the findings from them have been mixed. This type of research is not without its own methodological problems. As with victim surveys, there is the difficulty of matching offenders' definitions of criminal behaviour against official definitions or those of the researchers. There is also the risk that interviewees will invent incidents because of bravado. On the other hand, they might fail to disclose some offences through fear of prosecution. Dentler (1966) disapproves of self-report studies because they are intended to verify data from elsewhere, but the researcher ends up testing the method of verification.

Victim surveys and self-report studies have their weaknesses, but they have also given social scientists a valuable insight into the level of accuracy of official statistics. At the very least, they allow criminologists to reach more reasoned decisions about whether to use officially produced crime data and, if so, how.

PART TWO:
CRIMINOLOGICAL THEORY

3

Biological Theories

3.1 Introduction

All theories which put forward a biological explanation for crime are founded on the premise that physical structure determines function. Criminals are seen as biologically different from non-criminals. If such theories were accurate, they would have an obvious appeal for policy makers and crime prevention practitioners. Active or potential criminals could be identified by their physical appearance or through medical tests, and controlled in some way. Furthermore, the apparent existence of a separate dangerous or criminal class would support the maintenance of the *status quo* by diverting attention from possible social causes of crime. The latter ground has been put forward as one reason for the appeal of biological positivism at the end of the nineteenth century (Lindesmith and Levin, 1937; Radzinowicz, 1966). Biological theories have taken a variety of forms.

3.2 Physical type theories

Several varieties of theory suggest that criminals stand out because of their physical characteristics. Two of the very earliest versions tend to be omitted from text books, or to be regarded as somewhat eccentric. These are: physiognomy and phrenology.

Physiognomy is a study which has been in existence for thousands of years and which holds that a person's character is discernible from his facial features. It was the subject of a substantial work by Lavater in the late eighteenth century. Physiognomy might match with modern cliches about people's eyes being shifty or too close together, but it lacks scientific credibility.

Later in the eighteenth century, another doctrine, phrenology, received more systematic treatment, largely through the work of Franz Joseph Gall. Following extensive studies of the brain, Gall held a number of beliefs. He suggested that the brain was the centre of thought and was divided into separate areas which controlled different activities. The areas of more importance were of greater size. In some people certain brain areas were of disproportionate size and importance, and produced corresponding bumps in the skull. Irregularities in skull shape or size did not in themselves predict types of behaviour. They were indicators of the shape of the brain underneath.

Gall identified 26 separate functions of the brain, although these were subsequently added to by other writers. Those of most relevance in explaining crime included acquisitiveness, combativeness, destructiveness and secretiveness. The areas of the brain pulling in the direction of those functions could be held in check by others which involved moral sentiments and intellect, thus discouraging involvement in crime. These purely biological characteristics could be affected by social forces as it was thought that training could enhance or inhibit development of the different areas and their associated propensities. Notwithstanding this latter point, phrenology may well have failed to gain really broad acceptance because of its apparent deterministic bias. Furthermore, Vold and Bernard point out that it is impossible to scientifically test phrenology's conceptions of the brain's areas and their associated functions (1986:49).

Although phrenology is now usually regarded as *passé*, it would seem unfair to view Gall as a crank. It is noteworthy that in 1958 Vold described phrenology as an 'abortive absurdity', but that the third edition of Vold and Bernard misses out that term and calls Gall 'the eminent European anatomist'. Savitz *et al* (1977) provide a spirited defence of Gall's contribution to criminology.

3.3 Lombroso and the atavistic criminal

In spite of earlier contributions, Cesare Lombroso has been described as 'the founding father of the biological positivist school' (Taylor *et al*, 1973:41). He is best known for his notion of the born criminal, an individual who exhibited physical signs of atavism, that is, of being an evolutionary throwback. To some extent, such ideas had been given a better chance of acceptance by their closeness to the publication of Darwin's ideas about evolutionary theory.

Lombroso, a former doctor with the Italian army, claimed to have received a 'flash of inspiration' when he examined the skull of a notorious criminal. On seeing the skull, Lombroso realised that the nature of criminality lay in atavism. This explained the peculiar physical characteristics, such as enormous jaws, high cheekbones, and protruding ears, found in 'criminals, savages and apes' (Lombroso, 1911:xiv).

Spurred on by this insight, Lombroso produced an extended list of physical features or stigmata, typically possessed by the atavistic individual who was inclined towards criminality. These included asymmetry of the face; irregularities in the eyes, ears, nose, lips, teeth or chin; supernumary nipples, fingers or toes; and excessive arm length. Lombroso tested his ideas by examining a group of convicted criminals for the presence of such anomalies. Twenty-one per cent had one anomaly and 43 per cent showed five or more. Lombroso claimed that the presence of five or more of the specified characteristics identified a person as a born criminal. He also tested incarcerated criminals for anomalies of the skull and compared them against a sample of non-criminal soldiers. The criminals had all been convicted of homicide offences and were sub-divided into two groups, those who were simply imprisoned, and those who were serving a sentence of penal servitude. In each of the groups about 50 per cent of the sample had one or two anomalies of the skull. However, none of the soldiers showed five or more anomalies, whereas nearly 7 per cent of the prisoners serving penal servitude did. It is feasible that so many anomalies occurring together in one individual would appear so severe that the army would have rejected him.

The emphasis on atavism as an explanation for criminality is most explicit in *L'uomo Delinquente, (The Criminal Man)*, published in 1876. However, by the time the fifth edition was published in 1897, Lombroso had broadened his theory. It was clear that the born criminal was only one category of criminal type. Others included the insane criminal, the epileptic criminal, and a further broad category of occasional criminals who might be affected by atavism and who could be spurred into criminal activity by a variety of environmental factors, such as poor education, or the influence of criminal associates. Lombroso may well have been reacting to criticisms and to the more socially aware work of Garofalo and Ferri, fellow members of the Italian School.

3.4 Evaluation of Lombroso

Lombroso's theory and methods are open to various criticisms. His statistical methods have been described as 'totally inadequate' (Taylor *et al*, 1973:42). The objectivity of his research is questioned by his insistence that some defects were not measurable, but could be seen by a trained observer. It is also puzzling that Lombroso included tattooing as one of the features typical of the atavistic criminal.

An English doctor, Charles Goring, was highly critical of Lombroso's methods and at the beginning of the twentieth century was himself involved in a lengthy piece of research which, *inter alia*, assessed Lombroso's claims. Objective measurements were taken of the physical and mental characteristics of about 3,000 imprisoned recidivist criminals, and of unconvicted individuals in samples of university students, hospital patients, and soldiers of various ranks. Goring compared the results for the criminal group against the others, and also compared different types of criminals. He found no significant differences so far as most physical characteristics were concerned, and concluded 'there is no such thing as a physical criminal type' (Goring, 1913:173). However, Goring found that criminals were consistently shorter and lighter than comparative individuals. Linking this to his findings that the mental ability of criminals was lower, Goring claimed support for his thesis that hereditary inferiority was connected to criminal behaviour. Arguments about links between criminality and heredity will be examined in later sections.

Goring has been accused of overlooking aspects of his results which might have supported Lombroso's theories, because of his eagerness to challenge them (Driver, 1973).

Goring's own work was in turn strongly criticised by Hooton (1939). Hooton ran a study in which approximately 14,000 prisoners were compared with 3,000 non-criminals on the basis of physical characteristics. The subjects were drawn from ten American states. He reported significant differences, finding that features, such as the following, were more common among criminals: low foreheads; sloping shoulders; thin lips; and tattoos. Hooton suggested physical inferiority was significant because it was connected with mental inferiority. This inferiority was 'probably' due to heredity, and not to environmental factors (1939:306). However, crime occurred because of 'the impact of the environment upon low grade organisms'. Hooton took a further step by comparing the physical characteristics of different types of criminals. Thus small men were thieves, whereas stocky men would commit violent or sexual offences. Hooton overlooked the fact that on previous occasions many of the criminals had committed offences other than those for which the present sentence was imposed.

Several other criticisms can be levelled at Hooton. Although he noted differences between criminals and non-criminals, Hooton disregarded differences between samples from different states as well as variations between researchers. He did not substantiate his assumption that inferiority was inherited. Also, like Lombroso he regards certain characteristics as inferior because they apparently occur more frequently in criminals. Yet, without linking physical traits to criminal behaviour, there is no reason why a particular shape of nose, chin or whatever should be viewed as a sign of inferiority.

3.5 Theories related to body shape

Attempts to connect criminality with physique have continued until quite recently. Although these have tended to look at the significance of body shape rather than separate features, they have been referred to as 'neo Lombrosian theories' (Hall Williams, 1982:18). In 1921, *Physique and Character*, by E Kretschmer, a German psychiatrist, was published. Kretschmer attempted to show a relationship between body shape and types of mental illness. He divided people into three body types, referred to as somatotypes, and claimed that the tendency towards different kinds of mental illness varied between these types. It is not proposed to go into depth about Kretschmer's work. Although later versions of his book paid more attention to crime, his theory was related to constitutional causes of mental illness, and his research was weakened by a lack of comparison with non-criminals who were not regarded as mentally ill.

Sheldon presented a theory which related body types more specifically to varieties of criminal behaviour (1940, 1949, 1954). He described three basic types of physique and suggested the types of temperament which corresponded with them. His somatotypes are not identical to Kretschmer's and are named differently, but there are similarities. Sheldon's three somatotypes were:

1. Endomorphs, who would tend to be soft and round, and to be relaxed and extrovert.
2. Mesomorphs were athletic, and tended to act aggressively.
3. An ectomorph was thin and frail, and was introverted.

Sheldon held that an individual possessed features of each of the body types, but to varying degrees. The subjects of his research were given ratings between 1 and 7 to indicate the extent to which they possessed aspects of each of the different types. Therefore a person would be given a three-figure rating, such as 2–1–7, showing his possession of characteristics from each of the body types.

Sheldon compared such ratings for a group of 200 male delinquents against those for 200 students who were regarded as non-delinquent. He found that the delinquents were significantly higher in mesomorphy and lower in ectomorphy (1949).

In 1950 the Gluecks published the findings of a study in which they had compared 500 persistent male delinquents with 500 youths identified as 'proven' non-delinquents (Glueck and Glueck, 1956). The groups were matched for age, race, general intelligence and area of residence. Sixty-seven personality traits and 42 socio-cultural factors were taken into account. Part of their research involved assessing the youths for body type, on the basis of photographs. Sixty per cent of the delinquents were assessed as mesomorphs, compared with 31 per cent of the non-delinquents. Among mesomorphs in both groups there was a higher incidence of traits suited to involvement in aggressive activity, such as physical strength and insensitivity. They were also relatively free from characteristics such as submissiveness to authority, which might discourage delinquent behaviour. However, mesomorphs who actually became delinquent were more likely to display personality traits which were more characteristic of other body types, such as feelings of inadequacy. Socio-cultural factors, such as poor recreational provision, were also found to be related to delinquency among mesomorphs.

Cortes and Gatti (1972) also studied relationships between somatotypes and delinquency. Their samples were smaller than the Gluecks', but included a broader spread of delinquents. All of the Gluecks' delinquents had been placed in institutions, but Cortes and Gatti somatotyped 70 institutionalised delinquents, 30 delinquents on sentences not involving immediate custody, 20 institutionalised adult criminals and 100 non-delinquent high school students. The mean somatotypes of the groups, using Sheldon's rating of 1 to 7, were as follows:

Non-delinquents	3.9	–	3.5	–	3.5
Delinquents	3.5	–	4.4	–	3.1
Adult criminals	2.8	–	5.4	–	3.1

Remember that the centre rating measures mesomorphy. Fifty-seven per cent of the delinquents were found to be high in mesomorphy, compared with 19 per cent of the non-delinquents.

To test whether somatotypes and temperament were linked, 73 per cent of the youths who showed clear signs of a predominant body type were asked to identify which of a set of traits associated with the three types of temperament were applicable to them. A clear association was found between body-type and self-described temperament.

Cortes and Gatti concluded that delinquents differed from non-delinquents by being more mesomorphic in physique, more energetic and aggressive in temperament, and by having a greater motivation and need for achievement. They suggested the same might apply to criminals (1972:348).

Weaknesses in their research, and by implication in the conclusion, include the fact that assessments of temperament were not made objectively, and also a failure to match the samples on the basis of socio-cultural factors. Vold and Bernard point out that although the study shows associations between mesomorphy and delinquency, and links mesomorphy to types of temperament and motivation, it does not expressly support claims for a relationship between delinquency and types of temperament or motivation (1986:65). Clearly, other factors may explain the association between mesomorphy and delinquency.

3.6 Comments on physical type theories

One methodological failing is common to all of the research on which the physical type theories described here are based. All of the criminals tested had been convicted, and in most cases imprisoned. This is problematic for a variety of reasons. Firstly, if there is such a thing as a general criminal population, convicted criminals are not necessarily typical of it as they might represent only the most persistent (or unlucky) offenders. Secondly, the samples of non-criminals fall into that category because of a lack of convictions. Yet they might have felt inclined to offend, or even have committed crime without being caught. Thirdly, such a process of selection assumes that activities prohibited by the criminal law have some objectively defined quality of deviance. It also ignores any sifting processes within the criminal justice system which might result in certain categories of person being over-represented among convicts (Sarbin and Miller, 1970).

Physical type theories can be criticised for ignoring different aspects of the interaction between a person's physical make up and the environment.

At a fairly simple level, people from poorer backgrounds will tend to have a poorer diet and thus be smaller in stature. Youths in manual jobs are more likely to acquire an athletic build. The over representation of such people among convicted criminals may be explained by a variety of socio-cultural, rather than biological, factors. This casts doubt on early claims that physical inferiority and criminality are connected, and on later findings of an association between mesomorphy and delinquency.

Gibbons (1970) argues that the high proportion of mesomorphy among delinquents is probably due to social selection. The nature of their activities is such that delinquents will tend to be drawn from the more athletic members of their age group. Cortes found himself exasperated by that kind of criticism. He suggests it accuses biological explanations of being more exclusive and deterministic than they actually are, and asserts that because physical factors are essential to the social selection which occurs, human behaviour has biological and social causes (Cortes and Gatti, 1972).

Another sociological aspect which is ignored is the question of social reaction. Individuals with more extreme physical deformities have less access to legitimate social pursuits, or may be seen by others as aggressive in appearance. In such circumstances they may become deviant by default, rather than through positive selection.

3.7 Chromosomal anomalies and crime

In a normal human, each cell contains 23 pairs of chromosomes. One of these pairs determines a person's sex. The normal complement of sex chromosomes in a female is XX, and in a male XY, this description being derived from the shape of the chromosomes. However, an abnormal cell division prior to conception may result in an embryo of either sex having more than two sex chromosomes. As the presence of at least one Y chromosome will always result in a male child, an abnormal complement in a female could only consist of, say, an XXX combination. The majority of research in this area concerns males, who may exhibit abnormal chromosome complements such as XXY, XYY, or more rarely, XXYY or XYYY.

Interest in chromosome anomalies was sparked off by investigations of Klinefelter's syndrome, the presence of an XXY complement of chromosomes. This condition was said to be over-represented among inmates of institutions for the subnormal and to be connected with degeneration of the testes.

Later studies looked at institutionalised criminals and focused on individuals with an XYY complement of sex chromosomes, in order to test the hypothesis that they might be characterised by extra maleness and therefore be more aggressive. Several such studies were conducted at a Scottish maximum security mental hospital. Seven XYY men were found among the 196 inmates of the wing for the subnormal, and there were two XYY men on the wing for the mentally ill (Jacobs *et al*, 1965; Price *et al*, 1966). As the estimated occurrence of the XYY abnormality in the general population is 1.5 per 1,000 at the most, these findings were statistically significant. In this, and in other studies, XYY men were found to be exceptionally tall (Casey *et al*, 1966).

An early inference drawn from such results was that XYY males were more likely to be 'dangerous, violent or criminal' (Jacobs *et al*, 1965: 1351). However, Price re-examined the findings of the Scottish studies. The criminal records of the nine XYY inmates were compared against those of 18 inmates with normal chromosomes. On average the normal inmate had a higher number of previous convictions. Perhaps more significantly though, less than 9 per cent of the previous convictions of the XYY group were for offences against the person, compared with almost 22 per cent of those from the XY control group (Price *et al*, 1967). A study by Witkin, in Denmark, confirmed that men with XYY or XXY were not significantly more likely to commit offences involving violence. However, 41 per cent of the XYY men in Witkin's sample had at least one conviction compared with 9 per cent of the XYs (Witkin *et al*, 1977). The presence of extra chromosomes is not put forward as inevitably leading to criminal conduct. However, it does seem clear that a man with an extra Y chromosome is more likely to be institutionalised as a consequence of criminal behaviour. None of the studies has explained this finding, or isolated any link between chromosomal anomalies and actual behaviour.

This type of biological explanation is open to similar criticisms to those levelled against physical type theories. For example, Hunter (1966) has suggested that the abnormal size of XYY males might give them a frightening image which encourages courts and psychiatrists to place them in institutions in order to protect the public. This hypothesis was not supported by Witkin's study.

Theories of crime connected to chromosome anomalies have generated considerable discussion. However, since they can only apply to a very small proportion of the population, they are of limited value in explaining crime.

3.8 Genetic inheritance and criminality

A number of writers have suggested that criminality can be inherited in the same way as other characteristics. Such ideas concern normal genetic inheritance and not the effects of atavism or of mutations at the time of conception.

In the research by Goring (1913), described earlier, he regarded those prisoners with a history of long and frequent sentences as serious criminals. He found them to be inferior to other people, in both physical size and mental ability. Goring accepted that the environment had some impact, but considered these types of inferiority to be inherited. He had found strong correlations between the criminality of children and of their parents, and between the criminality of brothers. He argued that such correlations were not explained by environmental factors. Goring also asserted that his findings could not be explained by learning from the example of other family members. To support that claim, Goring pointed out that the correlation coefficient for stealing was similar to that for sex offences. It was assumed that parents would be open about their dishonesty, but cover their involvement in sex offences. With hindsight, the latter assumption appears naive in view of recent recognition of the widespread nature of child sex abuse. Also, children who were separated from parents at an early age because the latter were imprisoned were as likely, or more likely, to become criminals, when compared with other children not separated in this way. Thus, contact with a criminal parent did not seem to be a factor associated with criminal conduct. Goring therefore claimed that the primary source of criminality was heredity rather than environmental factors.

The major weakness of Goring's claims is that although he took some environmental factors into account, his attempts to control for the effect of environment were inadequate. The result is that environmental factors were not properly assessed, and consequently the influence of heredity was exaggerated (Vold and Bernard, 1986:86).

Any research which attempts to test hereditary influences on crime will be dogged by problems concerning the elimination of environmental effects. Attempts to overcome the problem of balancing heredity against environment have usually centred on two types of research: studies of twins and studies of adoptees.

Studies of twins

There is a clear difference, in genetic terms, between identical twins and fraternal twins. Identical twins occur when a single fertilised egg produces two embryos. They are genetically identical. Fraternal twins are the result of two eggs being fertilised at the same time. They do not have identical heredity and are in the same position as siblings born after separate pregnancies.

It is obvious that differences in the behaviour of identical twins cannot be explained by differences in heredity. It also seems fair to assume that similarities in their conduct might be attributed to inherited characteristics. A number of studies have tested this notion.

The results of one of the better-known studies, by Lange, are described in *Crime as Destiny* (1930). Lange identified a group of 30 men, comprised of 13 identical twins and 17 fraternal twins, all of whom had a record of being imprisoned. In checking the background of the men's twin brothers, Lange found that in 77 per cent of cases for the identical twins, the other brother also had a record of imprisonment. However, for the fraternal twins, only 12 per cent of the second twins had a prison record. This percentaged relationship is referred to as criminal concordance. More than 200 pairs of ordinary brothers, near to each other in age, were compared in a similar way. Where one brother had a record of being imprisoned, the same only applied to the second brother in 8 per cent of cases. Lange concluded from his findings that heredity played a major part in the causation of crime.

In a separate study, Newman (1937) compared 42 pairs of identical twins, and 25 pairs of fraternal twins. A criminal concordance of 93 per cent was found for the identical twins, compared with only 20 per cent for fraternal twins. Two German studies of the same period showed substantial variations in concordance between the two types of twin (Kranz, 1936; Stumpfl, 1936). Work by Scandinavian researchers has cast further light on this area. Christiansen (1968) examined official registers to discover how many of the 6,000 pairs of twins born in Denmark between 1881 and 1910 had a record of crime or delinquency. In the 67 pairs of male identical twins where at least one twin had a criminal record, the criminal concordance was 35.8 per cent. There were 114 pairs of male fraternal twins where at least one brother was recorded as a criminal, but here the criminal concordance was just 12.3 per cent. For females there were 14 pairs of identical twins and 23 pairs of fraternal twins where at least one had a criminal record. The concordance rates were 21.4 per cent and 4.3 per cent respectively. Although in both cases the rates were lower than for males, there was still a noticeable difference between identical and fraternal twins. For both types of twins, Christiansen (1974) found criminal concordance to be higher where more serious offences had been committed.

One difficulty about twin studies is a lack of clarity about the sorts of hereditary factors which are supposed to be passed on. This is important, as variations might manifest themselves in quite different forms of behaviour (Trasler, 1962). For example, some pairs of twins in Lange's study had committed entirely different types of offences from each other. Is it possible that a predisposition to offend is inherited, and that the ultimate form of that offending is determined by other factors?

It should be noted that Christiansen did not use his findings to claim that heredity was the sole or even the dominant factor leading to higher concordance for identical twins. It was his view that twin studies could increase our understanding of the interaction between the environment and individual characteristics. Indeed, he used variations in concordance rates between urban areas and rural areas in his study to suggest that environmental factors might play a greater part in an urban setting.

An easily observed criticism of studies of twins is that they cannot accurately assess the balance between the effects of heredity and those of environment. Twins are more likely than ordinary siblings to share similar experiences in relation to family and peers. It is feasible that such similarities will be greater in the case of identical twins.

Two Norwegian researchers studied 139 pairs of male twins, where at least one twin per pair had been convicted (Dalgard and Kringlen, 1976). Concordances of 25.8 per cent and 14.9 per cent were found for identical and fraternal twins respectively. However, the researchers claimed that when they controlled for mutual closeness, there was no appreciable difference in concordance rates between the types of twin. They stated that hereditary factors were not significant in explaining crime.

Research in relation to twins separated at an early age might prove illuminating (see Forde, 1978). However, the general population does not contain enough twins in that position to support a study from which the results would be generalisable.

Studies of adoptees

A different type of research, to assess whether criminality may be inherited, has involved the study of adoptees. In these cases, contact with a criminal parent has obviously been limited, so that any association between criminality in adoptive children and criminality in their natural parents could be attributed to heredity with a greater degree of certainty than in the case of twins raised alongside delinquent siblings.

Crowe (1972) studied 52 adopted children whose natural mothers had criminal records. He established a control group of 52 children matched against the adoptees for race, sex, and age at the time of adoption. Among the 52 children of criminal mothers, 8 had been arrested (some of them more than once), and 7 of them had been convicted. Only 2 of the control group had been arrested (each on one occasion) and only 1 had been convicted.

Hutchings and Mednick (1977) carried out a study of male adoptees born in Copenhagen between 1927 and 1941. A number of different comparisons were made, producing interesting results. Forty eight point eight per cent of boys with a criminal record, and 37.7 per cent of boys with a record of minor offences, had a natural father with a criminal record. Among boys without a criminal record, 31.1 per cent had a natural father with such a record. The study also discovered that an adoptee was more likely to have a record where both the natural and the adoptive father had previous convictions.

In a further comparison, 143 of the criminal adoptees were matched with 143 non-criminal adoptees according to age and occupational status of the adoptive father. Within this reduced sample, 49 per cent had criminal natural fathers, 18 per cent had criminal natural mothers, and 23 per cent had criminal adoptive fathers, compared with lower percentages for the control group of 28 per cent, 7 per cent and 9.8 per cent respectively.

On the basis of these findings there is a very strong suggestion of a link between hereditary factors and criminality. However, Hutchings and Mednick emphasised that they were not proposing a simple genetic explanation of crime. Instead they supported the likelihood of interaction between biological factors and the environment, by suggesting that some people are genetically endowed with characteristics which render them more likely to 'succumb to crime' (1977:140).

3.9 Biochemical explanations

The notion that behaviour can be affected by different foods or by hormonal imbalance is not new. Schauss (1981) cites examples of research during the early part of the twentieth century which indicated a link between diet and emotional disturbances, learning difficulties and dysfunctional behaviour. In recent times, the perceived connection between food additives and hyperactivity in children has attracted a considerable amount of media attention, as well as the interest of parents and some doctors.

At least one senior police officer takes the question of dietary influences on behaviour seriously and has collaborated with members of other agencies in seeking, first, to identify a link between juvenile offending and the eating of junk food and, secondly, to establish 'medicinal crime prevention' (Bennett, 1992:671). However, the topic has not yet grabbed the attention of mainstream criminologists.

Increased publicity has also been given to the subject of pre-menstrual tension, and some courts have accepted pre-menstrual tension at the time of an offence as part of the mitigating circumstances to be taken into account when sentencing women (Gregory, 1986).

Up to now, biochemical explanations of behaviour have not played a major part in either criminological research or criminology courses. However, a number of studies have provided convincing evidence that a greater display of interest could be worthwhile.

Early studies were inconclusive. Berman (1938) compared a group of prisoners in an American prison against a group of non-criminal males, on the basis of a glandular survey. He made a similar comparison between groups of delinquent and non-delinquent juveniles. In each case, the criminal group was at least twice as prone to glandular disturbances.

Molitch (1937) took a different approach. Two groups were selected from delinquents living in the same institution. Youths in one group suffered from glandular disorders but those in the other did not. The types of behaviour of the youths from the two groups were compared, it being thought that any link between glandular disturbances and behaviour would be manifested in different forms of delinquency. No significant differences were found. However, more recent work outside the field of criminology has suggested that the time may be ripe for a fresh consideration of biochemical factors. The essence of these findings, according to Hippchen, is that 'behaviour associated with delinquency and crime can be caused by chemical deficiencies or imbalances in the body or by brain toxicity' (1977:57).

An orthomolecular theory of behaviour holds that abnormally high or low amounts of natural substances in the brain can lead to irregular patterns of thought and behaviour.

The theory relates to behaviour generally, but some of the dysfunctional behaviour would be regarded as antisocial and sometimes as criminal (Pauling, 1968).

The causes of such chemical imbalances may be genetic or dietary. They are translated into antisocial behaviour in two main ways. First, vitamin deficiencies or food allergies may cause distortions of the perceptive senses, and result in actions which others may regard as delinquent. Secondly, hyperactivity may be caused by consuming food additives, or by hypoglycemia (low blood sugar). Symptoms of hyperactivity can include depression, hallucinations and violent behaviour. A child who is hyperactive may experience learning problems, and be regarded by parents and teachers as a problem child. Thereafter, as an adult, his educational and social skills will be inadequate.

It is noteworthy that orthomolecular theory is not biologically deterministic. The effects of interaction between the human organism and the environment are recognised. Shah and Roth (1974) argue that for too long scientists have tried to treat biological and environmental factors as mutually exclusive, by looking for an either/or explanation of human behaviour. They suggest the explosion of knowledge about biological influences on behaviour should be given greater recognition. Hippchen (1977) calls on criminologists to take part in collaborative work with orthomolecular researchers in order to strengthen criminological theory.

3.10 Intelligence and crime

Theories which try to link criminality to levels of intelligence are difficult to categorise, since it might be argued that intelligence is really an aspect of an individual's personality. However, they are being covered in this chapter because intelligence is often viewed as an innate or inherited ability (Gordon, 1976; Hirschi and Hindelang, 1977). Since the late nineteenth century a variety of different tests have been used to measure intelligence. The history of their development is involved, and even now there is controversy over what they actually measure (Vold and Bernard, 1986:69ff).

Early in the twentieth century, some American researchers were in no doubt that IQ tests were a reliable measure of intelligence, and that this was an inherited and static characteristic. Goddard (1914) tested prisoners himself, and reviewed various other studies of the intelligence of criminals. The median finding from these studies was that 70 per cent of criminals were feeble minded, that is, they had a mental age of 12 or less. Goddard's conclusion was that the majority of criminals were feeble minded. A change of opinion was forced upon him by the results of tests on American army draftees during the First World War. Thirty-seven per cent of whites and 89 per cent of black draftees were identified as feeble minded (Yerkes, 1921). Goddard (1928) now considered that feeblemindedness could be affected by education.

For some decades, interest waned in using intelligence as a factor for explaining crime. Woodward (1955) was adamant that low intelligence played little if any part in delinquency.

However, in the last 25 years or so there has been renewed interest. In their study of 400 London boys, West and Farrington found that low IQ was a 'significant precursor of delinquency' in much the same way as a number of social factors (1973:85). The boys were tested for a variety of characteristics including IQ. As this was a longitudinal study, boys were given scores before anyone could tell which of them would become delinquent. Thus the subjects were not in the same position as a pre-selected sample including only convicted criminals.

The mean IQ score of the boys who subsequently acquired criminal records was 91. For the remainder the mean IQ was 101. This difference was statistically significant.

The data was analysed in other ways. For the boys with only one conviction the mean IQ score was 100, only one fewer than for the non-criminal boys. Recidivists had a mean IQ score of 89. Twenty-nine per cent of boys with a score below 90 became delinquent, and 20 per cent of those were recidivists. West and Farrington noted that many of the boys without a criminal record had committed some delinquent acts, but had not been caught. Of the boys who were caught, not all were convicted.

Such findings cause one to speculate that less intelligent youths might be no more inclined towards delinquency than those of normal intelligence. It might simply be the case that they are more easily caught, and more likely to provide the police with evidence against themselves. This is the reverse of saying that bright delinquents are better equipped to avoid detection. Tennant and Gath (1975) compared 50 delinquents of above average intelligence with 50 delinquents of average intelligence. They were matched for age and race, and their social characteristics were similar. The brighter boys tended to be older than the others when they made their first court appearance and they apparently received more lenient treatment. During the three years after the original interviews, there was no significant difference in recidivism between the two groups.

Another source of objection to the use of IQ tests as a basis for suggesting a connection between low intelligence and criminality is that IQ tests do not measure innate intelligence anyway. It can be argued that a person's performance in such tests is affected by his cultural and educational background, because the tests have an inherent cultural bias (Mercer, 1972; Vold and Bernard, 1986). This objection could explain why, in America, blacks consistently receive lower IQ scores than whites. In relation to findings that delinquents receive lower scores than non-delinquents, Simons (1978) makes the astute observation that delinquents are generally regarded as lacking motivation at school, and there is no reason why they should feel motivated to do their best when taking an IQ test.

Notwithstanding objections to the possible biases of IQ tests, Hirschi and Hindelang (1977) examined various studies and concluded that low IQ was as important in predicting delinquency as were social class and race. Within different races and social classes they found a consistent relationship between low IQ and delinquency. In common with other writers on biological factors, they argue that an emphasis on sociological explanations has prevented IQ from receiving proper attention from criminologists.

3.11 Comments on explanations related to low IQ

Vold and Bernard say it seems clear that 'IQ is correlated with juvenile delinquency' (1986:78). West and Farrington's research supports a similar conclusion. What is not clear is why that correlation exists. It has been said that less intelligent criminals might be easier to catch and therefore be over-represented among recorded delinquents. Yet the correlation does not disappear even when self-reported delinquency is taken into account (Hirschi and Hindelang, 1977).

Trying to explain the correlation is complicated by uncertainty about what IQ scores actually measure. It appears that performance in IQ tests may be influenced by a person's social class, race and other environmental factors. It is also possible that the same factors lead to delinquency. If that were the case, any association between low IQ and delinquency might be coincidental. I prefer to compromise, by seeing intelligence as a partly innate characteristic which develops through interaction with environmental factors and which, through that interaction, may itself influence behaviour.

The last few paragraphs have mostly referred to juvenile delinquency. For adults, when social class is taken into account, there is no significant difference in IQ between criminals and non-criminals. Low intelligence is not a factor which helps us to explain adult crime. This is especially so in relation to organised or white collar crime.

3.12 Policy implications of biological theories

Explanations for crime are not usually sought just to satisfy academic interest. An explicit or implicit aim of many criminologists will be to suggest ways of reducing crime. A biological explanation could be well suited to this since the identification of actual or potential criminals could be very easy. However, this initial appeal might be superficial and the implementation of preventive measures could be a nightmare. The early theorists tended to recommend Draconian policies. Goring (1913) thought that inferior people should be prevented from reproducing. Goddard (1914) said the same about the feebleminded. Hooton (1939) recommended the extermination or complete segregation of organically inferior humans. Maybe we should be thankful that the cruder biological theories have lost popularity.

Orthomolecular theory is more sophisticated and shows promise, but what practical steps could it lead to? Should glandular screening and food allergy tests be made compulsory? Or should biological disturbances be accepted as a full defence to criminal charges? This possibility was once suggested for XYY males (Nielsen, 1968). None of these questions are meant to be frivolous or facetious. Finding an explanation for crime is only one step for criminology. Often, the next step will be to decide what to do about it.

3.13 Conclusion

When reading about some of the early biological theories you may have found it hard to suppress a smile. Some of the wilder, unsupported claims now seem unbelievably naïve. Nevertheless, each of the theories made its own contribution towards the development of criminology. As recently as 1971 Davies urged his readers to study phrenology with more than 'amused attention'.

A lot of the new research has been much more scientific, and some supports the notion that biological factors play a part in the causation of crime. It is refreshing to see that supporters of the more recent biological explanations recognise the effect of interaction between biological factors and the environment. Perhaps more sociologists should meet them half way.

4

Psychological and Psychiatric Explanations

4.1 Introduction

This chapter opens with a caveat. Having read the title, you may be looking forward to reading about the contributions of two clearly defined and separate disciplines towards our understanding of crime. Don't you believe it! If you thumb through various general criminology textbooks, or even some specialist books about psychology and crime, you may notice a tendency for the borders between psychology, psychoanalysis, and psychiatry to become blurred. Vold and Bernard (1986) include a chapter entitled *The Personality of the Offender* in which they state that the personality of offenders is generally included in psychological and psychiatric explanations of criminal behaviour. The remainder of that chapter then concentrates on psychoanalytical explanations, psychological tests of personality, and specific personality types. It is pointed out that other types of psychological and psychiatric explanations see criminal behaviour as originating in an offender's biology or environment rather than in his personality. However, even within such an excellent textbook, the divisions between the different types of theory are not crystal clear. The work of Hans Eysenck (see below) is often dealt with as a 'personality theory' (see Hall Williams, 1982:71), but Vold and Bernard divide it between chapters on biological explanations and on control theories.

The apparent confusion need not be a problem. Distinctions are often made on arbitrary grounds, but that is acceptable provided the limitations of such an approach are recognised. The present chapter will give only limited coverage of psychiatric theories, on the basis that they deal with abnormal behaviours with a pathological origin, and that they can therefore only explain a limited range of criminal acts. The major part of the chapter will take a selective look at psychological explanations, and in particular at those which concentrate on the ways in which people are socialised. The final sections will examine links between personality and crime, and psychopathy.

4.2 Socialisation, a brief explanation

Within psychology, there are several models for explaining human behaviour. However, for present purposes, it is not necessary to explore them all. Instead, a more straightforward division will be made. Feldman (1977) suggests that psychologists fall into two camps when accounting for criminal behaviour:

1. The first concentrates on the failure to acquire attitudes which oppose criminal activity.
2. The second is concerned with the positive acquisition of attitudes favourable to criminal behaviour.

According to each of these perspectives, attitudes are acquired through a learning process which has characteristics similar to any other form of learning. Supporters of the first camp, and some psychologists who fall into the second, tend to emphasise the effects of a person's early relationships, particularly with his or her parents. These types of explanation will be examined first.

One aspect of the second perspective is known as 'differential association theory':

it is really a social theory rather than an individually based one, and will be dealt with in Chapter 6.

4.3 Child/parent relationships, a psychoanalytic perspective

The psychoanalytical model

The field of psychoanalysis developed through the work of Sigmund Freud. A brief summary cannot do justice to the full range of his theories but for readers with a particular interest, Freud (1935) provides a useful introduction.

Within a psychoanalytical model, the human personality has three sets of interacting forces. These are:

1. the id (the primitive biological drives); and
2. the superego (which operates in the unconscious but is comprised of values which are internalised through a person's early interactions, particularly with his parents); and
3. the ego (the conscious personality). The ego has the task of balancing the demands of the id against the inhibitions imposed by the superego, as a person responds to external influences.

Aichhorn's concept of latent delinquency

In his book *Wayward Youth*, first published in 1925, August Aichhorn put forward an explanation (and proposed treatment) for juvenile delinquency. This took a psychoanalytical perspective and was developed through Aichhorn's work with delinquent children. Aichhorn's explanation involves the concept of latent delinquency. At birth a child has certain instinctive drives for which it demands satisfaction. It is unaware of, and obviously unaffected by, the norms of the society around it. Aichhorn describes such a child as being in an 'asocial state' and says that the task is to bring the child into a social state (1925:4). When a child's development is ineffective he remains asocial. If his instinctive drives are not acted out, they are suppressed and he is in a state of latent delinquency. Given outside 'provocation' the latent delinquency could be translated into actual delinquent behaviour (1925:41).

Aichhorn considered that many of the delinquents with whom he had worked had underdeveloped superegos. He suggested this lack of development was caused by the absence of an intimate attachment between such children and their parents, owing to a lack of parental affection. His technique for treating these children was to place them in a happy environment where they could identify with adults in a way they had not experienced with their parents. The aim of such identification was to help to develop the child's superego.

Aichhorn also found different categories of delinquent. Some delinquents had fully developed superegos but they had identified with parents who were themselves criminal. Others were used to being allowed to do whatever they liked by over-indulgent parents.

Healy and Bronner

Healy and Bronner (1936) put forward a psychoanalytic explanation which was broadly supportive of Aichhorn. This was based on research into the family backgrounds of 105 pairs of brothers in three American cities. In each case, one brother was a persistent delinquent and the other a non-delinquent. Healy and Bronner found that 19 of the delinquents and 30 of the non-delinquents lived in family conditions which were apparently favourable. Eighty-six delinquents and 75 non-delinquents lived in family circumstances which were apparently inimical (unfavourable). These findings show that within a household, circumstances may be favourable for one sibling but not for another. The authors found that the human relationships of the non-delinquent had been distinctly more satisfactory than those of the delinquent. The latter had not made an emotional attachment to a 'good parent'. This was said to have impeded the development of an 'ego-ideal' (1936:10). The same findings also indicate that siblings exposed to similar inimical circumstances may react differently. One may become delinquent whilst the other does not. The explanation offered by Healy and Bronner was that the delinquents were more emotionally disturbed and expressed their thwarted needs through activities regarded as delinquent. The non-delinquents' frustrated needs were channelled into other socially acceptable activities.

Healy and Bronner equated the superego with conscience and emphasised that the growth and effect of conscience are complicated matters which vary between individuals. Thus a person's conscience might condemn stealing but condone lying, or vice versa (1936:12).

Comments on the psychoanalytical approach

A number of other writers produced variations on the psychoanalytic theme. Redl and Wineman (1951) suggested that aggressive children possessed a delinquent ego. Such children had not identified with parents because of a lack of affection and security.

Psychoanalytic explanations have influenced modern psychiatric practice, and the views of those responsible for the care of convicted offenders (Jones, 1956; Vold and Bernard, 1986). There should be some concern about this, in view of the standard criticisms levelled at psychoanalytic theory:

1. Its concepts are so loosely defined and subjective that they cannot be tested (Trasler, 1967:36).
2. The effectiveness of psychoanalytic treatment is questionable (Schwitzgebel, 1974).

Hollin (1989) suggests the use of psychoanalytic explanations for crime is waning and cites the reason given by Rutter and Giller (1983) that such theories have neither helped to explain crime nor helped to provide preventive strategies.

4.4 Maternal deprivation

In 1944, John Bowlby proposed an explanation for delinquency which was more restricted than other theories related to early childhood experiences, in that it focused on maternal deprivation. Maternal deprivation occurred when a child had not enjoyed a 'warm, intimate and continuous relationship' with its mother (Bowlby and Salter-Ainsworth, 1965:14).

Bowlby had studied 44 juvenile thieves referred to the child guidance clinic where he worked. He compared them with a control group of 44 children, matched for age and intelligence, who had been referred to the same clinic, but not in connection with stealing. The sample of thieves was not randomly selected. Few had appeared in court, and there was variation in the frequency of past offending. Most of the children in each sample were referred to the clinic by parents. The control group was not checked for the presence of thieves. The study was therefore open to criticism on methodological grounds (Morgan, 1975; Feldman, 1977).

Bowlby found that out of the 44 thieves, 17 had been separated from their mothers for periods of at least six months, before the age of five. Only two of the controls had been affected in this way. Based on interviews with the children, Bowlby identified 14 of the thieves as 'affectionless characters'. None of the controls attracted that label. The term 'affectionless character' indicated a person who found difficulty in forming close personal relationships. It is noteworthy that two of the affectionless characters had not suffered maternal deprivation, and also that five of the 17 thieves who had suffered such deprivation were not regarded as affectionless characters.

4.5 Evaluation of maternal deprivation as an explanation of delinquency

Bowlby's theory had a substantial and long-lasting influence on the training of social workers (Morgan, 1975). It also provoked considerable interest among researchers, several of whom have tried to test it empirically. In general they suggest that separation of a child from its mother does not, in itself, significantly affect the likelihood of the child becoming delinquent. Research by Andry (1957) and by Grygier (1969) indicated a need to take account of the roles of both parents. Andry also emphasised that although more of the delinquents in Bowlby's samples had suffered maternal deprivation when compared with the non-delinquents, the majority of the delinquents had not experienced lengthy separation from their mothers, and most were not affectionless characters.

Naess's comparison of delinquents and non-delinquents showed that the former were no more likely to have been separated from their mothers than the latter (1959, 1962). A study by Little (1965) involved a sample of 500 boys sentenced to borstal training. Eighty per cent had been separated from at least one parent, for varying periods. Separations from the father were more common. Little found that the frequency of separation had no consistent correlation with the age of the children when first convicted, with the type of offence, or with the extent of recidivism.

So often, critics of particular theories paint an exaggerated picture of them, and then shower them with criticism. Both Andry (1962) and Prins (1982) point out that this may have happened to Bowlby, since he never claimed that maternal deprivation could account for all delinquency, and that in any event he has modified his early claims (Bowlby, 1979). Several writers have subjected Bowlby's theory to careful scrutiny.

For example, Wootton (1959, 1962) argues there is no evidence that any effects of separation of a child from its mother will be irreversible. She points out that only a small proportion of delinquents may be affected in this way. Wootton also refers to the lack of information about the extent of maternal separation in the general population (as does Little, 1965).

Clarke and Clarke (1976) review various studies and suggest that much of the earlier research concentrated too closely on the role of the mother and on the early years of childhood. They would prefer to see a greater focus on the quality of a child's upbringing.

Rutter's book *Maternal Deprivation Reassessed* (1981) is one of the better-known examinations of the maternal deprivation hypothesis. Like others, Rutter emphasises the short-sightedness of focusing on maternal separation *per se*. Instead, he says, the concept of adequate mothering must be broken down (1982:18). He identifies six different features of that concept:

1. a loving relationship;
2. attachment;
3. an unbroken relationship;
4. stimulating interaction;
5. the relationship should be with one person;
6. it should take place in the child's home.

Rutter considers the stability of the relationship to be more important than the absence of breaks. He believes a small number of substitutes can carry out mothering functions, without adverse effect, provided that such mothering is of good quality. Rutter also doubts the necessity of the relationship taking place in the child's own home. Although some of these features are important, the child has other needs, such as food, discipline, play and conversation. Rutter emphasises that privation is of more significance than separation on its own. By this, he means that the child's upbringing is lacking in quality in some way. Similarly, privation is related to the standard of the child's care or its relationships with people around it, rather than the single relationship with its mother. Following his own discussion of the theory, Hall Williams comments that 'the myth of maternal deprivation has been exploded' (1982:66).

Feldman (1977) suggests that maternal deprivation theory ignores social training and the methods associated with it. It is to a consideration of child-rearing practices that we now turn.

4.6 Child rearing practices

Chapter 3 included some discussion of the work of Glueck and Glueck (1950). Their study of 500 delinquents and 500 non-delinquents examined factors other than physique. For example, in relation to the child rearing techniques adopted by parents, Glueck and Glueck found that the fathers of delinquents provided discipline which was generally lax and erratic. For the delinquent group, the use of physical punishment by both parents was common, and the giving of praise rare. Parents of the non-delinquents used physical punishment less often and were firm but consistent in their use of discipline.

McCord *et al* (1954) obtained data on the family circumstances of 253 10-year old boys. They subsequently compared the backgrounds of those boys who had gone on to become delinquent with those of the boys who had not. Inconsistent and lax use of discipline, together with punitive treatment was found to be associated with delinquent behaviour. In this study, and that by the Gluecks, the consistency of discipline was regarded as more important than the degree of strictness.

A further example of inconsistent parental practices was provided by Bandura and Walters' comparison of 26 boys with a record of aggressive behaviour, against a control group of boys without such a history (1959). Fathers of the aggressive boys were more likely to punish the use of aggressive behaviour in the home whilst approving of such behaviour outside. They used physical punishments more often than the fathers of the controls.

A study by Hoffman and Saltzstein (1967) breaks down child training techniques in a slightly more sophisticated fashion. They identify three types of technique. These are:

1. *Power assertion.* The parent uses or threatens to use physical punishment and/or withdrawal of material privileges.
2. *Love withdrawal.* The parent withdraws or threatens to withdraw affection from the child, for example, by paying no attention to it.
3. *Induction.* By letting the child know how its actions have affected the parent, the latter encourages a sympathetic or empathetic response.

There is a fundamental difference between the first technique and the other two, so far as their influence on the child's subsequent behaviour is concerned. Power assertion is concerned with the development of an external orientation, connected to fear of being detected and punished by someone else. Withdrawal of love, and induction are concerned with the development of an internal orientation based on guilt. This latter orientation operates independently of external punishments (Feldman, 1977).

Hoffman and Saltzstein assessed the moral development of middle and working class children of both sexes, by means of a questionnaire. Interviews were conducted to discover the types of training technique used by parents. For the middle class sample, a high level of moral development was associated with parental use of induction, an intermediate level with withdrawal of love, and the lowest level with power assertion. In the working class group, the associations between moral development and training technique were less distinct, but induction had been used more rarely than in the other group. Earlier studies had suggested that techniques related to the withdrawal of affection or encouragement of empathy were more effective in developing an internal orientation towards the consequences of behaviour (Aronfreed, 1961; Burton *et al*, 1961).

Feldman (1977) summarises Hoffman and Saltzstein's own explanations for the association between moral development and use of different training techniques. These may be interrelated and, condensed even further, are as follows:

1. An open display of anger and aggression by a parent when disciplining a child increases the child's dependence on external control. Punishment connected with power assertion dissipates the parent's anger and the child's guilt more rapidly.
2. Love withdrawal and induction, and the anxiety associated with them, have a longer-lasting effect so that the development of internal control is more likely.
3. Where love withdrawal is used, the punishment ends when the child confesses or makes reparation (referred to as engaging in a corrective act), but in the case of physical punishment there is likely to be a lapse of time between its being carried out and the child performing a corrective act.
4. Withholding of love intensifies the child's resolve to behave in an approved manner in order to retain love.
5. Use of induction is particularly effective in enabling the child to examine and correct the behaviours which have been disapproved of.

People trained through the use of the love withdrawal or induction techniques are considered more likely to avoid proscribed acts and to redress those they have committed. This is because of the greater effect which internalised controls are said to have. As people trained by the power assertion method depend on the threat of external punishment to control their behaviour, they will only remain controlled so long as that risk is present, certain and sufficiently intense. Feldman remarks that internal controls are much more likely to be permanently 'on duty' (1977:52).

A number of studies have gone beyond child rearing practices to assess the relevance of more general features of the family unit in the aetiology of criminal behaviour.

4.7 Family circumstances

The broken home must be one of the most widely known reputed causes of delinquency. Research in both Britain and the United States has suggested that the broken home may be a factor in the development of delinquency, but caution is necessary.

Not surprisingly, the Gluecks' famous study measured the frequency of broken homes among its samples and found that 60 per cent of the delinquents came from such a home, compared with only 34 per cent of the non-delinquents (1950:122).

In Britain, Burt (1945) and Mannheim (1948) provide examples of research which finds that a high proportion of delinquents are from broken homes. However, Bowlby (1952) and Mannheim (1955) in Britain, and Tappan (1960) in America have all pointed out that the broken home cannot be regarded as a singular concept. The family unit must be broken down into smaller parts so that the effects of different factors can be examined. This seems obvious in the light of findings such as that by Nye (1958), which noted that delinquency was more likely to occur among children from intact but unhappy homes rather than among those from broken homes. Gibbens (1963) makes a similar point in his study of boys in borstal.

Wootton (1959) subjected explanations based on the broken home to a critical attack. For example, she highlighted the lack of information about the frequency of broken homes among the general population. She also pointed out that different researchers adopted different definitions of a broken home, so that comparisons of results would be unreliable.

West (1969) echoed Wootton's comment about the difficulty of defining what a broken home is. However, in his study with Farrington (1973), West found that about twice as many delinquents, compared with controls, came from homes broken by parental separation before the child was 10 years old. Comparing children from a home broken by separation with those from homes broken by a parent's death, more children from the former became delinquents. Furthermore, 20 per cent of delinquents in the former group became recidivists, whereas none of those from the second group did.

West examines various factors other than the straightforward existence of a broken home, including parental discipline, neglect and instability. As one might expect, unsatisfactory parenting was found to increase the likelihood of delinquency. The quality of family relationships and the existence of tension within the home are now considered to be of more importance than whether or not a child comes from a broken home. Part of the overall picture is summed up by West: 'Socially deprived, unloving, erratic, inconsistent, and careless parents tend to produce badly behaved boys' (1969:197).

4.8 Socialisation, concluding comments

Broadly speaking, each of the types of explanation discussed in this section has considered ways in which children learn to behave in acceptable ways, or put another way, how they learn *not* to offend. From that perspective, delinquent behaviour can be viewed as a consequence of inefficient training. Other types of theory suggest that people learn *to* offend. As these involve a wider social environment than the theories mentioned here, they will be dealt with in Chapter 6.

Some psychologists hold that a person's capacity to learn types of behaviour and to internalise norms is affected by biological factors. Therefore some people are more susceptible to attempts at socialisation than others. This is an important aspect of the theory of Hans Eysenck which will be covered in the next section.

4.9 Personality and crime

The writings of Hans Eysenck probably represent the most widely-known attempt to explain criminal behaviour by reference to personality. Eysenck's theory is not easy to categorise. Although it falls under the above heading in this book, it is sometimes described as a learning theory or as a control theory. The reasons for this will become obvious.

Although Eysenck accepts that external stimuli have a part to play in the occurrence of criminal behaviour, he believes the major role is played by individual dispositions which are largely inherited and long lasting.

4.10 Eysenck's dimensions of personality

Much of Eysenck's earlier work (eg 1959) describes two dimensions of personality:

1. Extroversion: this has two different components, impulsiveness and sociability, which are partly independent of each other.
2. Neuroticism.

In 1968, a third dimension was introduced, namely:

3. Psychoticism (HJ Eysenck and SBG Eysenck).

Each dimension takes the form of a continuum, running from high to low. Low extroversion is alternatively referred to as introversion. For neuroticism, a person with a high score would be regarded as neurotic, and someone with a low score as stable.

Few people would fall at the extremes of any of the dimensions. Most would fit somewhere between high and low on the continuum. Scores are usually obtained by the use of a personality questionnaire of which there are several versions. It is customary to abbreviate the descriptions of a person's score, for example, high N, low E, high P.

Different characteristics correspond with the personality dimensions. Thus, someone with a high E score would be outgoing and sociable, optimistic and impulsive. A high N person would be anxious, moody and highly sensitive. Low scores on these dimensions would show the opposite of those traits.

Uncertainty has been expressed about what the P scale measures (Howarth, 1986). However, the following traits are taken to correspond with psychoticism: insensitivity to others; a liking for solitude; sensation-seeking; and a lack of regard for danger (Eysenck, 1970). A similarity has been noted between this description of psychoticism, and psychopathy (Feldman, 1977). Psychopathy is explored in '4.12 Psychopathy defined' (below).

It is the way in which Eysenck links these personality dimensions to criminal behaviour that invites his theory to be regarded as a learning theory or control theory. Within Eysenck's theory, the successfulness of a child's socialisation towards acceptable behaviour depends on the extent to which it is conditioned (or learns) to avoid acts which attract disapproval, for example, from parents. An alternative interpretation is to say that conditioning leads to the development of a conscience. Where the conscience is strong, antisocial behaviour is associated with the punitive response it attracts, and is therefore avoided. The effectiveness of this conscience in causing avoidance of offending behaviour will be determined by the effectiveness of the conditioning process.

Eysenck suggests that each of the personality dimensions has a genetic origin. In relation to extroversion and neuroticism, he claims that each has a biological basis.

Extroversion is said to be related to an individual's level of cortical arousal. Stimuli are transmitted to the cortex via the nervous system. In extroverts, the cortex receives less stimulation, so that they are under-aroused. They seek excitement to make up for this. Introverts are more prone to cortical over-arousal, which is unpleasant. Therefore, they will avoid activities which generate unwelcome stimuli.

An introvert achieves cortical arousal more quickly, and maintains it for a longer period. An introvert is therefore more likely than an extrovert to develop inhibitions about certain types of behaviour, as a result of conditioning. In other words, extroverts do not learn non-offending behaviour as effectively as introverts. A high E score is therefore expected to be correlated with more frequent offending.

According to Eysenck, the biological basis of neuroticism lies in the autonomic nervous system. An individual with a high N score has an unstable autonomic nervous system which reacts powerfully to unpleasant stimuli. Levels of anxiety are generated which interfere with the process of conditioning because they are excessive in relation to the stimuli which provoked the reaction. Someone with a low N score conditions well because any feelings of anxiety are in proportion to the fear-producing stimuli which are important to Eysenck's notion of social training.

Combinations of the different personality dimensions within individuals will affect their ability to learn not to offend, and consequently their level of offending. Someone with a high E + high N score (a neurotic extrovert) will not condition well. A low E + low N scorer (stable introvert) will be most effectively conditioned. Stable extroverts and neurotic introverts come somewhere between the two extremes in terms of conditioning.

A positive relationship is claimed between psychoticism and the level of offending. Eysenck states 'we would expect persons with strong antisocial inclinations to have high P, high E, and high N scores' (1977:58).

It is important to note that Eysenck does not suggest that all crimes will be strongly antisocial. Nor does he claim that all, or even most, criminals will be psychotic. Eysenck has suggested that attempts to explain crime will be more successful if they focus on certain types of offenders rather than trying to encompass all types of crime (Eysenck, 1963).

A number of studies have attempted to test Eysenck's theory. A representative sample of these will now be briefly discussed.

4.11 Evaluation of Eysenck's theory

Little (1963) tested borstal trainees and compared their scores on the extroversion and neuroticism dimensions against scores for non-delinquents. There was no difference in relation to extroversion, but the borstal trainees scored slightly higher on the neuroticism scale. Neither dimension was found to be related to recidivism.

Hoghughi and Forrest (1970) gave scores for neuroticism and extroversion to a sample of youths in an approved school and compared them to non-delinquents. The detained youths were rated higher on neuroticism, but it is possible that the experience of being institutionalised causes people to become more neurotic than they were at the time of their offending. The approved school youths were also shown to be *less* extroverted than the controls, and Hoghughi and Forrest considered the former would be 'very amenable to social conditioning' (1970:244).

In a study by Hans and Sybil Eysenck, 178 borstal trainees were tested on all three personality dimensions. They were followed up after their release and it was found that 122 had been convicted again. The recidivists were found to score significantly higher in relation to extroversion. There were slight differences for the other dimensions, but they were not statistically significant.

A number of self-report studies have tested the relevance of E, N and P scores in relation to younger offenders. Feldman cites studies by Gibson (1967), and Allsopp and Feldman (1975, 1976) where school children reported their own involvement in antisocial behaviour. Not all the behaviours covered would amount to criminal offences – some involved breaches of school rules. Gibson found that self-reported offending was positively associated with extroversion and neuroticism (the higher the score, the higher the rate of offending). Allsopp and Feldman's 1975 study involved girls between 11 and 15 years old. They found a significant and positive association between scores for E, N and P and levels of antisocial behaviour. The strongest association was in relation to psychoticism. Their 1976 study of schoolboys made similar findings.

Comparatively less research has been done in relation to adult criminals. Feldman summarises the results (1977:145). Where E and N scores for prisoners have been compared with those for non-prisoners, prisoners receive higher scores for neuroticism. Recidivists were more neurotic than first offenders. As mentioned earlier, neuroticism might be influenced by the experience of detection and imprisonment rather than being biologically determined.

There is little evidence that adult criminals are more extrovert than non-criminals (Feldman, 1077:145). However, Eysenck has pointed out that extroversion has two components, sociability and impulsiveness. Eysenck considers impulsiveness to be associated with criminal behaviour, whereas sociability is of less importance in that respect (1970:143). Many personality tests provide a score for extroversion which combines scores for the two components. Therefore, a person who is highly impulsive but very unsociable will receive an intermediate E score.

The predicted association between psychoticism and criminal behaviour has only been the subject of a small amount of research. Eysenck and Eysenck (1970) compared English prisoners against controls and found support for Eysenck's own prediction in relation to psychoticism. Smith and Smith (1977) tested male probationers and found a positive relationship between psychoticism and the likelihood of reconviction. In a study by McEwan (1983), delinquents with a high P score had more previous convictions than the other delinquents.

The findings of McGurk and McDougall, shown in the table below, indicate that combinations or clusters of scores for the three dimensions are more important than scores for individual dimensions. For example, according to Eysenck's theory, the two clusters which are most likely to be associated with criminal behaviour are high E + high N and high P + high E + high N. These clusters only occurred among the delinquents in the study by McGurk and McDougall. Similarly, the only individuals with a low E + low N combined score were found in the non-delinquent group. Low E + high N and high E + low N clusters were found in both groups.

Table 3: *Cluster analysis of P, E and N scores per Eysenck's theory*

Cluster	Delinquents % in cluster group	Non-delinquents % in cluster group
Low E + high N	32	17
High E + low N	26	36
High E + high N	30	0
Low E + low N	0	13
High P + high E + high N	12	0
High P	0	34

(Source of data: McGurk and McDougall (1981).)

The work by Allsopp and Feldman (1975), mentioned earlier, also indicated the value of combining personality scores rather than concentrating on E, N or P in isolation.

A small amount of work has been done to test for a relationship between personality types and offence type. Hindelang and Weis (1972) classified 245 middle class, male, high school students into the four combinations of scores for E and N. Scores were then compared with the seven groups of offences which the students had reported committing. For general deviance (minor offences such as vandalism) and traffic offences, the descending order of offending was as predicted, namely, high E + high N; high E + low N or low E + high N, then low E + low N. However, this was not true of theft or offences involving aggression. SBG Eysenck *et al* (1977) found that groups of offenders involved in violence or property offences had lower N scores than other groups. Conmen had lower P scores. There was no variation for E scores. A study by McEwan and Knowles (1984) found no association between offence type and personality cluster.

4.12 Psychopathy defined

In England and Wales, the Mental Health Act 1983 defines psychopathic disorder as 'a persistent disorder or disability of mind (whether or not including significant impairment of intelligence) which results in abnormally aggressive or seriously irresponsible conduct' (s1(2)). That definition is not particularly helpful, as the various phrases within it are not themselves explained.

In any event, one would probably expect psychiatrists to look beyond a legal definition. One alternative is to identify the characteristics which a psychopath displays.

Cleckley (1976) produced a list of 16 characteristics, based on clinical observations. Hare (1980) provided a more concise summary, including five factors which characterise a psychopath. These are:

1. inability to develop warm, empathetic relationships;
2. unstable life-styles;
3. inability to accept responsibility for antisocial behaviour;
4. absence of psychiatric problems; and
5. weak control over behaviour.

The American Psychiatric Association (1968) provides a definition which emphasises such traits as an incapacity for loyalty, selfishness, irresponsibility, impulsiveness, inability to feel guilt, and failure to learn from experience. One feature which is common to most descriptions is a lack of empathy or affection for other people (Croft, 1966; Blackburn and Maybury, 1985).

Hare (1980) also produced a checklist of 22 items for assessing whether or not a criminal is a psychopath. Examples of those items include superficial charm; a parasitic life-style; pathological lying; and short-temperedness. Davies and Feldman (1981) collated 22 signs which psychiatrists use to recognise psychopathy. These include lack of control over impulses; inability to experience guilt; and being aggressive.

4.13 Psychopathic individuals or psychopathic behaviour?

Some of the items identified above are clearly forms of behaviour. Others might be regarded as personality traits but, if so, they are only discernible from behaviour. One of the difficult questions about psychopathy is whether there are people who are psychopaths, or whether a better view is that some people are sometimes involved in psychopathic behaviour. If the latter is correct, then it is circular reasoning to suggest that because a person exhibits certain types of behaviour, he therefore has a certain type of personality. Feldman argues that the notion of '*the* psychopath' as a separate type of person may be erroneous, and he favours the study of psychopathic *behaviour* (1977:169). Hare (1970) had made a similar point, but felt that research could be conducted without formally taking one side or the other. Feldman points out that most research and Hare's review (1970) assumes the existence of a psychopathic type.

Before we examine some of the relevant research, it is worth mentioning that American literature often uses the terms 'sociopath' or 'antisocial personality' as synonyms for psychopath (Vold and Bernard, 1986:122).

4.14 Empirical studies of psychopathy

The different types of research into psychopathy can be classified in various ways. However, in the interests of simplicity, the studies will be divided into those which deal with: background factors, physiological functioning and studies of learning.

Background factors

McCord and McCord (1964) suggested that a lack of parental affection was one of the factors contributing to later psychopathic behaviour. In a longitudinal study, Robins (1966) found that children who subsequently behaved in a psychopathic manner were more likely to have had fathers who were themselves psychopathic or alcoholic. However, Cleckley (1964) found that many of his psychopathic patients came from a family environment which was suited to happy development. Hare (1970) points out that most people from disturbed backgrounds do not go on to become psychopaths. In any event, childhood deprivation may increase the likelihood of a variety of behavioural disturbances other than psychopathy.

Physiological functioning

A number of researchers have studied the functioning of the central nervous system, by using the electroencephalogram (EEG) test for abnormalities in the electrical activity of the brain in psychopaths. The findings are far from conclusive. Syndulko (1978) suggests that irregularities are frequently shown in EEG testing of psychopaths. Hare and Jutari (1986) found that the EEGs of psychopaths were normal while they were active, but were abnormal when they were resting.

A different group of studies have examined the functioning of the autonomic nervous system in psychopaths. The level of activity in the autonomic nervous system is usually assessed by measuring the conductivity of the skin (electrodermal reactivity) and the level of cardiac reactivity. Some research has shown that while they are under stress, psychopaths show a high level of cardiac reactivity, but that when they are resting their level of electrodermal reactivity is exceptionally low (Jutari and Hare, 1983). Hollin (1989) offers a possible explanation for these findings. The fast heart rate may be a sign that the psychopath is lowering the level of cortical arousal by 'gating out' the sensory input related to unpleasant situational stimuli.

These findings can also be tied to earlier research. Quay (1965) postulated a link between low levels of autonomic arousal in psychopaths and a tendency to seek stimulation. Feldman (1977) reviews some of the research and suggests there is indirect evidence that psychopaths are more prone than non-psychopaths to seek increases in stimulation. We saw earlier that Eysenck argues that extroverts are apt to seek excitement, and in fact Eysenck (1964) also found that diagnosed psychopaths are mostly extroverted. This similarity between some of the features of psychopathy and those of extroversion highlights the possible relevance of the personality characteristics of psychopaths in explaining their antisocial behaviour.

Studies of learning

Extroverts are said to be more difficult to socialise because of difficulties in learning. This might also apply to psychopaths, and the difficulties may have a physiological basis.

If this is so, a related assumption would be that psychopaths will be very poor at learning to avoid the unpleasant stimuli associated with particular acts (referred to as passive avoidance learning). That assumption is supported by several studies (Lykken, 1955; Scura and Eisenman, 1971; Chesno and Kilmann, 1975). Hollin (1989) points out that results from this type of study can vary according to the type of unpleasant stimulus used. When poor performance in learning tests was met with physical pain (usually by means of an electric shock) or by disapproval, psychopaths obtained worse results than controls. However, psychopaths were better learners when the consequence of a mistake was a financial penalty (Hollin cites Schmauk, 1970).

Some studies have examined the responsiveness of psychopaths to reward learning. In these tests, correct responses are rewarded by social reinforcement, such as approval. Feldman reviews several studies (1977:174). He shows that the findings are mixed and do not clearly show psychopaths to be less amenable than non-psychopaths to reward learning.

4.15 Cautious conclusions about research into psychopathy

Feldman (1977) points out that the subjects of research into psychopathy may well be unrepresentative. In order for researchers to be aware of them, the subjects must have come to notice. This will frequently mean that they are incarcerated. It is argued that psychopathic behaviours may be widespread and that psychopaths might be found in legitimate professions, such as business, medicine and psychiatry (Cleckley, 1976). Unless their behaviour corresponds with legally proscribed activities, the individuals involved will not come to the notice of the criminal justice system. In addition, given the vague definition of psychopathic disorder, diagnoses will vary between practitioners and between areas. Therefore, samples of psychopaths and non-psychopaths may each include individuals who should be in the other group. Furthermore, the assessments of imprisoned subjects might reflect the experience of imprisonment (Feldman, 1977).

Nevertheless, putting together the results of the different types of learning studies, there is some evidence that psychopaths may be under-socialised because of the way they learn. In addition, those difficulties might stem from physiological factors.

4.16 Comments about psychopathy

Hollin comments that 'the psychopath remains something of a puzzle' (1989:122). Certainly, the term is poorly-defined. Vold and Bernard suggest that the term *psychopath* is useful as shorthand for psychiatrists who wish to describe a certain type of person who exhibits particular types of behaviour and attitudes. They argue that when it is applied to criminals, the term seems to be merely a label attached to especially serious offenders. It does nothing to help recognise such offenders in advance, or to explain their behaviour, or to prescribe suitable treatment (1986:124).

Psychopathy is a concept which has captured the attention of many practitioners in the fields of psychology, psychiatry and criminal justice. The psychopath is a frequently occurring *bête noire* in crime fiction. Nevertheless, these terms have done little to help explain crime or delinquency.

4.17 Conclusion

Not surprisingly, Eysenck takes a view of the potential contribution of psychology to the control of crime which is both optimistic about that discipline and dismissive about others: 'modern psychology holds out to society ... an approach geared only to practical ends, such as elimination of antisocial conduct, and not cluttered with irrelevant, philosophical, retributory and ethico-religious beliefs' (1977:213).

This chapter illustrates that, although psychology has provided some insights into the causation of criminal behaviour, it has not identified the means for bringing an end to antisocial conduct. Trasler (1962) seems more open minded and constructive when he emphasises the need for continual cross-fertilization between the work of psychologists and sociologists. He accepts the impossibility of developing an explanation of crime which ignores information about social class and about group values and attitudes. The next part of this book will examine sociological contributions to our understanding of crime.

5

Social Ecology

5.1 Introduction

5.2 Research by the Chicago School

5.3 Social disorganisation and cultural transmission

5.4 Methodological limitations of the Chicago School research

5.5 British area studies

5.6 Concluding comments about area studies of crime

5.1 Introduction

In the 1930s, a branch of urban sociology, often referred to as the Chicago School of human ecology, opened up a new approach to explaining crime. This school grew from the ideas of Robert Park, who suggested there were parallels between communities of humans and those of plants and animals (Park *et al*, 1925; Park, 1952). Park adopted some of his central concepts from biology. A city comprised several natural areas with characteristics blended from their ethnic composition, socio-economic make-up, and physical surroundings. A web of symbiotic relationships operated within and between these areas, and together they represented a super-organism, the city.

Patterns of change in the city paralleled changes in the balance of nature. They were influenced by economic competition for space, and the urban environment was affected by a process of invasion, dominance and succession. Park viewed the human population in American cities as being migratory, rather than fixed. New immigrants would move into the poor areas, replacing the previous inhabitants who were moving out. The latter were leaving partly because their economic standing had improved, enabling them to afford better accommodation, but also to escape the increasing dominance of the newcomers.

Burgess found that the city showed a tendency for radial expansion, in which a pattern of concentric circles moved outward. He described the areas within the circle as 'zones' and illustrated them in the form of a chart (see Fig 2):

Fig 2: *The growth of the city*

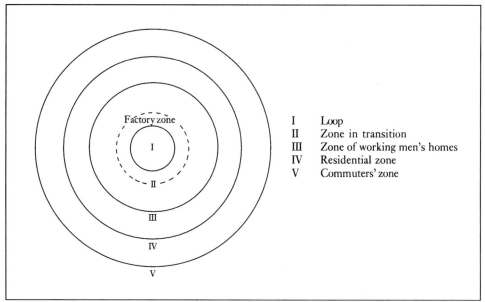

(Source: Park, Burgess and McKenzie (1925:51).)

Zone I was the central business district, where heavy industry and commerce were situated. Zone II was seen as a zone in transition, being invaded by industry and commercial usage from the core. Housing in this zone was allowed to deteriorate and the poorest city dwellers would be drawn there. The names given to the other zones are self-explanatory.

The notion of concentric city growth was challenged by some contemporaries of the social ecologists (Abbott, 1936; Robison, 1936). However, even supporters of the ecological approach accepted that the zonal hypothesis represented an ideal scheme to which no city would quite conform (Zorbaugh, 1925). Physical barriers, whether natural (eg rivers) or man-made (eg railway lines) would affect the growth pattern of a particular city.

5.2 Research by the Chicago School

Two members of the Chicago School, Clifford Shaw and Henry McKay developed the ecological model, using it as the basis for a wide-ranging study of juvenile delinquency in Chicago and other American cities (Shaw, 1929; Shaw and McKay, 1969). For Chicago, they divided the city into 140 areas of one square mile each, and mapped the residences of recorded delinquents. They also divided Chicago into concentric zones and calculated the percentage of the juvenile population resident in the areas and zones.

The findings of Shaw and McKay suggested that community problems were concentrated close to the centre of the city. The highest rates of delinquent residence were found close to the city's central core, and rates declined radially. The highest rates occurred in areas where buildings were in decay, where economic status was lowest, and where there were greater concentrations of recently arrived families. Similar results were found in other American cities, and subsequent research in Chicago indicated that delinquency areas persisted over time (Shaw and McKay, 1969).

Racial factors, taken independently of area, were not considered to be significant. Even when the population changed, crime remained concentrated in the same areas, at a similar level to before.

5.3 Social disorganisation and cultural transmission

In addition to the role of urban form, social ecology has another important element, in which levels of delinquency are influenced by social disorganisation. The process of invasion, dominance and succession is said to lead to a breakdown of social equilibrium. There is an absence of control over the behaviour of the young. At the same time, however, criminal attitudes and behaviour are said to be passed on through cultural transmission. Opportunities to steal preponderate. There is a continuity of contact with other delinquents and a tendency to pass down criminal techniques. The effectiveness of such contact is enhanced by an absence of training and encouragement towards lawful activity.

A major weakness of the ecological stance is that, having suggested that social disorganisation and subcultural methods of transmitting behaviour can co-exist, Shaw and McKay do not describe how this is possible. Furthermore, they do not explain how these two apparently conflicting concepts interact. Surely cultural transmission demands a degree of social organisation if it is to be successful? That paradox is all the more unfortunate since Brantingham and Jeffery suggest that by concluding that 'proximity to industry and commerce was really a proxy for the less directly measurable social variable, social disorganisation', Shaw and McKay placed too little emphasis on the spatial factors in their own findings (Brantingham and Jeffery, 1981:232).

5.4 Methodological limitations of the Chicago School research

Shaw and his colleagues relied quite heavily on officially recorded data, especially court records, and they have been criticised for this (eg Robison, 1936). As we have seen, the reliability of official statistics has long been questioned. Hence, Shaw's results may reflect inaccuracies in his data. Robison also questioned the use of a legal definition of delinquency, as sociologists often regard this as an inadequate test of deviant behaviour. A straightforward response to both criticisms is that official statistics and definitions represent an important starting point and a 'practical source' in the absence of more reliable data (Morris, 1957:36; also Baldwin, 1976:38). Robison pointed out that the mile square areas studied by Shaw and others were not necessarily related to natural neighbourhoods. This is a fair comment. Shaw and McKay recognised the difficulties of using such large areas, but adopted them to reduce 'fluctuations resulting from chance' (1969:56). However, some British research suggests that such an approach might also hide real differences. Rather than adhere to a city-wide analysis, some researchers have taken a more microscopic view of particular areas, and discovered notable differences in delinquency levels between apparently similar council estates (Jones, 1958; Baldwin, 1975), and even between neighbouring streets (Jephcott and Carter, 1954). British research has also provided a new perspective on various aspects of the Chicago School's work.

5.5 British area studies

Research in Britain has given rise to a certain amount of reserved support for the Chicago School's central theme. For example, in his survey of Croydon, Morris (1957) found that the central business district was a black spot, with 25 per cent of crimes occurring within a quarter of a mile of the town centre. Three of the four wards with the highest concentration of offenders' residences and the worst housing, bordered on the central business district. However, the support given is qualified. Morris questions the significance of his own findings, and suggests that an area's physical characteristics are relevant only insofar as they indirectly determine its social status (1957:130). Thus a deteriorating area may attract, rather than breed, individuals with social problems. The London study of Wallis and Maliphant (1967) found a high correlation between delinquency, and poverty and overcrowding but, on the other hand, these areas of high delinquency did not correspond significantly with areas plagued by other social problems, such as high rates of divorce and suicide. The 'delinquency areas' were substantially the same as those in a study 40 years earlier (Burt, 1925).

More recent research has indicated a failure by the Chicago School to fully exploit two important factors. For example, Shaw (1931) recognised that some delinquents travel to commit offences but this tendency was left unexplored. Furthermore, the ecologists did not differentiate between areas of crime commission, and areas of criminal residence. They also seem to have underestimated the importance of opportunities for crime (Morris, 1957; Baldwin, 1975:98). The differential distribution of criminal opportunities might explain the high concentration of crimes within the central business district.

Throughout the Chicago literature, the areas of highest delinquent residence are found in decaying, inner-city areas. In keeping with the ecological analogy, this is accepted as a natural phenomenon. British research again suggests the need for modification. Although such research has found delinquency areas within the inner city, it has also revealed a different feature, that is, high concentrations of delinquent residents in council-owned housing estates. Building patterns throughout much of the United Kingdom have meant that new estates are frequently built on the edges of towns rather than on cleared slum sites in the heart of the city (Morris, 1957; Jones, 1958; Baldwin, 1976). To a degree, the problem estate has replaced the ghetto as a crime area (see Mannheim, 1965:556). The zonal hypothesis needs to be altered, or possibly forgotten.

The picture drawn in Britain indicates the importance of housing policy. Clearly, moving tenants from slum areas to satellite estates does not cure delinquency. Indeed, there is some suggestion that a policy of segregation by some housing authorities perpetuates the existence of delinquency areas (Wilson, 1963). A study in Glasgow suggested that delinquency follows the migrating residents rather than staying in an area as Shaw had suggested (Ferguson, 1952).

The phenomenon of selective migration clouds the picture further. Put simply, it appears that 'birds of a feather flock together', thus creating pockets of delinquency (Taft, 1964:160; Morris, 1957:186). Migration will not always be a matter of choice, since some families will be drawn to poorer areas by low rents. Thus the overall picture may be affected by policy, personal preference, and economic necessity.

British research has provided a mixed assessment of the relevance of social disorganisation in contributing to levels of delinquency. Wallis and Maliphant (1967) thought it was significant, but considered that social disorganisation varied in the distribution of its factors and its effects between communities. Jones (1958) argued that the higher the mobility of residents on housing estates, the greater the degree of social disorganisation because opportunities to establish effective relationships and control were diminished. He claimed to find a positive relationship between mobility and delinquency.

Bagley (1965) claimed that the lack of social facilities increased delinquency. Baldwin and Bottoms (1976) have pointed out that neither Jones' nor Bagley's claims were corroborated by empirical data. Their own research, in Sheffield, found no significant link between social disorganisation and delinquency, except (and this was unexplained) on private housing estates (1976:122).

Morris questions whether social disorganisation exists in working class areas, arguing instead that the working class have their own culture and an alternative organisation (1957:177–8). Morris is right in suggesting that erroneous findings of social disorganisation can result from applying middle class norms to working class areas, but seems at times to fall into a similar trap by relying on stereotypical images of the working class.

5.6 Concluding comments about area studies of crime

The discussion above indicates that British research shows a need to modify the conclusions drawn by the Chicago School. Some difficulties reflect variations in urban composition between the two countries but, as we have seen, others are of greater significance.

Certain criticisms concern inadequacies of theory. In defence of the Chicago School, it is submitted that some of these criticisms are unfair. For example, Davidson (1981) describes the ecologists as being weak on theory. It appears, however, that Shaw and his collaborators never set out to be strong on theory.

Ecological analyses do not purport to provide a causal explanation in themselves. Morris stresses their importance 'as a method of calculating the contingency of delinquency' (1957:91). Area studies present the sociologists with 'information but not explanation' (Baldwin, 1976:16). It is important to recognise them as providing a means to an end, by highlighting the areas in which a researcher might profitably pursue more sophisticated enquiry.

Chapter 10 includes a description of environmental criminology, a relatively new perspective which examines the geographical distribution of crime and criminals in a more sophisticated fashion.

6

Class, Culture and Subculture

6.1 Emile Durkheim

Only a few paragraphs of this chapter will be given over to Emile Durkheim, but don't be misled by this. Durkheim's work has had a profound influence on sociology and criminology. Our major concern is with later developments of the concept of anomie, but traces of Durkheim's ideas can be seen in the social ecology model and in control theories. Durkheim's theories are complex and not limited to crime, so it is necessary to distil from them those points which are of most relevance to criminologists.

In *The Division of Labour in Society*, first published in 1893, Durkheim described the processes of social change which accompany the industrial development of society. The most primitive types of society were described as 'mechanical' and the more advanced types as 'organic'. No society was entirely mechanical or organic. Any given society would be in a state of development somewhere between the two extremes. Durkheim held that the functions of law and the origins of crime differed according to the predominant nature of the society. These variations are explained below.

6.2 Crime as a normal feature of a mechanical society

A mechanical society is made up of different groups, each of which is virtually autonomous and self-sufficient. There is a high level of uniformity among members of each group. They perform similar work to each other, share the same values and have similar life styles. Division of labour is rare, so there are few people with specialist talents.

Durkheim referred to the sum of the uniform characteristics of a social group as its 'collective conscience' (1965:80). He also recognised that, to varying degrees, individuals within each group would differ from the uniform ideal. As a mechanical society is characterised by uniformity, various means will be adopted to maintain that uniformity. One method is the use of criminal law.

Durkheim argued that members of a society have to make sacrifices to retain their membership. In other words, they have to behave in certain ways and refrain from acting in other ways. The way in which a society's norms are framed, together with the nature of human diversity, means that a certain number of people will always fail to make the necessary sacrifices. The existence of such an identifiable, but minority, group allows the conforming majority to feel superior. Durkheim considered that this feeling of moral superiority was supportive of social solidarity. Visible punishment of transgressors highlights their inferiority and reinforces the commitment of the majority to the collective conscience. In this sense, crime is a normal feature of a mechanical society.

Durkheim suggested that because punishment performed a necessary function, any reduction in behaviour already regarded as criminal would be compensated for by giving criminal status to other activities.

Furthermore, Durkheim claimed that a society with no crime would be abnormal. The imposition of controls so tight that they prevented any crime from occurring would also stifle progress. In order for progress to be possible, Durkheim considered that both the criminal and the idealist should be able to express themselves.

6.3 Anomie in an organic society

With greater industrialisation a society moves towards being organic. Division of labour is more common, and different groups become more dependent on each other. Social solidarity depends less on the maintenance of uniformity between individuals, and more on management of the diverse functions of the different groups. Of course, a certain degree of uniformity remains essential.

In an organic society, there is a greater emphasis on the use of law to regulate dealings between the different segments of society. Deficient regulation leads to different social problems, including crime. The likelihood of inefficient regulation was greater at a time of rapid modernisation, because new forms of control had not evolved sufficiently well to replace the older, and now less appropriate, means of maintaining solidarity. In such a period, society was in a state of normlessness which Durkheim described as 'anomie'.

The concept of anomie is developed in Durkheim's best-known book, *Suicide*. Durkheim analysed suicide rates and tried to explain why rates increased in times of economic growth as well as during depressions. It is important to note that Durkheim's interest was in variations in rates of suicide between different societies and groups. He did not attempt to explain individual causes of suicide. Durkheim's emphasis was on considering social integration. He looked at a person's ties to society.

For Durkheim, anomie was characterised by a breakdown in norms and common understandings within a society. He claimed that without external controls, a human being has unlimited needs. Society has to regulate man's needs by, *inter alia*, indicating the reward due to an individual worker. Except in times of crisis, everyone has at least a vague perception of what he can expect for his endeavours. However, at a time of economic upheaval, society cannot exert controls on people's aspirations. During a depression, people are forced to lower their sights, a situation which some will find intolerable.

When there is a sudden improvement in economic conditions, social equilibrium breaks down. There is said to be no limit on aspirations. Ultimately, there can be no sense of achievement.

Durkheim found that economic crises were associated with increases in suicide rates. Although his most prominent work concentrated on suicide, he made a number of valuable points in relation to crime. For example, he held that anomie or normlessness was an inevitable feature of the modernization of society, and that it would be most acute in times of rapid economic change. Durkheim claimed that industrialisation in nineteenth century France was accompanied by a marked reduction in regulation of personal aspirations. The influence of the church was said to have waned, and Durkheim pointed to the *laissez-faire* stance of the government. At the same time, however, Durkheim identified an upsurge in the implementation of functional laws to regulate the wheels of commerce. There is some dispute about whether Durkheim was right in suggesting that anomie was matched by an increase in crime in France. McDonald (1982) suggests that Durkheim and many of his contemporaries ignored the fact that crime rates actually dropped during the nineteenth century. On the other hand, Zehr (1981) suggests crime increased in France over that period, but still disputes the accuracy of Durkheim's explanation.

Although there is controversy about the accuracy of Durkheim's theory taken as a whole, his notion that crime was linked to a breakdown in social controls has inspired different sociologists in the twentieth century. His concept of anomie had a marked influence on a more recent theory developed by Merton, which will be examined next.

6.4 Merton's concept of anomie

In 1938 Robert Merton published a paper entitled *Social structure and anomie*. Although Merton's theory of anomie was influenced by Durkheim's model, there is an important difference in orientation between the two writers. According to Durkheim, aspirations or needs arose within an individual, and society sought to control them. For Merton, however, society induced or encouraged certain individual needs. The social structure produced the goals towards which people strove and also prescribed the means by which those goals could be reached. Merton wanted to discover 'how some social structures exert a definite pressure upon certain persons in the society to engage in non-conforming rather than conforming conduct' (1968:186). He concentrated on variations in crime rates, not on individual causes. Merton emphasised that his perspective was sociological.

Merton highlighted two elements of the social and cultural structure. These could be separated analytically, but they merged in practice. The first element was culturally defined goals. According to Merton, a society holds out and emphasises particular goals, or 'things "worth striving for"' (1968:187). Merton concentrated on American culture, and the culturally defined goals with which he was concerned centred on the American Dream or the pursuit of wealth as a sign of achievement.

The second element concerned the methods which are held out as being acceptable means of pursuing the goals. These might be reinforced by laws or by the mores of a particular culture. The acceptable methods were governed by institutional norms and were regarded as the institutional means for striving towards the goals.

Although group behaviour was affected by the interplay between the cultural goals and the institutional norms, the two elements varied, in nature and strength, independently of each other. Merton held that at times, certain goals would be emphasised, but little attention would be paid to the institutionalised means for attaining them. Any activities would be allowed provided they could bring about attainment of the goal. The opposite of that extreme situation would arise when activities which had once been indulged in for a particular purpose, became practices which were performed as a kind of ritual without any further objective. New forms of behaviour would be avoided, so that this type of culture is reminiscent of Durkheim's claim that excessive control of a society prevents progress.

Merton argued that equilibrium between these two elements of the social structure would only be maintained while individuals were able to gain satisfaction from conformity with both elements. As not everyone can reach the top in a competitive system, taking part in compliance with the institutionalised norms must itself provide satisfactions. If the only focus of concern is success, perpetual losers will seek to have the norms changed. If people at different levels in the social order are not given incentives to comply with the obligations imposed by the system, deviance will occur. Merton's central hypothesis was that from a sociological viewpoint, aberrant behaviour was a sign of dissociation between culturally induced goals and institutionalised means for pursuing them.

Merton was mainly concerned with the type of society where goals are heavily emphasised but institutional means are not. This is not to suggest that there will be no norms to control behaviour. Rather, Merton claimed that emotional support could be much higher for the cultural goals than for the means. In such a setting, an individual with an eye on goal attainment will be restrained only by selecting the means which are most efficient. If such a situation continues, the society becomes unstable and enters into a state of anomie (Merton, 1968:189).

According to Merton, American culture resembled the type of society just described, where there is great emphasis on the goal of success without a corresponding emphasis on institutional means. He claimed that in the American Dream there was 'no final stopping point' (1968:190). The importance of pursuing wealth, and the myth of equal success for all, were reinforced in the family, the school and the work place. Indeed, Merton went to some length to provide evidence of the promotion of unlimited ambition in American society.

At the same time, Merton claimed (without providing the same supporting evidence) that the legitimate means for achieving success were not emphasised to the same degree. Legitimate opportunities to pursue the American Dream were not evenly distributed, so many members of society would constantly be frustrated if they persisted in adopting the institutionalised means. Given the lower cultural emphasis on those means, it was inevitable that individuals would adapt in different ways.

6.5 Merton's types of individual adaptation

Merton described five types of adaptation induced by the pressures resulting from the lack of integration between cultural goals and institutionalised means. Although these are individual adaptations, they do not describe personality types. The five types were set out in tabular form, as below (a (+) indicates acceptance, a (-) shows rejection, and (+/-) indicates replacement by an alternative).

Fig 3: *Merton's typology of modes of individual adaptation*

Modes of adaptation	Cultural goals	Institutionalised means
1. Conformity	+	+
2. Innovation	+	-
3. Ritualism	-	+
4. Retreatism	-	-
5. Rebellion	+/-	+/-

(Source: Merton 1968:194. In the original the modes of adaptation were identified by Roman numerals. The table has been amended to match the layout of this textbook.)

The different forms of adaptation are explained below. Merton emphasised that individuals might adopt different types in relation to different social activities. His primary concern was with economic activity.

Conformity

Technically, conformity is not an adaptation. In a stable society it will be the most common type of conduct. The conformist adheres to cultural goals and the institutionalised means.

Innovation

This form of adaptation will be adopted when an individual has internalised the success goal but has not acquired a commitment to the institutional norms which prescribe the ways to achieve it. Obviously, this response will be encouraged when there is a powerful emphasis on the goal.

Merton suggested that the pressures towards innovation will affect people at all economic levels and he made reference to dubious activities indulged in by businessmen on the route to becoming rich. Although he recognised the existence of much undiscovered white collar crime, and the unreliability of official statistics, Merton still asserted that 'the greatest pressures toward deviation are exerted upon the lower strata' (1968:198).

The reason put forward for the concentration of pressures on members of the lower class was that they have far less access to legitimate opportunities for advancement. One result of the pressure was the use of illegitimate methods which were more effective than the legitimate ones.

Merton claimed that this theory could explain why varying associations are found between crime and poverty. There is a temptation to expect always to find a positive correlation between levels of poverty and rates of crime. However, Merton argued that crime levels will be higher when poverty, and the disadvantages associated with it, occur in the same cultural setting as a strong emphasis on financial success. Box (1983) suggests that in Merton's formulation, anomie is not a condition of normlessness, but one of relative deprivation.

Merton stressed that the individuals concerned might not make a conscious connection between their frustration and the social structure. Instead, because personal merit and hard work seemed to count for little, they might attribute their own lack of success to bad luck. This would further reduce their commitment to legitimate means of endeavour.

Ritualism

In this form of adaptation, the individual abandons the cultural success goal, and lowers his sights. At the same time, he continues to comply with institutional norms. Adapting in this way produces security, in that the anxiety associated with failure is avoided. According to Merton, members of the lower middle class were most likely to be affected, because of a background of parental pressure towards conformity coupled with poor prospects of gathering substantial wealth. Merton gave the example of the zealously conformist bureaucrat. He recognised that it is questionable whether this was really deviant behaviour, as the behaviour itself was permitted.

Retreatism

Someone who adapts in this way rejects both the cultural goals and the institutional means for achieving them, but does not replace them with alternatives. Merton gave examples such as vagrants, alcoholics and drug addicts. These people were, he said, 'in the society but not of it' (1968:207).

Merton argued that retreatism is most likely to be adopted by someone who starts out by valuing both the goals and the means, but who has followed institutional procedures without success. Internal inhibitions prevent him from using illegitimate means and the resulting conflict leads the individual to abandon the cultural goals and the legitimate practices for pursuing them. The individual is said to become asocialised.

Retreatism was seen by Merton as a privatised form of adaptation, rather than one connected with a separate subculture. Merton also suggested that retreatists are most likely to be viewed as pariahs by conventional members of society. In this respect they might be seen as filling the role of Durkheim's inferior minority, or of 'folk devils' (per Cohen, 1980).

Rebellion

Rebellion involves the abandonment of both the cultural goals and the institutional means. Substitutes are put forward for both elements. Merton saw rebellion as a collective activity, rather than an individual one. The stage is set for rebellion when the existing system is regarded as the barrier to achievement of culturally-induced goals. In order for political actions to follow, Merton said, allegiance must be taken away from the prevailing structure and transferred to other groups who promise to implement a new, more egalitarian structure in which the able will succeed.

6.6 Comments on Merton's theory

Merton's outline of anomie is peppered with provisos, such as 'This essay ... remains but a prelude'. Nevertheless, as so often happens, his critics tend to ignore these and challenge aspects of the theory which were never put forward as wholly accurate. Some of their criticisms are deserved, and examples will now be discussed.

Merton relied too heavily on official statistics

This criticism has to be qualified. Merton recognised the weaknesses of official crime figures, but he was still prepared to accept that most offences were committed by the lower class, on whom he believed the greatest pressures towards deviation were exerted. If he had had access to self-report studies, he might have modified his position.

Merton focused too much on crimes of the lower class

This seems to be a fair comment, linked to the criticism above. As Merton recognised that innovation could be behind forms of white collar crime, it is unfortunate that he so readily accepted that members of the lower class were most exposed to structural strain.

The theory does not explain non-utilitarian delinquency

Cohen (1955) put forward this criticism, stating that Merton sought only to explain acquisitive crimes. It is true that Merton did not seek to explain vandalism or similar activities in terms of anomie, but his essay clearly states that its current concern is with forms of economic activity and that the theory was not fully developed. Furthermore, although Merton did not say so, it is possible to view vandalism as one outlet for the frustrations produced by differential access to legitimate opportunities.

Merton's theory ignores group processes

Merton only referred to very large social groups, such as the lower middle class or the lower strata. Cohen (1955) suggests Merton gave the impression that the choice of adaptation is made in a social vacuum. The influence of subcultural or other social settings is ignored. In a separate article, Merton (1956) claims that he had recognised that the greater part of deviant behaviour was a group phenomenon.

Different individual responses are not explained

Merton insisted that the strain towards deviance was greatest on members of the lower class, but did not explain why most members of that class appear to conform. He did not address the question of why some people deviate and others do not. In part, this can be accounted for by Merton's statement that he was concerned with a sociological perspective and not with individual differences. More seriously though, it is connected with Merton's assumption that the same success goal permeates to all levels of American society.

Merton assumed the success goal was universally applicable

Merton's theory starts by assuming that people at all levels of American society had absorbed the goal of financial success. His different types of response to frustration are seen as adaptations from that initial position. Merton did not seem to consider the possibility that different classes might have entirely different cultural values, in which the American Dream did not feature. Lemert (1964) accuses Merton of ignoring the pluralistic nature of American society.

The theory ignores the possibility of positive commitment to deviancy

This point is linked to the one above. Clinard (1964) suggests that many deviant acts can be explained in terms of people living up to the expectations appropriate to their subcultural setting. This is in contrast to Merton's view that lower class deviance indicates a failure to follow norms which are supposed to apply to all social classes.

The theory applies only to the United States

It is true that in its original formulation, Merton's theory only set out to deal with deviant behaviour in the United States. Nevertheless, it is worth considering its relevance to other countries. Obviously, it can only apply in societies where status is achieved, rather than where it is given.

As can be seen, critics of Merton are able to point to various theoretical inadequacies in his concept of anomie. The theory has also been tested by a number of empirical studies.

6.7 Empirical findings in respect of Merton's theory

Toby's short paper, *Affluence and adolescent crime* (1969), provides limited support for Merton's theory. Toby refers to information put before two United Nations congresses in 1960 and 1964. This indicated that crime rates were increasing in most of the countries surveyed, and that this trend applied to rich countries as well as poor ones. Toby suggests that affluence was shown to be a causative factor in worsening crime problems. Toby had compared indices of affluence against juvenile crime rates in selected countries. He claims that a bettering of standards leads to wider desires for property ownership, and generates envy which may in turn lead to increased crime. Toby produces information, in case study form, about boys from Japan, Israel and Sweden. Each had been involved in delinquency. In view of their diverse cultural backgrounds, Toby argues that some common causal factor must be at work. In developing this argument, Toby does not claim that deprivation leads inevitably to crime. He refers to factors such as the increased opportunities provided in an affluent setting, a lessening of parental control, and peer pressure. In his conclusion, Toby suggests that pressure towards crime is more likely to develop among relatively deprived members of a rich society than among the objectively deprived in a poor society.

Lander (1954) studied more than 8,000 cases of delinquency occurring in Baltimore. He found delinquency to be essentially related to anomie. Delinquency was not directly associated with economic characteristics. Areas with high levels of anomie were characterised by relative normlessness. Bordua (1958) replicated Lander's experiment in Detroit and confirmed the latter's findings.

A test known as the Srole scale test has sometimes been used to measure anomia, which is a state of the individual, rather than of society. The scale measures an individual's perceptions of such factors as his capacity to achieve worthwhile goals through effort, and of the support available from community leaders and personal associates. In America, anomia is generally found to be more prevalent in the lower social strata (Cohen, 1955).

6.8 Extensions of Merton's concept of anomie

Parsons (1951) fitted Merton's formulation into a broader theory of interactional analysis. He added extra sources of strain, including one that occurs when a person cannot form sexual attachments which match institutionalised expectations. Another type of strain arises when a person cannot reconcile his own expectations of himself with those of others. Parsons suggested that deviant behaviour could follow on from an individual passively falling short of cultural expectations, or from his taking active control of a situation. His version credits some deviants with a greater degree of proactivity than is allowed by Merton.

Two notable extensions of Merton's theory were provided by Cohen and by Cloward and Ohlin. In common with Merton's work, their contributions are types of strain theory. As they also place much more emphasis on subcultural factors, they will be dealt with in sections 6.12 and 6.13 (below). We turn next to another important attempt to provide a sociological explanation for crime.

6.9 Sutherland's theory of differential association

Any survey of sociological contributions to criminology would be incomplete if it left out Edwin Sutherland. Sutherland is noted for his work on white collar crime, but equally importantly for his theory of differential association. In the 1930s, Sutherland set out to produce a general theory of crime. His first systematic attempt to explain crime in terms of differential association was published in 1939. Several revisions were made, but by the late 1940s the theory was in the form in which it now appears in the 10th edition of *Criminology* by Sutherland and Cressey (1978:80–2).

The theory sets out nine propositions, but for present purposes these have been consolidated into six statements:

1. Criminal behaviour is learned, in the same way as other forms of behaviour, through interaction with others.
2. Most of this learning occurs in intimate groups.
3. The matters learned include criminal techniques of varying complexity, and the specific directions of motives, drives and attitudes.
4. An individual becomes delinquent because he receives more definitions favourable to law-breaking than definitions unfavourable to law-breaking. *This is the central feature of differential association.*
5. Differential associations may vary in frequency, duration, priority and intensity. Clearly, the quality of interactions, and not just their quantity, is regarded as important.
6. Criminal behaviour is related to general needs, but it is not explained by them, because the same needs are also expressed in conforming behaviour. Sutherland uses this claim to challenge theories which link criminal behaviour to general drives, such as the pursuit of status, or reaction to frustration.

These aspects of differential association, particularly (5) and (6), can be regarded as a form of learning theory which has two main aspects (Vold and Bernard, 1986). These concern the content of what is learned (criminal techniques and attitudes), and the process of learning (interaction in intimate groups).

Sutherland suggested the theory was intended to explain the behaviour of individual persons. He added that the same explanation would be appropriate for explaining crime rates since they are simply the gross product of individual offending. However, Sutherland argued that a high crime rate could best be explained by the influence of social disorganisation. In preference to that term, though, he referred to differential social organisation. Sutherland asserted that most communities were organised partly for criminal and partly for non-criminal behaviour. Variations in crime rates between communities could be attributed to differences in the orientation of their social organisation.

Differential association and differential social organisation were complementary aspects of Sutherland's proposed general theory of crime.

6.10 Limitations of Sutherland's theory

Sutherland is open to criticism for seeing individuals as too passive. They seem to absorb definitions and to have little option but to react to outside forces.

Glaser (1956, 1978) has extended Sutherland's formulation to provide man with at least limited control over his fate. In Glaser's view a person will be prepared to take part in criminal acts if he believes such acts are acceptable to other people with whom he identifies himself.

Sutherland's concept of the way learning takes place, now looks very unsophisticated. The picture created is one in which learners absorb information, skills or attitudes which are poured into them as if they were passive receptacles. Although interaction is central, the theory does not seem to allow for a more active learning process in which ideas are exchanged.

By emphasising that most learning takes place within intimate groups, Sutherland seems to exclude the importance of learning from the media or other aspects of the wider culture (Burgess and Akers, 1968). The theory does not discuss the possibility that a person might commit crime without learning from anyone else (Radzinowicz and King, 1979).

Sutherland expressly denied the need to explain why a person has particular associations, saying only briefly that a 'person's associations are determined in a general context of social organisation' (1960:79). As he suggested that a boy may become delinquent because of the neighbourhood in which he lives and the quality of his contact with other boys, it would be helpful to have some further hint as to why people enter into particular associations.

Sutherland laid his theory open to a broader range of criticism by presenting it as a general theory. It does not seem to account for crimes which may be spontaneous responses to particular sets of circumstances, and which might be committed by almost anyone (Bottomley, 1979).

Like some other theories, if it were accurate, differential association would predict the occurrence of a greater amount of crime than actually takes place. In other words, it suffers from 'an embarrassment of riches' (Matza, 1964). It does not tell us why only some of the people exposed to similar experiences go on to deviate while others do not. This could have been avoided by allowing space for individual factors instead of adopting a wholly sociological approach (Tappan, 1949).

Notwithstanding these weaknesses, differential association theory provided a useful new perspective by suggesting that in some communities there could be a positive emphasis in favour of criminal conduct and that criminal behaviour could be normal learned behaviour. These aspects of Sutherland's theory have provided part of the influence for the subcultural theories which we turn to next.

6.11 Cultural and subcultural explanations of crime

Once again, we start with a caveat. The heading above seems to suggest that cultural theories and subcultural theories are two easily separable sources of explanation. That is not necessarily true. You will find that some textbooks use a similar heading, and follow it with a discussion of different theories or research studies, but never differentiate between cultural explanations and subcultural ones. This need not matter. What the different theories share is the notion that certain social groups have separate values and attitudes which allow or encourage delinquency. It is not easy or particularly helpful to define the difference between a culture and a subculture. Indeed, the two terms might mean the same (Heidensohn, 1989:50). It is possible to say, however, that most of the work in this area has dealt with juvenile delinquency or, in other words, with the subculture of youth. Much of the work has been inspired by early books about American street gangs (eg Thrasher, 1947; Whyte, 1943).

6.12 Albert Cohen

In 1955, Cohen wrote *Delinquent Boys: The Culture of the Gang*. He was critical of Merton's anomie theory, arguing that it could not explain non-utilitarian acts of delinquency. For Cohen, working class youths experienced strain, but of a different kind from that described by Merton. They suffered from status frustration. These youths came into contact with middle class institutions, such as the school, and the norms associated with them. Status was measured by middle class standards, so that a working class boy would find himself at the bottom of the status hierarchy. Some boys would suffer from problems of adjustment. As many boys would face these problems at the same time, a form of collective solution would arise. Boys would react in one of three ways:

1. *The college boy response*: the boy continues to aspire to middle class standards.
2. *The stable corner boy response*: he turns his back on institutions, such as the school, and looks to his own peer group for support.
3. *The delinquent response*: this is adopted by boys who initially attach themselves to middle class values, but because of their frustration at failing to achieve status by that route, turn such values upside down. This process is referred to as reactionformation. A delinquent subculture develops, in which working class boys can achieve status. Its values are non-utilitarian, malicious and negativistic.

Cohen's explanation did not have strong empirical foundations, in fact, it might be viewed as an armchair theory. It had a number of critics. Kitsuse and Dietrick (1959) argued that a lot of delinquency was committed by individuals, rather than being a collective response. Many gang activities could be regarded as utilitarian. Furthermore, Cohen's theory ignored the true extent of delinquency by middle class youths.

Miller (1958) challenged Cohen's claim that the values of a delinquent subculture were produced by inverting middle class values. Instead, lower class culture had developed focal concerns of its own. These included toughness, smartness, excitement and autonomy. Many of the gang members in Miller's study came from a single parent background with a dominant mother. Involvement in violence or tough activities could be seen as an assertion of masculinity. By occurring in conjunction with poor social conditions, this culture provided a 'generating milieu' for gang delinquency.

In later work, Cohen and Short (1959) divided the delinquent response into three subcategories:

1. the violent, conflict subculture; and
2. the drug subculture; and
3. the semi-professional thief subculture.

These categories bear similarities to ones suggested by Cloward and Ohlin (Downes, 1966).

6.13 Cloward and Ohlin

The subcultural explanation offered by Cloward and Ohlin extends part of Merton's theory and also incorporates some aspects of cultural transmission. Cloward and Ohlin considered that many young boys would suffer from problems of adjustment and frustrated ambition. Some would look for a deviant solution. Cloward and Ohlin added a new perspective to strain theory by suggesting that access to illegitimate opportunities was unevenly distributed. As a result, the types of delinquency and of associated subcultures in which those youths participated would be largely determined by the opportunities presented in the communities where they lived. Cloward and Ohlin said there were three types of delinquent subculture:

The criminal subculture

This would be found in working class areas where there was already a developed structure of illegitimate opportunities. It was mainly concerned with theft for profit.

The conflict subculture

This would develop in areas which lacked legitimate and illegitimate opportunity structures, and which were socially disorganised. Delinquent activities would revolve around gang fights.

The retreatist or double-failure subculture

This subculture would be adopted by youths, looking for a deviant solution, who did not become involved in one of the other subcultures, because of internalised inhibitions, or because they tried to do so but failed. Activities were mostly concerned with the use of drugs.

An important point about Cloward and Ohlin's theory is that for them a delinquent group was one which had delinquency as a central activity. Toby (1961) suggests that if they were right, gang delinquency would account for less than a tenth of juvenile prosecutions in America. Cloward and Ohlin also painted a picture in which gangs were tightly knit, organised groups. Like Cohen's, their model is largely based on armchair theorising. These theories have been subjected to empirical examination in a number of studies.

6.14 American studies of juvenile gangs

Yablonsky (1962) studied juvenile gangs in New York. His work challenged the notion that such gangs were tightly woven. Yablonsky preferred to see them as 'near groups', which had three types of member. The first type were core members who, Yablonsky claimed, were psychologically disturbed and led the gang into violence because of their own aggressiveness. A second type regarded themselves as members, but were casual rather than consistent participants in its activities. The third type would occasionally take part in the gang's violent excursions but did not purport to be members.

In so far as they matched earlier typologies at all, the gangs studied by Yablonsky resembled the conflict type. Criminal gangs were not seen as a distinct phenomenon. A more realistic picture was that members of ordinary juvenile groups sometimes took part in delinquency, but as individuals rather than as part of a group activity. The retreatist subculture did not appear to exist, as drug abuse was more often carried out as a solitary activity.

In Chicago, Short and Strodtbeck (1965) studied 16 gangs with almost 600 members. Their findings were not supportive of the theories of Cohen or of Cloward and Ohlin. For example, they found little evidence of reaction formation or the rejection of conventional values. Boys for whom the strain between ambition and opportunities appeared to be greatest were not necessarily the most delinquent. Short and Strodtbeck did consider that boys used the gang to provide an alternative status system, in that it gave them a valued identity which was not otherwise present in their lives. Nevertheless, delinquency was a by-product of membership, not a central activity. Sykes and Matza (1957) also argued that delinquents often had a high regard for law-abiding people and for conventional values.

6.15 British studies of delinquent groups

Downes (1966) studied groups of working class youths in Stepney and Poplar, London. He found that a considerable amount of delinquency took place, but that this mostly happened in street corner groups, rather than organised gangs. Status frustration did not occur to a significant degree among these youths. Instead, their typical response to lack of success at school or work was one of 'dissociation'. The process was one of opting out rather than of reaction formation. Among these youths there was an emphasis on leisure activities, not on school or work. They tended to be interested in commercial forms of entertainment, not in youth clubs with their middle class orientation. Access to leisure pursuits was limited, for example, by lack of money. Instead, youths would congregate on street corners, and take part in delinquency to find excitement. Downes found little evidence of the specialized subcultures suggested by Cloward and Ohlin.

Parker (1974) conducted a survey of unskilled adolescents in an area of Liverpool which official statistics suggested had a high rate of delinquency. He found there was a pattern of loosely knit peer groups, not one of tightly structured gangs. Delinquency was not a central activity. Youths shared common problems, such as unemployment. Leisure opportunities were limited. Some youths had developed a temporary solution in the form of stealing car radios. The community in which the boys lived was one which largely condoned theft, provided the victims were outsiders.

Ken Pryce (1979) studied West Indian youths in the St Paul's area of Bristol. He suggests that the first West Indians to arrive in the 1950s came to Britain with high aspirations, but found they were relegated to a force of cheap labour. They and their children were subject to racism and discrimination, which contributed to a pattern of 'endless pressure'. Pryce suggested there were two types of adaptation to this pressure. One was to be stable and law abiding, the other was to adopt an expressive, disreputable attitude. Second and third generation West Indians were more likely (but not bound) to adopt the second response. Pryce suggested two further divisions within this second category. The first, 'hustlers', would reject low status work if it was available. Instead they would take part in robberies, deception, drug-dealing or pimping. Such activities would support a lifestyle which gave a feeling of mastery and autonomy. The second subcategory contained 'teeny-boppers'. They were typically school-leavers with few qualifications, for whom any available work would be unrewarding. The typical pattern was to lose jobs quickly, to fall out with parents, and then to drift into petty crime and homelessness.

6.16 More recent theories of youth subcultures

Several British writers have considered a variety of youth subcultures, such as teddy boys, skinheads, mods and rockers. There is a tendency to view participation in such subcultures as coded responses to changes affecting working class communities. The task of the researcher is to crack the code.

Examples are: *Resistance Through Rituals: Youth Subcultures in Post War Britain*, edited by Hall and Jefferson (1976) and *Working Class Youth Culture* edited by Mungham and Pearson (1976).

Robins and Cohen (1978) focus on the break-up of the East London community in post-war years. The local economy was destroyed, large areas were demolished, many locals were rehoused elsewhere, and there was a high rate of immigration. In other words, fundamental features of the working class community, including jobs and leisure opportunities, were destroyed. The ensuing problems registered more acutely on the young. Subcultures, such as skinheads, were viewed as an attempt to retrieve some of the elements destroyed by the changes. Control was being reasserted, not in real terms, but symbolically. Clarke (1976) also argues that the skinhead style was an attempt to recreate the working class community. Violence was part of the machismo associated with the working class image. Activities like 'Paki-bashing' and 'queer-bashing' were interpreted as a ritual defence of the community against outsiders (Clarke, 1976; Pearson, 1976).

Elsewhere, Taylor (1971, 1976) describes football hooliganism as a kind of resistance movement, saying it represents an attempt to restore working class control over football.

Whatever the validity of these explanations might be, it is worth bearing in mind that skinheads, mods and punks do not necessarily take part in delinquent behaviour. It is quite probable that the majority of people who attract such labels are not involved in delinquency. Cohen (1980) argues that the media help to distort the image of youth subcultures and to exaggerate the amount of crime in which they are involved. He also suggests that everyday delinquency is mostly concerned with property crime and has little to do with codes or ritualism.

6.17 The subculture of violence

Wolfgang and Ferracuti (1981) put forward a subcultural theory which breaks away from the tendency to focus on juvenile delinquency. They examine studies of criminal violence and generalise the results in an attempt to explain homicides which occurred without premeditation as a result of often minor provocation. Wolfgang and Ferracuti suggest there are significant differences between the values of the dominant culture and those of the subculture of violence. People in the latter subculture place a higher value on honour, and a lower value on human life. Different norms are respected. Within the subculture of violence, jostles or trivial insults are expected to be met with violence. Failure to respond in this way is met with social censure. Although Wolfgang and Ferracuti suggest the development of the subculture is rooted historically in social conditions, they do not consider it is necessary to identify the development process. The original social conditions may have ceased to exist, but the values and norms at the centre of the subculture are passed on from generation to generation in the form of ideas.

Curtis (1975) has adapted this theory of the subculture of violence to explain violence among American blacks. Maintenance of a manly image is important in the subculture, and individuals who are unable to resolve conflicts verbally are more likely to resort to violence in order to assert their masculinity. Similarly, men in this subculture who lack the social skills to obtain consensual sex are more likely to commit rape. Curtis' version of the black subculture of violence places greater importance on the influence of existing social conditions than does the theory of Wolfgang and Ferracuti. Behaviour is partly a response to social conditions, and partly the result of an individual's acceptance of the ideas and values which he has absorbed from the subculture of violence.

Vold and Bernard (1986) state that some studies support the subculture of violence theory, but that others regard economic inequality as a better explanation in the areas studied.

6.18 Concluding comments about subcultural theories

Subcultural explanations of crime have a strong common sense appeal, particularly when they are linked to theories involving cultural transmission. If criminal attitudes and behaviours are acquired through learning, or are regarded as normal, it is logical to assume such processes will be more effective within a subcultural milieu where other types of values are shared. Unfortunately, these common sense assumptions have not been supported by research. Subcultural theories have provided neither concrete explanations, nor reliable preventative measures for coping with crime or delinquency.

In his critique of the criminal justice system, David Rose (1996) unravels what Helena Kennedy QC calls 'the complex relationships and philosophies which sustain a system in crisis'. Rose calls for a radical rethink, and in his most recent publication, *In the Name of the Law*, he discusses the issues which Judge Tumim classifies as 'police, crime, race, class', analysing many major specific cases.

Rose was given unrestricted access to Kilburn police operations for seven months. During that time, he took part in raids, patrolled on foot and watched the treatment of prisoners. His findings give a clear insight into the criminal justice system.

In Chapter 2, Rose examines 'Race, Class and Justice' embracing three clear areas of criminology. He examines a number of racial and class-based crimes, and concludes that to examine racist violence 'on the touchstone of class' is a conclusion the criminologist might prefer to ignore. He views those who live outside council estates as conceding that a consideration of racial violence is seen only in 'skin politics' terms requiring no deeper analysis of the causes of crime.

Rose also examines 'right wing' opinion where he claims that crime in general is blamed on the individual evil of 'demonised young thugs'. He gives a number of actual cases to justify his contention. For the 'left', he concludes that racist violence is perceived as simply the act of the 'demonised racist thug', writing that 'the contradictions and paradoxes multiply'. He ends the chapter by stating that 'once we bring class back into the picture, the crisis comes into sharper focus. If criminal justice is collapsing, it is only a part of a deeper social palsy'.

It is clearly Rose's aim to merge a number of specific criminological theories into one cohesive attack on the failure of the criminal justice system to work adequately. He challenges the ebbing shibboleths of the liberal left and the terrifying revenge justice of the right. His book is not merely confined to theoretical criminology, for he suggests that criminal justice 'provides the starkest pointer to a twenty-first century hell' with a two-thirds/one-third society. He sees the comfortable defending themselves against a desperate minority with guns and fortifications 'and ever more drastic forms of imprisonment' as he concludes with a comment on applied criminology.

7

Control Theories, Interactionist Perspectives and Labelling Theory

7.1 Introduction

Most of the theories examined so far are based on the premise that criminal behaviour is unusual, and that something special has to occur before someone will commit crime. That something special may have biological, psychological or social origins. Control theorists adopt a different starting point. They suggest everyone would commit crime if certain forces did not operate to prevent them from doing so. These forces are seen as 'social controls', or as bonds to society, which insulate a person from deviance. The various forms of control theory which will be covered in this chapter, and the empirical studies used to test them, have tended to focus on juvenile delinquency. You should note that the personality based theory of Hans Eysenck, which was dealt with in Chapter 4, can also be viewed as a control theory.

7.2 Early versions of control theory

The first control theory of delinquency to claim that label, was published by Reiss in 1951. Reiss studied the court records, including psychiatric reports, of about 1,100 white males, aged between 11 and 17, who had been placed on probation. He found that youths possessing weak ego or superego controls, and for whom intensive psychotherapy or institutional treatment was recommended, were more likely to have their probation revoked. Reiss suggested the psychiatrists' findings were based on an appraisal of the juvenile's capacity to refrain from satisfying his needs by means which clashed with the expectations of the community. That capacity was described as the juvenile's 'personal controls'. Reiss regarded these and other factors, such as good conduct at school, as indicators of a juvenile's acceptance of the control imposed by socially approved institutions. Vold and Bernard point out that Reiss's research and arguments provided only weak support for control theory since other factors relating to family and community controls were not found to be related to the probability of revocation of probation (1986:234). In any event, personal controls were being tested against the ultimate actions of the authorities, and not against the juveniles' initial or continued involvement in delinquency.

Six years later, Toby put forward the notion that all youths have the inclination to break the law but that some resist because they have more to lose if they do so and are caught (1957). He described this variable control mechanism as a youth's 'stake in conformity'. Thus a youth who is doing well academically may resist involvement in delinquency because of the risks to his career prospects. Toby also suggested there could be a cumulative effect, because in communities with many youths having a low stake in conformity, there is a greater likelihood of peer pressure towards delinquency.

7.3 Travis Hirschi

The writer most associated with control theory is Hirschi, principally because of his book, *Causes of Delinquency*. According to Hirschi, 'we are all animals' and the capacity to commit crime is part of our nature (1969:31). However, he argued that the tighter an individual's social bonds to institutions, such as family or school, the less likely he is to offend. Hirschi identified four main sources of social control: attachment, commitment, involvement and belief.

Attachment refers to a person's sensitivity to other people, especially family and friends. Whether or not he takes their opinions into account will depend on the quality of their relationship. Attachment influences the degree to which an individual internalises norms and values. It can vary within a person's lifetime, so that the possibility of deviant behaviour may also vary.

Commitment is very similar to Toby's 'stake in conformity', in that it concerns the losses an individual is likely to incur through participation in delinquency.

Involvement is related to the notion that 'the devil makes work for idle hands'. Adolescents who are involved in constructive activities are considered less likely to take part in delinquent acts.

Hirschi held that people vary in the extent to which they believe they should obey society's rules. Delinquency is made possible by an absence of beliefs that forbid it.

7.4 Empirical support for Hirschi's theory

Hirschi used a sample of 4,000 youths, in a self-report survey, to test his theory. A questionnaire sought information about their family, peers, and school. They were asked whether they had committed any of six different delinquent acts in the previous year (in fact three of the six acts involved stealing, but differed according to the value of the items stolen). Police data and school records were also examined.

One of the more notable findings was that there was no relationship between social class and delinquency.

Hirschi also found that youths with a closer attachment to their parents were less likely to report committing delinquent acts than others who were less closely attached. That finding applied regardless of race or class, and was not affected by the delinquency of respondents' friends. Hirschi also found that youths who had negative attitudes to school, and who were poor achievers there, were more likely to report a large number of delinquent acts. Delinquents were found to have lower educational and career aspirations than non-delinquents. Hirschi's research seems to support the notion that attachment and commitment act to discourage delinquency. Findings in relation to involvement were equivocal, except to the extent that involvement in academic study appeared to exercise control away from delinquent conduct.

Putting together Hirschi's findings in relation to social class, and those concerning the aspirations of his sample, class of origin is not important in control theory, but class destination is.

7.5 Limitations of control theories

One of the limitations of Hirschi's study and of other research on control theory (eg Nye, 1958), is that the samples contain very few delinquents who have admitted serious offences. Theories based on them may therefore be more useful in explaining youthful mischief, rather than serious criminal behaviour. It would not be good enough to simply extend Hirschi's assertion that we are all animals by saying that some are more animal-like than others and therefore more likely to take part in violent crime.

Control theories have frequently relied on self-report studies, which tend to challenge the previously assumed link between social class and involvement in delinquency. It is possible that the control theorists make too much of this, as one of the weaknesses of control theory is an excessive emphasis on individuals and a lack of attention towards group processes at a variety of levels. This is backed by an implicit concept of human nature which is simplistic and untested.

7.6 Matza and delinquent drift

In *Delinquency and Drift* (1964) David Matza put forward a variation of control theory which you may see referred to as a 'neutralisation theory'. He challenged the assumption of most positivist theories that delinquents are different from non-delinquents and that factors associated with that difference drive them to commit delinquent acts. Matza called this latter notion 'hard determinism' and he argued that if this were an accurate picture, these youths would indulge in delinquency far more frequently than they actually did. Such theories could not explain the maturation effect or the episodic nature of delinquency. Matza preferred the idea of 'soft determinism', which viewed most delinquents as standing somewhere between constraint and freedom. He did accept, however, that there is a small minority of delinquents who are committed to delinquency, and whose behaviour might be explained by traditional theories. Matza suggested that most delinquents were much the same as everyone else, and that they were more free to choose between different types of behaviour than traditional theories allowed. According to Matza, delinquency became possible when social controls were loosened. He used the term 'drift' to describe this state in which an individual was open to involvement in delinquent conduct (1964:27ff). Matza suggested delinquents were not really committed to values favouring delinquency. They accepted that some types of behaviour were wrong, but justified some behaviour in a way which allowed them to avoid guilt. To do this, they adopted various techniques of neutralization (described in Sykes and Matza, 1957). Some of these techniques bear similarities to legal defences or to the mitigating circumstances often put before courts. They include:

1. Denial of responsibility: 'something came over me', or 'it was an accident'.
2. Denial of injury: 'they can afford it'.
3. Denial of the victim: 'he asked for it'.
4. Condemning the condemners: 'what's wrong with a bit of dope, the magistrates get drunk don't they?'
5. Appealing to higher loyalties: 'I had to look after my mates'.

Although such remarks may be made to rationalise behaviour after it has occurred, they are used here in advance of deviant conduct in order to neutralise the values which forbid it.

Matza suggests that forces which encourage delinquency would come into play once a juvenile was in a state of drift. He could experience a feeling of desperation, where he had no control over his life. At the same time, his male adolescent peers might be emphasising the importance of manliness and physical courage. In such a situation, the juvenile may decide to regain a sense of potency by committing acts which might be delinquent (1964:181ff).

By allocating some space to group culture, Matza is less open to the criticism that control theories tend to focus on individuals and to ignore group processes.

7.7 Interactionist perspectives and labelling theory

A feature of most of the theories covered so far is that they generally assume crime to be an objectively defined concept. As a result, the central question for criminology is: 'Why does X commit crime?' and not 'Why is this behaviour regarded as crime?', or 'What is the effect of society's reaction to such behaviour?'.

The types of perspective which will be examined next represent a change of approach, in which crime or deviance is considered from the point of view of the actor. They will be dealt with under the headings 'Symbolic interaction' and 'Labelling theory'. Such terms (and others like 'interactionism' and 'social reaction theory') are sometimes used interchangeably, but will be treated separately here..

7.8 Symbolic interaction

At the core of symbolic interaction theory is the idea that your actions should be considered according to what they mean to you, not what they mean to others. You give meaning to your own conduct, but obviously you do not do so in a vacuum. Interpretation comes about through interaction with others. Your own perceptions of yourself and of what you do will be affected by other people's reactions. The actions and words of persons involved in these interactions have symbolic significance. According to this perspective, an individual's self-image and his perception of reality are not given, but are constructed through a series of interactions with others. As a result, where a person acts in a way which other people label as deviant, his view of himself will be affected and he might come to see himself and his actions as deviant. This may encourage commitment to deviance.

Symbolic interaction is not a new idea. More than 70 years ago it was represented in the writing of Cooley (1902) and Thomas (1927), but perhaps more notably in the work of George Herbert Mead (1918). For the latter, the consistent punishment of criminals did not control crime, but instead 'provoked intransigence and hostility in the criminal ... [Mead] seemed to take it for granted that such reactive antagonism led to further crime' (Lemert, 1967:42).

More recently, this type of social psychology has influenced the work of sociologists. Becker (1963) looked at the processes by which marijuana users became alienated from the wider society after breaking its rules, and came to view themselves as different, as outsiders. In his work on closed institutions, Goffman (1961, 1963) illustrated the stigmatisation attaching to individuals because of mental illness or criminality.

The symbolic interactionist perspective has had a considerable influence on the development of labelling theory, and a number of writers draw attention to the close theoretical ties between the two (Davis, 1975; Gibbons, 1979; Hall Williams, 1982; Schur, 1969). It is to labelling theory that we now turn.

7.9 Labelling theory

Social reaction to deviance was not a source of concern for a positivist model of criminology which concentrated on the search for causes of crime (Taylor *et al*, 1973:28; Gibbons, 1979:144). In contrast, labelling theory adds characters to the equation by calling for consideration of reaction against the deviant and of the deviant's interpretation of such reaction. The approach asks 'deviant to whom?' or 'deviant from what?' (Schur, 1971:29).

Within the labelling viewpoint, deviance is not a quality inherent in particular acts, but is conferred on certain acts by society (Erikson, 1962). However, a person does not become a deviant simply by indulging in rule breaking conduct. His conduct must be recognised by others and made the subject of official sanctions.

According to Becker, 'The deviant is one to whom that label has been successfully applied; deviant behaviour is behaviour that people so label' (1963:9). Similar points are made by Erikson (1962) and Kitsuse (1962).

Being found out and stigmatised, as a consequence of rule breaking conduct, may cause an individual to reconstruct his self-image, to see himself as deviant, and to become committed to further deviance. The labelling approach identifies deviancy as 'a process rather than a static condition' (Hall Williams, 1982:143). Lemert suggests, 'the original causes of the deviation recede and give way to the central importance of the disapproving, degradational and labelling reactions of society' (1967:17).

It was Lemert who proposed one of the central distinctions made by labelling theorists, between two stages of deviation:

1. Primary deviation. Supporters of the approach see little point in searching for the causes of primary deviation which are 'assumed to arise in a wide variety of social, cultural and psychological contexts, and ... to have only marginal implications for the psychic structure of the individual' (Lemert, 1967:17).
2. Secondary deviation. This is seen as 'deviant behaviour ... which becomes a means of defense, attack or adaptation to the overt and covert problems created by the societal reaction to primary deviation' (Lemert, 1967:17).

As mentioned earlier, the influence of symbolic interactionism on labelling theory is readily apparent. Similarities can also be seen between the labelling approach and the claims discussed in Chapter 2 that the actions of the police or society can lead to deviancy amplification. The former deals with the labelling of individuals whereas the latter refers to the stereotyping or isolation of groups.

7.10 Evaluation of labelling theory

Labelling theory has been complimented for greatly enriching our appreciation of deviant behaviour by 'standing the question on its head' (Hall Williams, 1982:145; note also Taylor *et al*, 1973:139). It is ironic that those features which attract favourable comment are also the targets for criticism.

By seemingly denying choice on the part of the rule breaker the approach arguably slips into the same determinism which is a feature of the type of positivism it seeks to challenge. One critic has said that the writings of labelling theorists sometimes suggest that: 'people go about minding their own business, and then – "wham" – bad society comes along and slaps them with a stigmatised label ... the individual has little choice but to be deviant' (Akers, 1967:455).

Labelling theorists are to be applauded for challenging an absolutist view which sees deviancy and crime as static, objectively defined entities (see Schur, 1971:14), but their counter approach has led Taylor *et al* to argue that much of the work in this area lapses into 'relativistic idealism' by virtually claiming there would be no deviance if there were no labels (1973:144).

Furthermore, the central distinction between primary and secondary deviation, and the almost exclusive concentration on the latter, severely limit the credibility of the labelling perspective. Mankoff suggests the approach 'fails to seriously consider the possibility that deviant behaviour may be persisted in even when the rule-breaker has every opportunity to return to the status of non-deviant, because of a positive attachment to rule-breaking' (1971:211).

Taylor *et al* say the labelling approach overplays its claim that the explanation of deviancy lies in the effects of social reaction. Like Gibbs, they argue that the deviant status of many acts will be obvious, from existing social meanings. Such acts do not depend on subsequent social reaction to define them as deviant (Gibbs, 1966:13; Taylor *et al*, 1973:147ff). Someone who stole, or used illicit drugs in our society, would be aware at the time that his conduct was regarded as criminal.

Another criticism of labelling theory is that it portrays the deviant as the underdog or as a victim. Taylor *et al* propose a shift in focus so that he is seen as a 'decision maker who often violates the moral and legal codes of society' (1973:147). Although continued involvement in deviance may be explained by social reaction in some cases, in others it may have the same causes as the actor's original motivation. Any attempt at gaining a full picture of why individuals first become involved in crime and continue their involvement requires consideration of both initial causes and explanations for secondary deviance. To separate the two is artificial.

Attention is sometimes drawn to inconsistencies in labelling theory. For instance, Becker implies that people who commit deviant acts are no different from others who do not: 'There is no reason to assume that only those who commit a deviant act actually have the impulse to do so. It is much more likely that most people experience deviant impulses frequently' (1963:26).

Yet there is no real attempt to explain why only some individuals follow such urges or, more significantly, to explain different responses to social reaction. Taylor *et al* suggest that implicit in labelling theory's fascination with why some people become committed to deviance whilst others do not, is an assumption that deviants are radically different from conformists (1973:153).

Becker is also accused of another form of inconsistency. For example, he refers to the 'secret deviant' (1963:20). Given the alleged importance of the discovery of deviant conduct and of social reaction, this appears to be a contradiction in terms. However, it should be recognised that elsewhere Becker says that labelling 'cannot possibly be conceived as the sole explanation of what alleged deviants actually do' (1974:42).

7.11 Conclusion

The labelling approach has come in for some hard criticism. Davis says it has been 'largely astructural, ahistorical, and noncomparative, and tends to promote a sociology of the segmental, the exotic, and the bizarre' (1972:453).

Such comments would seem more justified if the approach had really been promoted as a developed theory, but in reality it is 'an extremely loose set of themes ... To some extent it turns out to be a phantom theory' (Gibbons, 1979:146).

Writers often refer to 'labelling theorists' as if they belong to some clearly defined group and share identical ideas. In a paper entitled *Misunderstanding labelling perspectives*, Plummer discusses this tendency and shows the diversity of interests of those writers who are described as labelling theorists (1979:86ff). Once a variety of loosely connected writings have been mixed together, it becomes all too easy for critics to construct hypotheses and to identify assumptions allegedly adhered to by the authors, and to go on to demonstrate their weaknesses (Lemert, 1976:244). For these reasons, it is safer to view labelling as a perspective rather than as a coherent theory or paradigm (Gibbons, 1979:147).

Social interaction and labelling theory were among the developments which inspired the growth of the 'new criminology', which will be dealt with in the next chapter.

8

The New Criminology

8.1 The origins of the new criminology

During the 1960s an approach to criminology began to emerge which challenged many of the assumptions of mainstream theories. There were a number of threads within this approach but collectively they tend to be referred to as 'the new criminology'. Although this perspective has by no means obliterated what by implication must be the 'old' criminology, it has generated considerable interest among theorists as well as teachers and students of criminology, and has spawned a substantial body of literature.

The conditions which encouraged or even necessitated the development of a new approach existed both within the discipline and in the outside world. For example, a number of writers assert that in the United States the growth of radical criminology was closely related to social events, such as activity by the civil rights movement (Platt 1974; Gibbons, 1979; Greenberg, 1981). As one of the reasons for embarking on an analysis of the relationship between power, social conflict and crime, Turk (1969) cites embarrassment because of the unreality of traditional studies in the light of actual events involving law enforcement.

Undoubtedly, some of the initial impetus behind the new criminology was provided by slightly earlier challenges to mainstream criminology. Young (1988) suggests that in the United States radical criminology had its origins in labelling theory, but that in Britain it was inspired by subcultural theories. Vold and Bernard (1986) trace the American origins to conflict theory, and those in Britain to social reaction theory.

Supporters of the new approach point to several shortcomings in the then dominant positivist model of criminology. For one thing, most traditional theories were based on a consensus view of society which, putting it simply, held that all of a society's members had a shared opinion as to which types of behaviour should be labelled as criminal. However, during the last half century that view has been challenged by several forms of conflict theory (eg Sellin 1938; Vold, 1958). Conflict theory recognises that society is made up of a variety of groups with different and often competing interests, and that the most powerful groups will be in a better position to control the functions of the state, including the making and enforcement of law. Vold and Bernard suggest that Marxist criminology is really a form of conflict criminology which looks deeper than the exercise of power towards political and economic systems to explain crime (1986:299). This is just one reason to wonder how new the 'new' criminology is.

8.2 The challenge to 'value-free' criminology

Perhaps the most fundamental point about the radical approach is its emphasis on praxis, that is, the notion that theory should be translated into practice. As the causes of crime are rooted in the economic, political, and social fabric of our society, crime can only be tackled through major change to that fabric (Taylor *et al*, 1973; Downes, 1979; Young, 1988). From this viewpoint, the kind of social tinkering advocated by some positivist theories cannot succeed in controlling crime. Similarly any attempt to reduce crime by rehabilitating individuals is like 'trying to empty the ocean with a bucket' (Greenberg, 1981:18).

Leading proponents of the radical school suggest that traditional criminology supports the *status quo*, and argue that instead criminologists should take an active role in bringing about social change (Platt, 1974; Taylor *et al*, 1973). Quinney (1978) calls on criminologists to be advocates of working class interests.

Radicals do not stop at challenging the role of criminologists, they also seek to broaden the scope of criminology by calling for a new definition of crime. Those in power are said not only to decide which behaviours will be identified as criminal but also to control the social definition of crime, by ensuring that criminals and crime are seen as something separate from themselves and their activities. A broadening of the definition would encourage criminologists to look under stones which are usually left unturned. For example, Schwendinger and Schwendinger would amend the definition to include activities which violate human rights (1970) or damage working class interests (1977). Turk suggests that criminology must look at issues like racism and sexism but that a legalistic focus must be maintained if it is to continue as a separate discipline.

The radical approach challenges other features of traditional criminology such as its deterministic bias, but not through a straightforward quest for intellectual or scientific development. Aspects of the traditional model had already come under scrutiny anyway. Rather, the source of radical criminology's opposition to the mainstream school and of its own newness, is to be found in its ideological underpinnings.

8.3 What's in a name?

The new approach has been given a number of titles such as 'radical', 'critical', or 'Marxist'. Cohen (1979) uses those titles in referring to criminologies which emerged during the 1970s, so it is clear that separate strands can be found within the new school. That said, it is not unusual for the terms to be used interchangeably, or for 'radical' and 'critical' to be used as brackets for a type of criminology which may be based on a 'socialist, libertarian/anarchist, socialist or radical feminist' viewpoint (Young, 1986:160). A similar approach will be used here as it would be pointless to construct distinctions between titles which some writers treat as identical. First of all, though, the influence of Marxism on the new perspectives should be examined.

8.4 The influence of Marxism on the new criminology

The different strands in radical criminology are 'usually dependent on a fiercely socialist root' often inspired by the work of Marx and Engels (Hall Williams, 1982:147). Furthermore, Marxist criminology is often discussed as a separate model (eg Greenberg, 1981; Vold and Bernard, 1986). A brief look at how Marxist theory influences the study of crime is necessary.

It will be assumed that you already have a basic awareness of Marxist theory. As Vold and Bernard point out, the work of Marx and Engels represents a theory of society and social change which is highly complex and which is still evolving (1986:299). Current supporters give differing interpretations and to summarise Marxism in a few paragraphs would lead to gross over-simplification.

A fundamental point that must be remembered is Marx's assertion that 'The mode of production in material life determines the general character of the social, political, and spiritual processes of life' (1904:11). Marx's claim should not be read as simple economic determinism since it is clear from his other writings that the law, and other institutions, interact with a society's economic base in a dynamic relationship (eg Marx and Engels, 1969). Hence the law is at least partly independent, but within a Marxist perspective it can never be seen as a wholly autonomous entity free of class-based influence.

Neither Marx nor Engels had much to say about crime specifically, and in the words of one commentator 'Their scattered observations do not add up to a criminology' (Greenberg, 1981:11). Nevertheless, it is interesting to note that some of the rare mentions are echoed in more recent work. For example, Marx and Engels described crime as 'the struggle of the isolated individual against the prevailing conditions' (1965:367).

During the early part of this century, Willem Bonger applied Marxist concepts to the study of crime (1916, 1936, 1943). As with Marx, the demoralisation of individuals under a capitalist system is important in explaining the presence of crime. According to Bonger, by involving the production of excess goods, a capitalist system discourages men from sharing with their fellows and instead encourages them to exchange those goods for their own benefit. In his words, capitalism 'has developed egoism at the expense of altruism' (1969:40).

Owing to the lack of explicit direction offered by Marx in relation to crime, criminologists wishing to work within a Marxist framework are forced to interpret Marx's thoughts and to supplement them. Bonger was no exception. For Bonger (1916), the egoism fostered by capitalism enables the 'criminal thought' to arise in man. Closer reading of his work indicates that not all men will experience the criminal thought; that within some of those who do, forces will operate which prevent the thought being translated into action; and that persons suffering from psychic defects are more likely to indulge in criminal acts.

Taylor *et al* suggest that Bonger's emphasis on the individual characteristic of the criminal thought, is equivalent to the individual and sociological factors which are given causative significance in the works of positivist criminologists (1973:223). More fundamentally, Taylor *et al* criticise Bonger for ignoring questions about how the criminal law is framed and enforced in a capitalist society (1973:223–4). However, according to Vold and Bernard, Bonger recognised that the criminal justice system criminalised the selfishness of the poor but gave legality to the greed of the rich (1986:303).

Bonger appears to have been ahead of his time in including ideas not dissimilar to aspects of differential association and anomie but, by doing so, he brought into question his own fidelity to Marxism. It is not surprising that his approach has been called 'eclectic and, at times, urbane' (Taylor *et al*, 1973:235).

Marxist criminology faded after the mid 1920s, and it was in the early 1970s that a new radical approach began to emerge. On both sides of the Atlantic, some sociologists looked to Marxism to help them achieve a deeper understanding of social processes (Greenberg, 1981:10). Writing in this field has been so prolific that it is virtually impossible to provide an accurate summary. The approach adopted will be to take a brief, selective look at some of the early writers, followed by an examination of the work of several noteworthy contributors.

8.5 Some American contributions to radical criminology

Gordon (1971) suggested that in capitalist societies, opportunities to attain economic security are not evenly distributed. People are left to fend for themselves and, inevitably, some laws will be broken in the quest for economic survival. From Gordon's viewpoint, crime in a capitalist society was a perfectly rational response to that society's institutional structure. Gordon looked at ghetto crime, organised crime, and corporate crime, arguing that each was a rational response to economic pressures. The type of response varied according to the circumstances of the people involved. Gordon went on to suggest that differential processing by the criminal justice system (ignoring corporate crime whilst prosecuting everyday offences with vigour) could be traced to the fact that the state serves the interests of owners of capital.

Michalowski and Bohlander (1976) asserted that the criminal law is used as an instrument to repress certain groups in order to serve the interests of those who own or control the means of production. The oppressed classes tolerated this use of the criminal law and the commission of corporate crime because the powerful class was able to control the social definition of crime, thus creating an illusion of consensus about the legal order of society.

Spitzer (1975) put forward a theory of deviance drawing on Marxian ideas. Assuming that the power-holders in capitalist societies are concerned to uphold the existing social relations of production, individuals or groups who threaten those social relations will represent a threat. According to Spitzer, such people become 'eligible for management as deviant' when they threaten features of the capitalist structure, such as the modes of appropriating profit or the social and ideological patterns that support it (1975:642). His categories are so broad that almost anyone might fit in at one time or another (Gibbons, 1979:175). For example, Spitzer suggested that individuals who were unable to perform wage labour might become targets for the control machinery. Critics of Spitzer argue that there are many unemployed people in Britain who never fall foul of the criminal law. However, such people can be marked out as deviant by attracting the label 'scrounger'. Perhaps the radicals could argue that the use of such tactics is more subtle than invoking the criminal law and allows the illusion of consensus to be maintained.

Chambliss, whose earlier work was written within the conflict perspective, also drew on Marxist theory to put forward a radical explanation of crime (1975). The central points of his propositions were that acts are criminalised in such a way as to reflect the interests of the ruling class; crimes by the ruling class will go unpunished; the attention of the lower classes is drawn away from the exploitative acts of the capital-owners towards the crimes of other members of their own class; crime is a rational response to conditions characteristic of one's social class; crime will vary between societies as their economic and political structures vary; crime rates should be lower in socialist societies because there is less inter-class conflict.

All of these versions of radical criminology are open to criticisms, which will be discussed later. It should be noted, however, that a lot of the earlier material was intended to promote discussion rather than to represent fully developed theories.

Other writers have shown a greater degree of thought and sophistication, and attract more coverage in discussions of radical criminology.

Richard Quinney stands out among American writers in the radical field. After producing several works in the mainstream tradition, he moved into conflict theory (1970), and then went on to write or collaborate in several works with a strong radical influence (1974; 1974a; 1975). Quinney's *Critique of Legal Order* is not vastly different from other crude versions of a Marxist approach. For example, it includes a set of propositions centring on the notion that the criminal law is an instrument of class oppression, enforced via the criminal justice system in such a way as to keep control in the hands of a ruling elite, and that the only way to end crime is to replace capitalist society with a new socialist society (1974:16).

Quinney's most developed description of a radical criminology appears in his *Class, State and Crime* (1977). Like other writers, Quinney sometimes relies on supposition rather than concrete evidence to support his claims, but this book does at least avoid some of the more obvious limitations of other radical works. For example, it recognises that rather than society being comprised of two groups, namely, the owners of capital and the working class, there are sub-divisions within those classes. It also recognises that with increased unemployment and the need to manage welfare programmes without taking too much money from the capitalist economy, the state has a far more complicated role than simply acting as the instrument of a unified ruling class. In addition, the book avoids the tendency of some writers to treat ordinary criminals as romantic rebels. Whilst certain types of crime committed by members of the lower class arise from economic deprivation or from circumstances endemic to capitalism, Quinney sees such acts as an unconscious opposition to capitalist domination rather than as deliberate acts of rebellion. *Class, State and Crime* has been described as 'a contemporary version of Marxism' (Gibbons, 1979:181).

8.6 The growth of radical criminology in Britain

In Britain in the late 1960s there was growing dissatisfaction among sociologists with traditional approaches to criminology. Young (1988) suggests there was a crisis of aetiology. Mainstream theories were unable to explain why an improvement in standards of living was accompanied by an increase in crime instead of a decrease. Sociology had been given a back seat because criminology was being dominated by other disciplines, such as psychology, medicine and law. The criminological establishment (represented by the Home Office and the Cambridge Institute of Criminology) was thought to be unduly concerned with controlling crime rather than explaining it. The renewed interest in the sociology of deviance which grew out of this dissatisfaction manifested itself in several developments.

For instance, in 1968 the first National Deviancy Conference was held as a breakaway movement from the British Criminological Conference and was followed by the publication of a large body of literature. One example is *Images of Deviance* edited by Stanley Cohen. The membership of the National Deviancy Conference was comprised of various factions, with diverse viewpoints.

The year 1973 saw the publication of *The New Criminology* by Taylor, Walton and Young. The greater part of this book represents a ground-clearing exercise, with earlier theories of crime being described and subjected to critical analysis. In the concluding chapter the authors spell out their requirements for a 'fully social theory of deviance' (1973:270–8). By 'fully social' they mean that the theory would not be hindered by assumptions of a biological or other non-social nature. Such a theory must cover seven dimensions, and the connections between them, as follows:

The wider origins of the deviant act

The act must be placed in its wider structural origins. This means not only looking at factors such as the physical environment, subcultural influences and the availability of opportunities for crime, but also placing these in the broader context of the inequalities characteristic of capitalist society. Taylor et al call this the requirement for a 'political economy of crime'.

Immediate origins of the deviant act

The theory must explain how people at different levels in the social structure interpret and react differently to structural demands in such a way as to make deviant choices. The authors say this is a requirement for a 'social psychology of crime' which recognises that crime may be consciously chosen as a solution to problems posed by society.

The actual act

The fully social theory of deviance must be able to explain how an individual's capacity to exercise his choice to act is affected by his place in the social structure. This is described as the need for an account of the 'social dynamics' surrounding criminal acts.

Immediate origins of social reaction

The theory needs to explain how and why the social audience reacts to a deviant act in different ways. For example, why a witness decides to report or not to report suspicious behaviour to the police. Taylor *et al* call this the requirement for a 'social psychology of social reaction'.

Wider origins of social reaction

(If you read the original you will notice that 'deviant' has mistakenly been substituted for 'social'.)

There is a need to examine the economic and political initiatives which lead to certain activities acquiring (or losing) criminal status. In other words the theory requires a 'political economy of social reaction'.

The outcome of the social reaction on the deviant's further action

The fully social theory of deviance must recognise and explain the connection between the deviant's response to social reaction towards his deviant act and the conscious choices which led to the act itself.

The nature of the deviant process as a whole

The fully social theory envisaged by Taylor *et al* must not only include all of the six factors described above it must also reflect the real world by involving those factors in a complex interactive relationship with each other.

Taylor *et al* argue that the new criminology must be a normative theory – it should not just explain crime, it should tell us what to do about it. They suggest the causes of crime are intimately bound up in the existing social arrangements and that therefore the only way to abolish crime is to implement fundamental social change. They submit that deviance is normal, and that it is an assertion of human diversity. Finally, they call for the creation of a society in which human diversity is not 'subject to the power to criminalise' (1973:282).

Taylor *et al* do not go on to describe this new socialist society.

8.7 Comments on the radical approach

Several criticisms can be levelled at the type of perspective described above. Its supporters make sweeping generalisations, often supported only by impressions or assumptions. It is Utopian in outlook. For example, just as Marx held that in a socialist society the state would wither away, so the new radicals claim that the implementation of socialism would remove the circumstances inherent in capitalist society which create crime. Certain activities formerly regarded as deviant would come to be tolerated as expressions of human diversity.

There are fatal flaws in such assumptions. Cohen describes the claims about the possibility of a crime free society as an 'implausible plank' in the radical approach (1979:41). He points out that the radicals produce no realistic alternatives to criminalisation for negative acts, nor do they set out the recipe for a truly socialist society.

Another criticism is that the radicals tend to paint a picture of capitalist society in which there is one monolithic ruling class. Thus they raise a naïve type of conspiracy theory which lacks credibility.

Similarly, the radicals ignore signs that imperialism is not exclusive to capitalist societies. Downes (1979) reminds us about the tanks rolling into Czechoslovakia and Hungary. Now we could add Tiananmen Square.

A further weakness is the radicals' assumption that working class fear of crime or support for law and order is based on false consciousness. Given that members of the working class face a greater risk of victimisation for many categories of crime, surely they have a real interest in the prevention of crime and the detection of offenders? Furthermore, as the perpetrators are often from the same class, a suggestion by Young (1975) that communities could police themselves seems very optimistic.

It would also be possible to argue that the perspective is weakened because its ideological foundations prevent its supporters from being objective. However, Greenberg suggests that Marxist criminologists seem no more prone to value-based bias than anyone else (1981:21). It would be difficult for any criminologist not to allow his views to influence his work, and at least the radicals are open about their political leanings.

In making these comments about radical criminology, it has been necessary to create a stereotypical picture. It must also be admitted that the perspective outlined here was more typical during the 1970s. Some of the writers involved have modified their positions, and we now turn to an examination of such developments.

8.8 A realist criminology

The need for a radical realism

Some of the most persuasive arguments for overcoming the weaknesses in radical criminology and creating a radical realism, have come from Jock Young, one of the leading lights of the new criminology during the 1970s. In a more recent work, he points out that left idealism caused the new criminologists to ignore some of the useful aspects of earlier theories, and to avoid some methods of research because they were part of the positivist tradition against which they were reacting (1986:13). Young suggests that for two decades radical criminology had ignored the victim of crime. He also says that left idealists encouraged a focus on the law and why the state criminalises people, but ignored the question of why certain people commit crime. In this way, they 'managed to construct a theory of crime without a criminology' (1986:19).

Young says the romantic conceptions of radical criminology must be disposed of, and that a left realism must be substituted. This would reflect the reality of crime, including why it occurs, what it is and what its effects are. Holding true to the radical commitment to praxis, Young asserts that realism would inform its supporters' notion of what can be done about crime.

Crime really is a problem

The starting point for Young's left realism is to recognise crime as a problem. Young calls on realists to steer between two extremes. On the one hand, the problem could be exaggerated. On the other, the true extent of crime could be played down. There is a need for accurate research into victimisation. This would confirm that most crime is focused on the most vulnerable sections of the community. It would also show how much crime occurs between members of the working class, and how much is committed in a domestic setting. Not surprisingly, the left realists would not ignore crimes of the powerful. Young contends they would show that the working class falls victim to crime from all directions. He maintains that 'crime is a potent symbol of the anti-social nature of capitalism' (1986:24).

The position of the criminal

A more accurate picture of crime and criminals could avoid the idealistic conception of the criminal as a hero, but could also counter media-generated images of criminals as something apart from normal society. Young suggests that painting criminals as folk-devils allows them to be targets for feelings of unfairness produced by capitalism (1986:24).

In terms of explaining crime, a realist perspective would recognise the complications in the question of why particular individuals commit crime. It is not helpful to view the criminal as a rebel against an unjust system. Whilst the forces created within a capitalist society have to be taken into account, realists would recognise that individual pathology might matter for some individuals. For others, guilt and even rational choice will play their part to varying degrees (Young, 1975; Cohen, 1979).

The tasks for a realist criminology

Young claims the basis of a widespread support for a realist approach has been emerging, particularly in Britain, Canada, the United States and Australia (1986:25). However, a realist criminology has yet to be constructed, and for Young there are two key tasks to be performed:

1. The first is the carrying out of theoretically grounded empirical work. Victimisation surveys are a key area of interest for radicals, but Young does not rule out the use of ethnographic studies or various uses of qualitative or quantitative research.
2. The second task is to develop a practical policy, for Young admits that socialists lack a developed strategy for dealing with crime.

Realist criminology is still the newest of the new criminologies and has yet to be developed, but if it acquires sufficient supporters with the imagination and the will to overcome earlier romanticism, Rock might be correct in commenting that 'radical criminology may leave a legacy which will be useful' (1988:84).

8.9 Feminist criminology

Criminology and the feminist movement

We have seen that the growth of radical criminology during the 1960s and 1970s was linked to real social events. During the same period, the feminist movement acquired greater visibility as more women struggled to free themselves from the subordinate role assigned to them in a male dominated society. It should be no surprise that this development was mirrored in attempts to establish a feminist criminology.

Criminology's neglect of women

As you will have noticed, criminologists have generally concentrated on finding explanations for male deviancy. Women and girls are rarely considered, and on the few occasions when they are, they are assigned a marginal place. Lombroso and Ferrero published *The Female Offender* in 1895, but could not explain female criminality in terms of the atavistic features supposedly found in many male criminals. Female offenders were said to be 'almost normal' when compared with criminal men, but not when compared with normal females. In addition to being devoid of typical female attributes, they possessed an excessive amount of the shortcomings found in normal women (1895:107). This seems to define female criminals as 'biological abnormalities' (Gregory, 1986:60).

More recent attempts to explain crime have tended to ignore the importance of gender. For example, Leonard (1982) criticises Merton for formulating his theory of anomie in a way which ignores the different goals and opportunities offered to American women when compared with men. Studies of youth culture have occasionally considered females, but the majority have concentrated on young males (Gregory, 1986). Leonard (1982) also argues that labelling theorists have not explained the ways in which power structures affect women differently from men, so that women seem to be less involved in crime.

Radical criminologists also stand accused of virtually ignoring women. Greenwood (1981) says that in *The New Criminology*, Taylor *et al* create an image of the criminal as a male. Leonard (1982) emphasises that the same book contains nothing about women. Gregory suggests that the gender-blindness of a Marxist criminology can be traced to its central concerns. As men relate more directly than women to the means of production and exchange which are studied by Marxists, the latter are unable to explore the power relationships which affect women differently on the grounds of gender rather than class (Gregory, 1986:62).

Gregory suggests that by the mid 1980s, a trickle of feminist criminology had become a 'steady stream' (1986:53). The reaction of most teachers and theorists has been to bolt female criminality on to the syllabus or the criminological agenda, rather than making any major changes. Heidensohn (1987) has criticised this as a 'lean to' approach.

Possible reasons for criminology's male bias

It seems natural to ask why criminology has suffered from this male bias for so long. An obvious answer is that criminologists have merely been reflecting the society in which they work. Schwendinger and Schwendinger suggest the early sociologists were 'sexist to a man' (1973:310).

Another possible cause may be the fact that women appear to commit far less crime than men. In England and Wales in 1995, 1,383,000 men were found guilty or cautioned, whereas the figure for females was 326,000. (Home Office 1996a p94).

Chapter 2 questioned the accuracy of official statistics, and it has been argued that if true levels were recorded, the gap between male and female crime rates would disappear, or at least be much smaller (Pollak, 1950). Self-report studies have often been used to measure real levels of offending. In relation to serious crimes, such studies tend to indicate that females commit far fewer offences than males (Hindelang, 1979; Smith and Visher, 1980). Box (1983) claims that women have hardly any involvement in organised crime, corporate crime, or governmental crime.

As the comparatively low rate of female offending appears to be genuine, it is feasible that male criminologists consider this to be an area unworthy of exploration. Furthermore, female crime may not appear to be a serious enough social problem for governments or other sponsors to provide funds for research into it.

The implications of ignoring female crime

Whatever the cause, a refusal to consider female criminality is short-sighted, and according to Gregory it leads to a double failure:

1. No analysis is made of the factors which may bring about female conformity or non-conformity. (An interesting possibility is that because of the low rate of crime by women, feminist criminology would be more concerned with explaining conformity rather than deviance).
2. Proper examination of female criminality would allow comparisons which could enhance our understanding of why criminality seems to be an almost exclusively male preserve (Gregory, 1986:59). Smart asserts that criminology 'must become more than the study of men and crime if it is to play any significant part in the development of our understanding of crime, law and the criminal process' (1976:185).

Branches of feminism

The arguments above seem to be beyond challenge. A logical next step is to consider the sort of questions a feminist criminology would ask. That task would be made easier if there were only one branch of feminism and of feminist criminology. Unfortunately, that is not the case. There are three main branches:

1. Socialist-feminists, who are committed to developing a perspective which embraces both feminism and Marxism.
2. Radical feminists, who recognise that sexual oppression pre-dates capitalism and who investigate and challenge the effects of sexual divisions without adopting a Marxist framework.
3. A third type of feminism, which is older than the other two, and might be described as bourgeois feminism. Its members seek to improve women's rights, but do not challenge the capitalist structure of society.

As the different strands become entangled, the way forward for feminist criminology 'remains obscure' (Gregory, 1986:65).

The concerns of feminist criminology

Smart (1981) suggests a wide variety of theoretical positions have been taken within feminist criminology, and says the critical question is one of distinguishing between 'women studying criminology', 'criminology of women', and 'feminist women studying criminology'. No one seems to have done this satisfactorily, and little assistance is given by Brown's suggestion that feminist criminology can be recognised by its critique of traditional theory and practice (1986).

Greenwood (1981) describes feminist criminology as a coalition of studies of female offenders which offer varied perspectives on:

1. Conventional views of female criminality (Simon, 1975).
2. The invisibility of women in traditional criminology (Bunker, 1978).
3. Apparent sexism within the criminal justice process.

However, it is arguable that such studies would fit more closely with the concerns of bourgeois feminists than with those of radical or socialist-feminists. Kress (1979) suggests feminist criminology has failed to consider the distinction between the experiences of women of different races and classes.

The emphasis on gender, rather than sex

It seems that feminist criminology must be concerned with gender, which is a socially-constructed concept, and not simply with a biologically determined difference in sex (Gelsthorpe, 1987). Work which attempts to explain female criminality in terms of biological differences between men and women, and between criminal and non-criminal women runs the risk of condemnation by feminists (eg the comments about the work of Cowie et al, 1968, by Gregory, 1986:60).

Further essential qualities of feminist research (not limited to criminology) have been identified by Stanley and Wise (1983). These include the requirements that research must be by, on and for women; that non-sexist methodologies be employed; and that the research must be useful to the women's movement. In relation to the first requirement, Morgan (1981) expresses curiosity as to whether men could appreciate feminist perspectives, or whether the issues involved can only be understood by women.

A future for feminist criminology?

For whatever reasons, it is clear that feminist criminology has neither formulated a single voice, nor made a significant impact on the general field of criminology. Some of the leading supporters of feminist criminology have expressed disappointment and even, it may be said, despair. Carlen (1985) doubts the existence of a true feminist criminology. In 1968, Heidensohn called for a crash programme of feminist study to catch up with decades of research and theory about male crime. By 1985, she thought that day was 'further off then ever and less exciting as a prospect' (1985:200). Even more recently Heidensohn has asked 'has anyone been listening ... have they changed their minds, their research studies or their institutional practices?' (1987:21).

This lack of progress is disappointing. It seems to be beyond argument that the virtual exclusion of gender from criminology represents the omission of a significant, and even essential variable. A full and meaningful consideration of women as both offenders and victims of crime would surely help to produce a more rounded and scientifically defensible criminology.

9

Corporate Crime

9.1 Introduction

More than 80 years ago, Ross (1907) sought to focus attention on the threat presented by white collar crime and to cast light on the apathy with which such crime was regarded. He urged academics and others to be: 'Zealous to reconnoiter and instant to cry aloud the dangers that present themselves in our tumultuous social advance'. This chapter aims to assess the way in which criminologists have picked up the gauntlet thrown down by Ross, in relation to corporate crime. It will be argued that criminology has not yet faced the problem head on, and that much of the discussion in the intervening years has concerned itself with assessing the terms on which the challenge should be met.

From 1940 onwards, Sutherland made pioneering efforts in the study of corporate crime, supplementing theory with empirical work (1940, 1945, 1949). Although he usually referred to 'white collar crime', Sutherland's main concern was with the crime of corporations (Kramer, 1984:16). Box describes Sutherland's efforts as 'a legacy scorned by its putative beneficiaries' (1983:18). Of 3,700 publications listed in an index of criminological work between 1945 and 1972 (Wolfgang, Figlio and Thornberry, 1975), just over 1 per cent dealt with corporate crime (Wheeler, 1976).

However, there are signs that the study of corporate crime is now growing, and the literature 'burgeoning' (Kramer, 1984). Ninety-six per cent of all the social problems textbooks published by 1980 and which mentioned corporate crime, were published after 1971 (Clinard and Yeager, 1980). Nevertheless, there remains a tendency for much of the work in this area to be atheoretical, and to concentrate on corporate crime as a phenomenon. The apparent failure of criminologists to address corporate crime has not been entirely wilful, as there are a number of obstacles to its concerted study.

9.2 Obstacles to the study of corporate crime

Obvious hurdles include a shortage of research funds, an absence of official statistics, problems of access, and the lack of an adequate theoretical framework on which to build (Kramer, 1984). However, several preliminary issues frequently dominate discussions of corporate crime. They concern:

1. Apparent public ambivalence.
2. Assessment of the seriousness of corporate crime.
3. Defining corporate crime.

As those issues often dwarf or even exclude theoretical content in such discussions, they must be examined in order to emphasise their relevance to the current state of theory and research. The examination will be kept as brief as possible.

Apparent public ambivalence

There is some evidence that in the past, the public were indifferent to corporate crime (Newman 1957), but recent attitude surveys have indicated growing public concern about corporate crimes, especially where there is a physical impact (Scott and Al-Thakeb, 1977; Sinden, 1980; Cullen *et al*, 1982).

As Schrager and Short (1980) have pointed out, even if the public were indifferent to corporate crime, that would not be an excuse for criminologists to rule it out as an area of behaviour demanding deep and urgent study.

Assessment of the seriousness of corporate crime

Corporate crime inflicts three types of damage:

Economic damage
Conklin estimates that in the United States in 1977 the economic losses from various white collar crimes were about 40 billion dollars, as against 3 to 4 billion dollars

from ordinary economic crimes (1977:4). The financial burden imposed by corporate crime is enormous, both in relative terms, and absolutely.

Physical damage
In terms of physical consequences, corporate crime 'kills and maims more ... than any violence committed by the poor' (Liazos, 1972:111). In the United States an estimated 100,000 people die each year from occupationally related diseases, most of which are contracted because of wilful violation of laws designed to protect workers (Swartz, 1975; Kramer, 1984:20). Defective products kill 30,000 Americans annually (Kramer, 1984) and an untold number of injuries and deaths must surely stem from the willingness of American manufacturers to dump drugs and medical equipment in third world countries after they have been banned in the domestic market (Silverman, 1977; Dowie, 1979; Braithwaite, 1984).

Social damage
According to Wilson, conventional street crime 'makes difficult or impossible the maintenance of meaningful human communities' (1975:XX). In reality, corporate crime inflicts similar damage on the moral fabric of society. By reducing commercial confidence, and thwarting fair competition, corporate crime lowers moral standards in the business world (President's Commission, 1967). Conklin (1977) adds that crime by the upper class enables the lower classes to rationalise their own criminal behaviour. The activities of the corporate criminal are not only greater in impact than those of his ordinary counterparts, but they are also longer lasting in effect (Edelhertz, 1970:9).

Defining corporate crime
Traditionally, the toughest 'intellectual nightmare' facing the student of corporate crime has been that of defining the concept (Geis and Meier, 1977). A valid and meaningful definition must be found in order to mark out the boundaries of study. Labels can be very confusing, especially when they are applied inconsistently. It has to be noted that corporate crime and white collar crime are not identical. In an early attempt at a definition, Sutherland said: 'White collar crime may be defined *approximately* as a crime committed by a person of respectability and high social status in the course of his occupation' (1949:9, my emphasis).

White collar crime, then, can be committed when an individual commits crime against the organisation within which he works, for example, the accountant who embezzles company funds. Equally, a self-employed person who evades income tax would be regarded as a white collar criminal. Corporate crime involves illegal acts carried out in the furtherance of the goals of an organisation. In the sense that these acts are performed by people in positions of authority within that organisation, corporate crime is a particular form of white collar crime. However, white collar crime is not always corporate crime. A further point to be aware of is that although corporate crime is sometimes referred to as organisational crime, it should normally be distinguished from organised crime. The former term refers to crime committed on behalf of a legitimate organisation and the latter to crime carried out by a criminal syndicate. Admittedly, the dividing lines are often blurred and from a moral standpoint a company which knowingly exposes its employees to the risk of fatal industrial diseases might seem far worse than a straightforward gang of racketeers. As will be seen below, more sophisticated attempts have since been made to re-define white collar crime, and to refine earlier definitions to fit corporate crime. It is not proposed to examine them all here, for while the criminologist is toying with semantics, he is not grappling with more tangible problems. Sutherland's inclusion of the word 'approximately', and subsequent inconsistent uses of his own definition, suggest that he considered the study of the concept itself to be more important than the definition.

Schrager and Short put forward the following definition of organisational crime:

> 'Illegal acts of omission or commission of an individual or a group of individuals in a legitimate formal organisation in accordance with the operative goals of the organisation which have a serious physical or economic impact on employees, consumers or the general public.' (1978:409)

That definition can be profitably applied to corporate crime as it avoids the restrictions of some other models. For example, Schrager and Short go beyond economic impact. They also include omissions as well as action.

A question which has taxed criminologists since Sutherland is whether corporate crime is really 'crime'. Many of the laws governing corporate activity are regulatory in nature, and of recent origin, without roots in the common law. Enforcement is often in the hands of agencies other than the police, and violations may attract civil or administrative action rather than criminal prosecution.

Schrager and Short, in referring to illegal acts, seem to include those attracting civil or administrative sanctions. Others would go further and include serious harms which, though not proscribed, are in breach of human rights (Schwendinger and Schwendinger, 1970). As Box (1983:22) points out, doing so raises enormous philosophical issues, and minimises the range of possible support for the serious study of corporate crime.

Tappan (1947) supported a narrow legalistic viewpoint, encompassing only breaches which attract criminal sanctions, but according to Vold, excessively rigid definitions 'are of little assistance in helping to understand problems of crime causation' (1958:268).

For the criminologist interested in exploring corporate deviance, the importance of such conduct lies not in the type of law by which it is prohibited, but in its source within the violator's corporate status. If it is necessary for him to do so in order to examine significant behaviour, the criminologist would seem to be no less entitled than some lawyers to follow Humpty Dumpty and say ' "crime" means what I want it to mean'.

9.3 Attempts to explain corporate crime

A number of different theories have been used to try to explain corporate crime, and some of these will now be examined. Research efforts will be treated not separately, but concurrently, by illustrating discussion of theories with particular examples. Anyway, research has been 'frugal when compared to conventional crime or delinquency' (Newman, 1958). As corporate crime has only recently begun to catch the serious attention of scholars, there is little wonder that empirical work is under developed.

9.4 Differential association

Sutherland (1940) pointed out that criminological data had in the main been compiled in relation to criminals from the lower class. As massive amounts of crime were committed by businessmen, he considered that traditional explanations were based on a false premise and therefore misleading. Sutherland tried to apply differential association theory to explain white collar crime. There is some empirical support for Sutherland's argument, in respect of corporate crime. Geis (1967) examined evidence given during hearings into the illegal price-fixing activities of some American companies, and found that people taking up new posts tended to find price-fixing to be an established practice, and picked it up themselves as part of learning their new job. Baumhart (1961) found that businessmen's unethical behaviour was influenced by superiors and peers. Both studies suggest the learning process is reinforced by 'rewards' and 'punishments'. Personality differences are not important to Sutherland's theory. Clinard (1952) argued that the theory did not explain why some individuals exposed to the same processes did not deviate, and that it must be adapted to take personality traits into account.

9.5 Anomie

Attempts have been made to explain corporate crime in terms of the concept of 'anomie'. In this context, it becomes clear that explanations based on individual motivations are inadequate. They must be seen against a background of corporate goals. The goal of a business corporation 'is to make the maximum possible profit over a long period' (Etzioni, 1961; Box, 1983). Box identifies five potential sources of 'environmental uncertainty' for the corporation which represent obstacles to the lawful attainment of its main goal. These are: competitors; the government; employees; consumers; and the public, especially as represented by protectionists. The corporation faced by such obstacles adopts tactics which frequently involve breaking the law, in order to achieve its goal.

Staw and Szwajkowski compared the financial performance of 105 large firms subject to litigation involving illegal competition, against those of 395 similar firms not so involved (1975:353). They concluded that 'Environmental scarcity does appear to be related to a range of trade violations'. For Box, the profit motive renders the corporation inherently criminogenic (Box, 1983:36, 39).

At the level of the individual, Box suggests that the bulk of corporate crime is initiated by high-ranking officials (1983:38). He sees a need to consider whether the factors connected with career success in corporations, and the consequences of such success, are themselves criminogenic.

A survey by Gross (1978) of several research projects on corporate career mobility supports Clinard's assertion, mentioned earlier, about the relevance of personality differences. Senior managers were found to be ambitious, to accept a non-demanding moral code, and to regard their own success at goal attainment as being linked to the success of the organisation.

Box argues that the promotion system of corporations means those who reach the top are likely to have the personal characteristics required to commit corporate crime (1983:39). The greater the success they achieve, the more free they feel from the bind of conventional values. In that respect, Box's interpretation of anomie seems closer to Durkheim's formulation than to Merton's.

When Box asked Jock Young for his explanation for corporate crime, he answered simply 'greed' (Box, 1983:IX). In one word Young seems to have hit the nail very nearly on its head, yet it would be simplistic to assert that the only goal relevant to anomie was financial profit.

Braithwaite describes fraud as 'an illegitimate means to achieving any one of a wide range of organisational and personal goals when legitimate means ... are blocked' (1984:94). For example, he found a widespread willingness among pharmacologists to fabricate the results of safety tests (1984: Chapter 3). Sometimes this was attributable to financial greed, but there were other explanations. Braithwaite points to the intensity of commitment of some scientists to their work, and to a tendency by some to regard a new discovery as an offspring (1984:93). The scientist who sees the value of his discovery threatened by test results could be inclined to cover up in order to defend his professional prestige.

9.6 Neutralisation

Those executives whose consciences are not placated by material comforts may apply some of the 'techniques of neutralisation' described by Sykes and Matza (1957) to rationalise their deviant acts. Shared decision making in an institutional setting allows people to contribute 'to cruel practices ... without feeling personally responsible' (Bandura, 1973:13). 'Denial of the victim' may also be used. Pharmaceutical marketeers are separated by thousands of miles (and social class) from the Third World consumers on whom they dump their unsafe drugs (Braithwaite, 1984). Company spokesmen have been prepared to blame industrial accidents on 'careless and lazy' workers or the development of brown lung in negroes on their 'racial inferiority' (Swartz 1978:125). The corporate crook sometimes denies that any harm has been caused. An executive described his price-fixing activities as, 'Illegal ... but not criminal ... I assumed that criminal action meant damaging someone, and we did not do that' (Geis, 1968:108). The corporate official can 'condemn the condemners', by pointing to political corruption, or describing laws as unwarranted fetters on free enterprise. A final technique is to appeal to higher loyalties. Acting for the good of the company, or following widespread (but illegal) business practices is seen as more important than obeying the law.

9.7 Subcultural theory

Aubert (1952) examined the attitudes of certain Swedish businessmen towards violation of rationing regulations. Although the businesses studied were not corporate, the points made are relevant. Aubert saw each subject as being pulled by two sorts of obligations. 'Universalistic' obligations affected him as a law–abiding citizen. They should motivate him to obey the law, but sanctions against the breach were usually weak. 'Particularistic' obligations were felt towards business colleagues, and were supported by an ideology which only demanded avoidance of certain blatant offences.

Aubert's research suggested that business concepts had the greater influence. He describes the groups to which white collar criminals belong as having 'an elaborate and widely accepted ideological rationalisation for the offences and ... great social significance outside the sphere of criminal activity' (1968:177). White collar crimes are sometimes accepted and endorsed by group norms and certain types of illegal activity come to represent a normal response. Thus 'paying off health inspectors ... was normal and acceptable business practice' (Braithwaite, 1984:12).

It must be appreciated that any subcultural influence is not fully deterministic. The executive who violates laws is not simply swimming with an irresistible current. Deviance may be encouraged and condoned, but it is not automatic. Studies of certain large American corporations seem to illustrate a Svengali-like domination by senior executives (eg Farberman, 1975; Denzin, 1977; Blundell, 1978). However, those industries were all in a similar market position, and Box (1983) suggests the findings are not universally valid. Even within such industries, some employees were prepared to boycott unlawful practices in spite of pressure from above (Geis, 1967; Farberman, 1975:447).

Individual characteristics, variations between groups within a subculture and degrees of exposure to subcultural values seem to be relevant.

9.8 Crime as an endemic feature of corporations

Elsewhere, there are suggestions that crime is endemic to corporations, and that there is something about organisations, other than the simple profit motive, which invites deviance. A corporation cannot itself plan, think, or act, except through human agents (Box, 1983:38). Therefore, any analysis of the 'why' of corporate crime must include individuals. Nevertheless, while a corporation lacks living grey matter, Galbraith (1967) suggests it does have a 'brain' of sorts. French says a firm can hold a corporate intention which is more than a simple composite of the intentions of its directors, managers and employees for:

> '... the melding of disparate interests and purposes gives rise to a corporate long range point of view that is distinct from the intents and purposes of the (original contributors)' (1979:214).

Braithwaite (1984) claims that in performing their organisational roles, individuals form part of a whole to which they would not choose to belong if they could see it for what it was.

It seems that a corporation equals more than the sum of its parts, and that the adding up process somehow facilitates deviance. This point does not itself represent an explanation, but highlights the need for any theory of corporate crime to recognise and explore the complex interplay between the corporation and individuals.

9.9 A critical perspective

Some discussions refer to the ability of powerful interest groups, such as corporations, to influence the law-making process (eg Box 1983; Carson, 1980). Aubert argues that the aetiology of law-breaking and the aetiology of law-making and enforcement concern the same theoretical concepts and he calls for the careful study of both. Swartz suggests that because capitalism involves the maximisation of corporate profits, 'its *normal* functioning produces ... deaths and illnesses' (1978:115, my emphasis). If Swartz is right, corporate crime is unlikely to be affected by changes in law enforcement or the treatment of offenders.

Adopting the research tactics which are apparently called for would require the criminologist to make value judgements, and in the past it could have been submitted that doing so would compromise his scientific integrity. For some, such a view is no longer tenable. As a social scientist, the criminologist is obliged not to be taken in by what Box (1983) calls mystification, a process which, *inter alia*, perpetuates the myth that corporate crime is not serious, and protects the powerful segments of society who benefit from such crime.

9.10 Conclusion

Criminology has tentatively picked up the gauntlet thrown down by Ross, and some progress has been made. However, much remains to be done if the correct weapons are to be chosen and the challenge squarely faced. The comments of one of those picking up that gauntlet remain highly relevant:

> 'No longer is the criminologist a middle class observer studying lower class behaviour. He now looks upward at the most powerful and prestigeful strata, and his ingenuity in research and theory will be tested indeed!' (Newman, 1958:753.)

10

Crime Prevention

10.1 Introduction

Obviously, crime prevention is not a theory. However, it seems proper to include it here because there are a number of theoretical assumptions underlying the use of any preventive measures. According to Hough *et al*, 'crime prevention is a rather elastic term, which at its broadest encompasses any activity intended to reduce the frequency of events defined as crimes by the criminal law' (1980:1). Such a definition would include techniques for diverting potential offenders from crime, as well as the use of the criminal justice system to discourage recidivism. Such methods are described, respectively, as secondary and tertiary prevention (Brantingham, 1986:103).

This chapter is concerned with situational crime prevention, a concept very similar to Brantingham's notion of primary prevention. Situational measures have been vigorously promoted in recent years, largely because of a growing recognition that the criminal justice system is of limited effectiveness in reducing crime (Martinson, 1974; Brody, 1976; Walker, 1979; Brody and Tarling, 1980). It has also been argued that efforts to change the criminal dispositions of offenders have been unproductive (Hough *et al*, 1980:3; Wilson, 1975).

Reppetto suggests that if they could succeed, preventive measures which removed the individual motivation of offenders would be preferable to techniques which merely seek to reduce opportunities for crime, as the former could reduce crime in an absolute sense. However, he goes on to say that individual motivation derives from 'a complex of economic, social, and psychological factors that are often difficult to ascertain and even more difficult to alter'. In contrast, situational measures offer a 'pragmatic advantage' (1976:167).

It may be that advantage, the offer of results now, instead of later, which attracts policy makers and practitioners towards the situational approach. In referring to the rapid spread of Neighbourhood Watch schemes in Britain during the early 1980s, Bennett and Wright comment that 'there is a new optimism that perhaps something does work after all' (1984:3). It is to be hoped that this new optimism does not prove to be short-sighted, in view of the high profile which crime prevention is currently enjoying.

10.2 Situational crime prevention, a definition

In a nutshell, situational prevention 'attempts to prevent crime by changing the situations in which crime occurs' (Poyner, 1983:5). Within the situational approach, opportunity is a key concept. The notion of opportunity affecting crime will be revisited later, but for present purposes it can be said to have several shades of meaning. Firstly, it can refer to the material conditions in which a potential offender may commit a crime. Secondly, in crimes resulting from impulse, the opportunity is said to consist simultaneously in those conditions and in the inducement to commit the crime. In an even broader meaning, the element of chance is included, that is, the opportunity exists not only where the material conditions are conducive to crime, but also where benefits can be gained at minimal risk (Hough *et al*, 1985:5; Clarke, 1980).

It follows that situational measures should be tailored to the types of opportunity which they seek to foreclose. Bennett suggests that situational preventive methods are intended to operate at three levels (Bennett, 1986:42). Those levels relate to:

1. the individual;
2. the community;
3. the physical environment.

In Home Office literature, situational measures are generally grouped under eight headings (Hough *et al*, 1980). By and large, these operate at either an individual or a community level and they will be discussed accordingly in this chapter. Techniques which have a substantial effect on the physical environment will be referred to as 'crime prevention through environmental design'.

10.3 Measures operating at the level of the individual

Target hardening

This involves increasing the physical security of potential targets, for example by the use of locks, grilles and strong materials. In some cases the method has proved successful. For instance, in West Germany in 1963 steering locks were made compulsory on all cars, including those already registered. Car thefts are said to have dropped by 60 per cent (Hough *et al*, 1980:6). In the United Kingdom, in 1971, steering locks were required to be fitted to all new cars. A survey drew two samples of cars stolen or taken without consent in the Metropolitan Police District in 1969 and 1973. Comparison showed that in 1969, new cars represented 21 per cent of all cars taken, but in 1973 the proportion had dropped to 5 per cent (Mayhew *et al*, 1980:21, figures rounded). The survey suggested that fitting locks to new cars had a specific displacement effect in that potential offenders were re-directed towards older, unprotected cars. At the time of the survey there was no overall reduction in the unauthorised taking of vehicles. In the Metropolitan Police District, recorded offences of this kind rose by 80 per cent between 1970 and 1974. Mayhew *et al* suggest that such locks might prove more effective as the proportion of protected cars increases.

Relative security levels do not seem to exert much influence on the choice of targets by burglars, according to data from offenders (Bennett and Wright, 1984:50) and from site surveys (Winchester and Jackson, 1982:21). Bennett and Wright asked a sample of burglars whether, during their last period of offending, they would have been put off a building that had or did not have certain types of situational factor, including security locks. Responses were coded according to whether the burglar would be deterred unconditionally, deterred conditionally, or not deterred. Only 10 per cent would definitely be put off burgling a house by the presence of security locks, while a further 20 per cent might be deterred (1984:77).

In other studies, offenders' verbal claims have been at variance with their actions. For instance, one of the methods in a recent study by Wright and Logie was a recognition test. This involved showing convicted burglars and a control sample the same series of photographs of houses on two occasions. On the second occasion, half the photographs were left untouched, a quarter had a factor added, and the remainder had a factor removed. Where that factor was a lock, burglars recognised the change correctly in 75 per cent of cases, compared with 50 per cent for the control group. Yet, in a different test, only 17 per cent of the burglars said locks would put them off. An explanation offered for the inconsistency is that although locks may not render a house unattractive as a target, burglars may consider them when deciding how to gain access (Wright and Logie, 1988:102). In Reppetto's study only 5 per cent of the burglars said they would be put off by locks, but most fared badly at overcoming security devices in practical simulations (1974:85).

Since at least some burglars admit that good locks deter them, there is some argument for making houses reasonably secure. In 1987, about 8 per cent of recorded burglaries were attempts, and some of those will probably have been thwarted by physical security (Home Office, 1986: Paragraph 2.19; Mayhew, 1984:35).

Carelessness by householders often makes it unnecessary for burglars to overcome physical security. In two recent English surveys, entry was via an unlocked door or window in about 20 per cent of burglaries (Winchester and Jackson, 1982:19; Home Office, 1986:14).

. The fitting of particularly strong security measures may be considered unacceptable because of fears of creating a fortress society. Security can also conflict with safety. During 1989, two fires in London resulted in deaths when firemen were unable to break through steel security doors fitted to flats (The *Evening Standard*, 27 January 1989).

Target removal

These measures involve removing targets from the environment to which potential offenders have access. Examples include replacement of prepayment fuel meters with card-operated systems or quarterly billing (Hill, 1986; Forrester *et al*, 1988); and switching to paying wages by bank credit instead of in cash (Hough *et al*, 1980). Target removal may sometimes be combined with target hardening, as in the case of schools where televisions are kept out of sight in a protected strongroom. Hough *et al* suggest another variation involves removal of the target from the subjective worlds of potential offenders, for example, where damage is repaired quickly so that further attacks will not be encouraged (1980:6).

Removing the means to commit crime

An example commonly used to illustrate this type of measure is the introduction during the 1970s of screening procedures to detect bombs and weapons at airports. This was followed by a reduction in incidents of 'skyjacking' (Wilkinson, 1977; Hough *et al*, 1980). At a more mundane level, householders are urged to store ladders securely, and not to leave keys in locks.

Reducing the pay-off

Measures under this heading are generally only applicable to property offences, as they seek to reduce the benefit gained by offenders. For example, cash in transit will be less attractive if the potential thief knows that if it is stolen, its container will contaminate the contents with dye.

Property marking also comes under this heading. Car windows are etched with the registration number to make 'ringing' less profitable. Portable items are indelibly marked with the owner's postcode or another unique reference. The idea behind the method is that property will be less valuable to thieves or fences if its owner can easily be traced. The fact that property is marked must be brought to the attention of potential thieves, and this is usually attempted by displaying window stickers.

Property marking is vigorously promoted by crime prevention panels and police forces, and is a feature of most Neighbourhood Watch schemes. However, evaluations of this method have not been too encouraging. Hough *et al* cite American studies which indicated that some protection against burglary was gained in areas with a high level of participation in property marking schemes, but that it was difficult to persuade householders to take part (1980:7). Laycock's evaluation of a property marking project in South Wales found that the burglary victimisation rate for participants dropped by 38 per cent, with no discernible displacement on to non-participants, but she admits the results may not be generalisable (1985:11). The rate of participation was very high, at 72 per cent (1985: Table 1).

Poyner claims property marking schemes could only be effective if police made extensive routine checks of property, and he points out that marks are frequently easy to remove or alter (1983:7).

Against these criticisms, it should be emphasised that property marking will often be combined with other measures, such as target hardening, and it is feasible that techniques may be more effective where they are used in combination and where the attention of potential offenders is drawn to them.

10.4 Measures operating at the level of the community

Formal surveillance

A belief in the effectiveness of formal surveillance rests on the notion that potential offenders will be deterred by the threat of being seen, and that the agencies which perform formal surveillance represent such a threat. The first assumption corresponds with common sense and appears to be accurate (Mayhew, 1981:119).

The provision of formal surveillance through preventive patrolling has traditionally been regarded as a central police function, yet such patrols, whether on foot or mobile, have been shown to be fairly ineffective in reducing crime (Bright, 1969; Kelling *et al*, 1974: Clarke and Hough, 1980).

Several writers point to the very low proportion of recorded crime which is discovered by police on patrol (eg Reppetto, 1974; Pope 1977; Bottomley and Coleman, 1981).

Notwithstanding these findings, attempts are sometimes made to supplement the patrol function of the police. Citizen patrols are rare in Britain, but a few exist (*The Times*, 11 October 1988). Evaluations in the United States suggest such patrols help to reduce fear of crime, but that they have a minimal effect on levels of offending (Reppetto, 1974:81; Yin *et al*, 1977).

Natural surveillance

Behind this form of surveillance lies the notion that by observing their environment as they go about their everyday business, people can provide themselves with some protection against crime.

This idea finds it way into Jacobs' arguments for mixed land use to increase activity on the street (1961), and surveillance is an important part of Newman's concept of defensible space (1976). The relationship between crime and the built environment will be discussed in more depth in sections 10.6 – 10.9.

A third of Bennett and Wright's sample of burglars said they were deterred by the proximity or presence of neighbours. One-third said they would not burgle buildings that were overlooked by others, and another third might be deterred in those circumstances. A quarter would be put off by passers-by or people standing near to a potential target.

The presence of vegetational cover and lack of visibility to passers-by were both rated as important by more than 50 per cent of the burglars interviewed by Nee and Taylor (1988:109).

Using site surveys, Winchester and Jackson conclude, 'houses that are burgled tend to be those characterised by poor surveillance opportunities and good access' (1982:15). Other studies show the most common entry points to be at the rear of premises, or to be obscured by fences or shrubs (Pope, 1977; Home Office, 1986). There may be preventive value in increasing opportunities for surveillance, both through design and by mobilising neighbours (Brantingham and Brantingham, 1984; Forrester *et al*, 1988).

Surveillance by employees

Hough *et al* suggest there is promise in exploiting the capacity of certain employees to take on a surveillance role (1980). For example, apartment blocks with doormen are less vulnerable to burglary than those without them (Waller and Okihiro, 1978); two-man buses suffered less vandalism than those with a driver only (Sturman, 1980); and after the installation of closed circuit television in four London Underground stations, thefts and robberies were reduced (Burrows, 1980).

Environmental management

Some of the measures under this heading involve tending the physical environment. For instance, alterations to fences, alleyways and so on can maximise the opportunities for surveillance. It is also suggested that if public areas are kept free of litter and graffiti, vandalism is less likely to occur (Lawrence, 1979; Zimbardo, 1973). On the other hand, Trasler (1986) argues that erasure of graffiti is unlikely to have any long-term impact on the process of urban decay.

Such measures overlap with others discussed above, and Hough *et al* (1980) suggest that activities under this final heading tend to involve manipulation of the social environment. Two of the examples that they suggest are that opportunities for football violence can be reduced through good liaison between the police, football clubs and supporters' clubs and that housing allocation policies can avoid high concentrations of children on estates where this could lead to problems.

10.5 Neighbourhood Watch

The eight headings described above do not fully cover the range of activities which could properly fit under the umbrella of situational prevention.

If crime prevention measures are going to be adopted at a community-wide level, some form of catalyst is required. During the 1980s, Neighbourhood Watch was a popular medium for achieving wider involvement in crime prevention. Shortly after its introduction, Neighbourhood Watch was described as 'gripping the attention of the police and the public as a major new hope in the control of residential burglary' (Bennett and Wright, 1984:3). Schemes were started in four police areas in 1983, and by 1989 there were 60,000 operating in the United Kingdom (*Crime Prevention News*, Spring 1983, Spring 1989).

The basic idea of how a Neighbourhood Watch scheme operates is that the residents of a group of houses organise themselves and appoint one or more co-ordinators, depending on the number of houses involved. Householders are encouraged to adopt individual measures, such as improving home security and marking property. They are also urged to become more watchful and to report suspicious incidents to the police, directly or via the co-ordinator. In many cases, the police assist residents to set up schemes, but the amount of continuing police involvement varies considerably.

During 1994, the government launched 'Partners Against Crime', an initiative aimed at revitalising interest in Neighbourhood Watch and at encouraging members of the public to take part in Street Watch. Members of the latter scheme are expected to walk specific routes in their areas, to look out for suspicious activity and to contact the police if such behaviour is observed. Notwithstanding the cool response which a proposal to introduce Street Watch had received from the police staff associations in 1993, the Home Office's promotional booklet advises potential participants to contact the police before they establish a scheme and to obtain their guidance about how to behave. This booklet estimates there to be 130,000 Neighbourhood Watch schemes in existence, covering five million households.

Research into whether the traditional scheme actually reduces crime is limited and inconclusive. An evaluation of a project in Seattle indicated that blocks where residents participated in watch schemes enjoyed reductions in burglaries of between 48 per cent and 61 per cent. There was no significant displacement of crime (Cirel *et al*, 1977). In contrast, Rosenbaum's evaluation of schemes in Chicago found no consistent effect on levels of crime, and indicated an increase in fear of crime (1986, 1988). Titus (1984) reviews a number of American studies and whilst questioning the methological validity of some of them, finds a consistent pattern of reductions in burglary. There is also some evidence of increased reporting of crimes in progress, of more interaction between neighbours, and of reductions in fear of crime. Research elsewhere suggests that the more quickly a crime is reported, the more likely it is to be detected (Pope, 1977).

In the United Kingdom, during the heyday of Neighbourhood Watch some bold claims were made about its effectiveness. For example, one scheme in Bradford was said to have reduced crime by 80 per cent (*The Times*, 11 November 1987). However, systematic evaluations of Neighbourhood Watch are rare. Not all of the earlier police-initiated schemes were evaluated, but where research was conducted it was normally performed in-house and often amounted to simple before and after comparisons with little attention to displacement (Husain, 1988).

In one of the few scientific evaluations, Bennett suggests: 'Overall the strongest conclusion that can be drawn on the basis of available evidence is that Neighbourhood Watch has no discernible impact on crime, its reporting or detection' (1987:33).

It should be noted that Bennett's study focused on only two schemes in London, and that he did find an increase in social cohesion and a reduction in fear of household crime (1987:44).

Once a scheme has been initiated, enthusiasm may be short-lived. At least 12 of the 300 schemes studied by Husain were discontinued, and in half of those apathy on the part of residents was seen as a contributory factor (1988:38). Earlier studies in the United States also showed a waning of interest (Cirel *et al*, 1977).

A review of relevant literature by Brown (1992) confirms the finding that schemes can diminish in effectiveness after an initial honeymoon period. Some schemes exist in name only. Although participants in some Neighbourhood Watch schemes would vouch for the benefit gained in their areas, the concept now seems to have passed the peak of its popularity.

10.6 Crime prevention through environmental design

Through the work of writers like Jacobs, Jeffery, and Newman, the concept of crime prevention through environmental design has captured the attention of academics, architects, planners, crime prevention practitioners and interested members of the public. Jeffery, in his book which adopts the phrase as its title, is at times self-contradictory, but in places he adopts a broader than usual definition of crime prevention through environmental design, by including aspects of the social environment, such as parental control, as well as physical factors (1971:184).

Here we are mostly concerned with the more usual meaning of the expression, the rationale of which is that the nature of the built environment can affect the level of crime both by influencing potential offenders and by affecting a citizen's ability to exercise control over his surroundings (Home Office Crime Prevention Centre, 1989).

Jacobs undoubtedly heralds much of the later work in this area in *The Death and Life of Great American Cities*. Jacobs identifies a tendency for public spaces and private spaces in residential areas to 'ooze into each other', and calls for a clearer demarcation of the two. She also insists that buildings must face in such a direction that there may be 'eyes upon the street, eyes belonging to [its] natural proprietors'. Jacobs suggests that if pavements are well used, they will be well watched, both by the users and by people looking out from buildings. She supports the mixed use of land, that is, juxtaposition of commercial and residential uses in order to keep areas busy (1962:35). These themes indicate a powerful belief in the capacity of surveillance to help control crime.

10.7 The ingredients of defensible space

Oscar Newman is probably the best publicised writer in this field and it is his early writing (1972, 1976) which has gained the most attention. Newman suggests that part of the explanation for urban crime lies in a breakdown of social mechanisms which once kept crime in check, and that the inability of communities to come together in joint action hampers crime prevention. The solution he offers is one of 'restructuring the residential environments of our cities so they can again become livable and controlled ... not by police but by a community of people sharing a common terrain' (1976:2).

Newman describes four elements of the physical design of environments which can contribute, positively or negatively, to their security. These are: territoriality, surveillance, image and milieu.

Territoriality

Territoriality is the 'capacity of the physical environment to create perceived zones of influence' (Newman, 1976:51). It is claimed that the design of buildings and their sites can encourage residents to adopt proprietary attitudes, and also that certain layouts inform outsiders that particular areas are for the private use of residents.

Newman suggests that within the built environment there is a hierarchy of types of space ranging from private space at one end to public space at the other. Private space is that area of space under the total control of a resident, typically the inside of a house or apartment. Semi-private space is the area under an occupant's control, which is visually and physically accessible to the public, such as the garden of a house. Semi-public space represents the area of space which is under the control of a group of residents or in their area of responsibility. Examples would be the corridors of high-rise buildings, and shared areas for recreation and parking. Public space is an area to which the public has open access. An obvious example is a public street.

The explanations and examples suggested here are clearly simplistic. The points at which one type of space ends and another begins are blurred and will vary between different settings. For example, Newman suggests that in a high-rise building with low-income tenants and no doorman to control access, only the interior of an apartment will be private space, and everywhere else is a no-man's land.

Newman goes on to argue that residents can extend their responsibilities beyond their front doors. He puts forward a number of suggestions which seek to increase the territorial influence of residents. One expected result is that strangers will be more easily recognised as such, and will therefore be discouraged from entering.

It is not proposed to describe all of the measures, but Newman's devices for defining boundaries include various types of barrier, both real (high walls, locked entry points) and symbolic (open gateways, steps, changes in texture of walking surface). Both are said to inform users of space that they are passing from a public domain to a private one where their presence must be justifiable.

Surveillance

A second element of defensible space design is the capacity to provide opportunities for surveillance. Windows should be positioned in such a way that semi-private and public areas can be kept under natural observation by residents. Newman argues that such surveillance reduces residents' fears and enables areas to be regarded as more secure, thus encouraging greater legitimate use and thereby making them still more secure (1976:78).

Newman accepts that surveillance is not a panacea for a complex problem. To be effective, it must be combined with techniques of territorial definition, since the ability to observe will not automatically cause an observer to come to the aid of a person or target being victimised. The decision whether or not to act may be affected by several conditions, including the extent to which the observer believes the activity to be happening within his sphere of influence; whether he regards the behaviour as normal within that area; whether he identifies with the victimised person or property; and the extent to which the observer feels he can have an effect on the events he is watching (1976:78).

Image

In relation to image, Newman argues that if a building is of a distinctive height and texture it can be singled out for particular attention. Where the distinctive image is negative 'the project will be stigmatised and its residents castigated and victimised' (1976:102). Newman suggests that public housing projects are particularly affected because they are so designed as to stand out. This image combines with other design features which reduce territoriality and surveillance opportunities and with the socio-economic characteristics of the population to make this type of housing particularly vulnerable to crime.

Milieu

With reference to milieu, Newman says that if certain areas are identified as 'safe', other areas which adjoin them will benefit from their safety. He argues for the juxtaposition of residential areas with other areas seen as safe.

However, Newman challenges Jacobs' suggestion that residential areas should be sited alongside commercial areas in the expectation of enhancing safety because of increased activity. It is Newman's contention that the success of a particular mixture of land uses 'depends as much on the degree to which residents can identify with and survey activity in the related facility as it does on the nature of the users of that facility and the activities they indulge in' (1976:116). Newman does not rule out the mixing of commercial and residential uses of land, but he insists there must be a critical evaluation of the nature of a commercial area and of its intended users before it is located next to housing.

10.8 Comments on defensible space

Mayhew suggests that one of the reasons for the wide appeal of Newman's writing may have been the apparent 'respectability of being backed by seemingly extensive empirical research' (1979:152). Newman's opening description of his study looks impressive. The research techniques adopted by his team included interviews with housing project residents, project managers and police officers. They had access to 'detailed reports' compiled by the police on criminal or vandal activity (his distinction), and to a 'massive amount of data' from housing records. This provided, Newman claims, 'an incomparable laboratory for measuring the effects of different housing environments on crime and vandalism' (1976:xiv).

Nevertheless, several commentators have drawn attention to methodological weaknesses in Newman's early work. Mawby describes Newman's style as 'predisposed towards political oratory rather than serious scientific endeavour', and suggests the research findings are 'rather expertly obscured within the text' (1977:169). The use of multi-variate analysis in relation to the data obtained is accused of yielding little, and of including inaccurate calculations (Bottoms, 1974; Mayhew, 1979).

The same authors criticise Newman for paying insufficient attention to socio-demographic factors, such as income, and for ignoring offender rates which may have influenced variations in offence rates. It has to be said that in his later work, Newman gives greater recognition to the relevance of social factors (eg Newman, 1980).

One serious cause for criticism of the earlier material is that Newman chose to concentrate on a comparison of just two housing projects, thus attracting suspicion that the two chosen were those which best suited his hypothesis (see Bottoms, 1974:204).

Newman refers to the high-rise residential block as 'the real and final villain of the peace' (1976:24), and his use of data emphasises the alleged influence of high-rise buildings on crime rates, so it is not surprising that this aspect of the defensible space concept tends to cast a longer shadow than the buildings it indicts.

Mawby used data from a study of crime in Sheffield to test whether area crime patterns varied with physical design features. He compared the crime rates of four residential areas, all council owned. Two consisted of flats, and two of conventional housing. For each type of housing, one area had a high rate of offender residence, and the other a low rate. Although some differences were found, high-rise buildings were not found to be at a disadvantage when compared with conventional housing (1977:173). In fact, for the two areas with high offender rates, the rate of residential offences was considerably higher in the area with conventional housing.

Mawby points to a number of inherent contradictions in the notion of defensible space. Firstly, the concept is so wide that the same design can incorporate both good and poor defensible space qualities. Perhaps more seriously, Mawby suggests that Newman fails to consider the possibility that the four main elements of defensible space may themselves include features which threaten security, as well as others which enhance it.

For example, as well as highlighting strangers, an increase in territoriality will also legitimise the presence of residents, and may increase the possibility of crime by them against neighbours.

In terms of surveillability, the same building might give a good view of some areas, such as the ground below, but poor views of others, such as corridors. Mawby suggests that, using Newman's criteria, it is arguable that most private housing has poor defensible space qualities since an enclosed garden creates a private area with a visibility barrier for potential onlookers. He goes on to suggest that a flat may be less open to burglary than a conventional house because there is less choice of entry points and because although the corridor may be relatively invisible, it is still a public place and therefore more open to possible interruption. This is said to make it possible to turn Newman's hypothesis on its head by suggesting that flats will be less prone to crime (1977:176). This particular suggestion seems to be criticism for criticism's sake, since Newman's recommendations include increasing visibility of as many areas as possible, and maximising the use of shared areas to increase natural surveillance. Also, literature which makes practical recommendations based on defensible space ideas tends to recognise the detrimental effect of cover around conventional housing (Poyner, 1983).

So far as image is concerned, Mawby argues that rather than increasing the extent to which a housing project is victimised, isolation could mean that non-residents are less likely to cross its boundaries. He also disagrees with claims by Jacobs and Newman that increasing the number of people using public areas will reduce the number of offences occurring. On the contrary, he argues, the number of potential victims will grow, and offenders will be less conspicuous, so that an increase in crime is more likely. Mawby refers to another study by himself in which he found that telephone kiosks in more public situations were vandalised more often than secluded ones (Mawby, 1977a).

Mawby's appraisal of the Sheffield crime data was not totally condemnatory of Newman. It included an analysis of the type of person reporting offences, by victim type (corporate or individual) and by area. This showed that a higher proportion of offences against corporate victims was reported by witnesses as opposed to victims, police, or other parties, in the areas with high-rise housing. Most of the offences against corporate victims were highly public. In the high-rise areas they occurred at sites which were overlooked by flats, whereas in areas of conventional housing they were isolated. In relation to this finding, Mawby admits, 'far from undermining Newman's theory, it may support it' (1977:174).

Not surprisingly, Mawby does not allow this piece of possible supporting evidence to overcome his reservations about Newman's claims, and he argues strongly for careful treatment and analysis of defensible space before the concept is implemented on a wide scale.

10.9 A brief appraisal of design-based approaches to the prevention of crime

Interest in crime prevention through environmental design has spawned a number of projects on both sides of the Atlantic. A prominent American example is the Hartford Demonstration Project, focusing on the city's Asylum Hill district. Preventive activities took a three-pronged attack including changes to the physical environment, alterations in the organisation of policing, and encouraging residents to form community groups. We are concerned only with the first approach.

Physical changes included closing some streets and using large planters as symbolic barriers in order to limit access, partly with the intention of promoting territoriality. During the first year, data from police reports and resident surveys were used to plot distributions of offences and of arrested offenders. The evaluation indicated that the project was achieving some success in reducing crime. Burglaries and robberies were lower, but the figures were so small that it was impossible to reach definite conclusions (Fowler *et al*, 1979).

A follow-up evaluation, two years later, showed disappointing results. Crime levels matched the rates expected if no changes had been made. However, it appeared that residents used the neighbourhood more, were better able to recognise strangers, and were more willing to intervene in suspicious incidents. Fear of crime had not been lowered, but had not risen at the same rate as elsewhere in Hartford (Fowler and Mangione, 1982).

Poyner points out that the physical changes made in Asylum Hill may actually have increased pedestrian traffic, thus putting more potential offenders and victims on the street (1983:24). Identification of which factors, if any, were effective in the Hartford project was complicated by the fact that policing activity decreased as the project developed.

Hunter describes an improvement project to a development of three-storey houses in Liverpool, where some of Newman's basic principles were applied. Within weeks, external doors and entry-phones had been wrecked, graffiti reappeared, and the contents of planters were stolen or damaged. Hunter comments:

> 'Architectural symbolism in terms of territorial definition may be fine for professionally qualified, sensitive persons but doesn't cut much ice with vandals, criminals and boisterous children' (1978:677).

Elsewhere, Newman's notion of territoriality has been described as being based on an 'ignorant view of human nature which has largely been discredited by anthropological research' (Hillier, 1973:539).

Defensible space concepts have been examined in relation to existing housing developments. Wilson studied levels of vandalism in 285 residential blocks of different designs in 38 Inner London council estates. No direct relationship was found between vandalism and design features. Child density was identified as the factor most linked to levels of reported vandalism (1980:52).

In their study of residential burglary in Toronto, Waller and Okihiro considered the validity of defensible space concepts, and their findings 'seriously question the importance of defensible space to prevention of burglary in *apartments*' (1978:60, my emphasis).

A recurring comment is that accurate evaluation of projects which seek to reduce crime by manipulating the physical environment is almost impossible because of other uncontrolled factors or the simultaneous adoption of other measures, as in the Hartford project (Mayhew, 1979:152; Bennett and Wright, 1984:29). This is ironic because it is reasonable to assume that a project which combines different measures has a greater chance of success (Forrester *et al*, 1988:11).

Care has been taken, except when citing other authors, not to refer to Newman's ideas as his 'theory' of defensible space. It would seem from many of the comments made about his work that the concept, as described in Newman's early work, was not sufficiently well defined to be regarded as a developed theory. Waller and Okihiro prefer to view defensible space as 'an approach, a way of looking at things, rather than a systematic theory' (1978:55).

10.10 The reaction against dispositional theory

It was suggested earlier that increased interest in the situational approach indicates a move away from previous methods of attempting to control crime. At the same time, a growth of research into situational influences on crime shows a shift in criminological thinking.

Trasler describes *Designing Out Crime* (Clarke and Mayhew, 1980) as an 'atheoretical book' (1986:17). For a collection of empirical reports compiled by the Home Office Research Unit (as it then was), such a label is not necessarily a criticism. However, recent Home Office-sponsored research is described elsewhere as being at the centre of 'an administrative criminology ... which has abandoned all interest in the causes of crime and is concerned solely with devising *ad hoc* measures to reduce opportunities for criminal acts' (Smith, 1988:197).

Certainly, reliance on the situational approach seriously questions the value, for crime reduction purposes, of the dispositional bias which previously predominated in much academic criminology. Supporters of the exploration and use of situational measures challenge the notion that a deeper understanding of the causes of crime would lead to remedies, or at any rate to viable ones: 'causal explanations expressed in terms of broad social parameters may offer little help to the problem of preventing crime' (Nee and Taylor, 1988:115; note also Clarke, 1980; Wilson, 1975).

It has also been suggested that adherents of theory with a dispositional bias see little merit in situational techniques because they tend to view displacement as an inevitable consequence of such methods, on the basis that 'bad will out' (Hough *et al*, 1980:10).

Comments such as these add fuel to the inference that the situational approach might be excessively pragmatic and somehow not grounded in theory. Given the amount of energy being committed to situational measures in recent years, the approach must, one hopes, be informed by its own theoretical underpinnings or at least by reasonable assumptions. Some of these will now be examined.

10.11 Environmental criminology

The major expansion in the use of situational preventive measures during the 1970s occurred at the same time as a growth of academic interest in environmental criminology.

Brantingham and Brantingham suggest that a crime happens when four elements 'are in concurrence: a law, an offender, a target, and a place' (1981:7). They refer to those elements as the four dimensions of crime, and describe environmental criminology as the study of the fourth dimension. Environmental criminologists consider where and when crimes occur. Their questions concern the physical and social characteristics of crime sites; the movements that bring the offender and target together; the perceptual processes that bring about the selection of crime sites and the social processes of ecological labelling; the spatial patterning of laws and how this affects the creation of crime sites; the spatial distribution of offenders and targets in different settings; and how the fourth dimension interacts with the other dimensions of crime in order for crimes to occur (Brantingham and Brantingham, 1981:7).

The growth of environmental criminology during the last 20 years has largely been influenced by the work of Newman and Jeffery, which generated greater consideration of the effect of the environment on crime levels. However, recognition of the relevance of geographical setting to levels of crime is not new. It is suggested that modern criminology has been substantially influenced by the findings of predecessors of today's environmental criminologists (Brantingham and Brantingham, 1981).

The Brantinghams discuss two separate waves of research. The first wave occurred in the nineteenth century. In France, Guerry (1833) and Quetelet (1842) analysed conviction rates for crimes in the different departments and made a number of important findings. Firstly, crime rates varied greatly among the departments. Secondly, when violent crimes and property crimes were separated, a further variation in patterning was found. Thirdly, these patterns remained stable over time. Similar comparisons were made in England, and these also showed spatial variations in crime rates, at county level (Plint, 1851; Mayhew, 1862).

Further English research followed, in which crime was studied at lower levels of aggregation. For example, Glyde (1856) looked at how crimes were distributed across different towns and villages of Suffolk. Comparing different locations, major variations were found. Villages were found to have higher rates of crime than towns, and a greater proportion of rural crime involved violence. Mayhew's study of parts of London pointed to the existence of areas (known as rookeries) with a high proportion of criminal residents (1968). The tendency of these areas to persist over time was confirmed by later studies.

The findings of this first wave of research are valuable for academics and policy makers. For example, they highlight the significance of geographical settings to the incidence of crime. The tendency for spatial patterns to persist suggests an element of predictability and therefore the possibility of adopting preventive policies.

The second wave of interest which the Brantinghams describe involved the work of the Chicago School and more recent area studies of crime. These were discussed in Chapter 5.

Although the Brantinghams suggest that the findings and explanations of this second wave of research have been central to the subsequent development of North American criminology, they say it would be a mistake to equate the earlier period of work with contemporary environmental criminology, which they describe as 'a dynamic and expanding field' (1981:18). Contemporary environmental criminology is said to be separated from earlier research by at least three types of shift in perspective:

> 'The first shift is a move away from the tendency for academics to keep their research into crime within the parameters of their own specific discipline. The environmental criminologist is said to "borrow techniques and knowledge from many different disciplines in order to understand ... crime"' (Brantingham and Brantingham, 1981:19).

The second shift has been alluded to earlier and involves resisting the traditional search for causes of criminal motivation. Environmental criminologists assume that some people are criminally motivated. They focus instead on the criminal event, to find patterns in where, when and how crimes occur (1981:19).

The third shift involves moving from the sociological imagination to the geographic imagination. The following examples help to explain the different views which will be obtained about events, depending on which type of imagination is applied. They are anglicised versions of examples provided by the Brantinghams (1981:21). Two burglaries committed in London and Manchester on different days of the week by different youths, both of whom are unemployed, could be identical according to the sociological imagination, in that the same law is broken, the offenders are of the same age, and they are both out of work. To the geographic imagination, the burglaries would be seen as different from each other because of the gaps in time and setting. From another angle, a burglary committed by an unemployed youth within a quarter of a mile of his home in the inner city, and a theft from a car by a middle class youth within a quarter of a mile of his suburban home (both committed in the early hours) might be regarded as identical by the geographic imagination, but as quite diffferent by the sociological imagination. Significance is given to different properties of the events, according to the perspective which is adopted.

Environmental criminologists do not replace the sociological imagination with the geographic one. They use the two together in an attempt to gain a better picture and understanding of crimes, and ultimately an increased capacity to control them.

In a short summary it would be impossible to do full justice to environmental criminology. However, to give a very brief picture, the field includes studies of: the spatial patterning of crime at different levels of aggregation; the 'journey to crime'; the processes by which potential offenders recognise potential crime sites and specific opportunities; and the creation and maintenance of areas of criminal residence.

It would be wrong to equate environmental criminology with environmental determinism. Rather, the sequence by which potential criminals recognise and act on criminal opportunities is seen as a 'multistaged decision process situated within a more general environmental learning and evaluation process' (Brantingham and Brantingham, 1981:25).

10.12 Rational choice theory and the relevance of opportunity

Environmental criminology is complemented by another development in criminological thinking, described as 'rational choice theory'. This deals with the decision-making process adopted by offenders, and in an earlier, more crude version that process tended to be compared with straightforward economic choice. It was suggested that:

> '[A] useful theory of criminal behaviour can dispense with special theories of anomie, psychological inadequacies, or inheritance of special traits and simply extend the economist's usual analysis of choice ...' (Becker, 1968:170).

For the 'economist of crime', a potential offender calculates the legitimate opportunities of earning income open to him, the amount of reward they offer, the amounts offered by illegal methods, the probability of arrest, and the likely punishment.

He then chooses the activity (legal or illegal) which offers the highest discounted return. Preventive strategies would involve reform of the law and its administration in order to alter the equation and make crime less attractive. It is ironic that the economic approach to explaining crime reflects classical theory, when the methods of economics are probably the most scientific of any social science (Sullivan, 1973).

Not surprisingly, these early theories have been accused of implying too high a degree of rationality by comparing criminal choices too closely with market-place decisions, and of failing to deal with expressive crimes (Trasler, 1986). However, in their defence, it has been submitted that the amateurish criminal who makes wildly inaccurate estimates is no less rational than a consumer who runs up huge debts (Sullivan, 1973). Clarke (1987) points out that although the motivation behind some expressive crimes may be pathological, their planning and execution may be highly rational.

Rational choice theory has developed considerably, largely through the work of Clarke and Cornish whose writings in this field have been somewhat prolific (eg Clarke, 1980, 1987; Cornish and Clarke, 1986, 1986a, 1987). The theory 'sees crime as the outcome of the offender's choices or decisions, however hasty or ill-considered these may be' (Clarke, 1987:118).

In Clarke's formulation, the offender is not seen as acting with full rationality. Instead, the level of rationality which he applies to decision-making is said to be limited or bounded. It is accepted that the offender will not always obtain all the facts needed to make a wise decision, and that the information available will not necessarily be weighed carefully. This avoids the tendency of dispositional theory to treat criminals as a class apart, in that the perspective allows much crime to be regarded as 'rational action performed by fairly ordinary people' in response to particular pressures, opportunities and situational inducements (Hough *et al*, 1980:5; and note Trasler, 1986:22).

Interestingly, a rational choice approach to explaining crime does not dismiss dispositional theory as totally invalid. Clarke describes a move in criminology and its parent disciplines away from a deterministic, static approach towards a complex, dynamic formulation which has regard to an individual's immediate environment, learning, and perceptions as well as his background and personality. He suggests that most of the factors seen as predisposing an individual to crime can be re-interpreted in terms of their influence on offender decision-making (1987:124). This notion of the interplay between background factors and cues presented by the environment seems to be shared by Jeffery, who suggests that individuals respond to situations in different ways because they bring with them a different history of conditioning (1971:177).

Bennett reminds us that an offence rarely happens because of a single decision. In fact, a series of decisions will probably be made, starting with the original choice to offend, somewhere at some time, and ending with the final decision to act against a particular target (1986:48). Both background and situational factors are involved.

Other writers point to the operation of a conscious selection process at the scene of burglaries (Brantingham and Brantingham, 1984; Mayhew, 1984).

In any formulation of a rational choice model of offender decision-making, situational factors would be expected to exert more influence later in the chain, that is, in relation to decisions closest to the criminal event (Bennett, 1986; Heal and Laycock, 1986). If that is correct, there are clear implications for crime prevention practitioners in deciding when and where to intervene in the potential offender's sequence of decisions.

Clarke's ideas about rational choice theory developed as a result of his research into absconding from approved schools. His findings led him to abandon the notion that absconding was the result of personality factors. In fact, absconding was found to be 'powerfully related to opportunity' (1987:119).

Opportunity was identified earlier as a key concept so far as situational crime prevention is concerned, and its various shades of meaning were explained. During the 1970s, the Home Office Research Unit put considerable energy into exploring the relationship between criminal opportunities and levels of crime.

Depending on the observer's point of view, crime prevention strategies which focus on the reduction of opportunities may be cynically regarded as a tactic of administrative criminology (see Smith, 1988), or justified as the most practical approach available (National Crime Prevention Institute, 1986:3).

Rational choice theory has a common sense appeal, and it is to be hoped that it bears a strong resemblance to reality, since, as Bennett emphasises, the wisdom of pursuing situational crime prevention depends partly on the validity of the rational choice perspective. The analysis of offenders' accounts by Bennett and Wright offers support for the rational choice model proposed by Cornish and Clarke, including a suggestion that most offenders were conscious of actively making a decision to offend in response to specific situational cues (Bennett, 1986:51).

10.13 The nature of displacement

Displacement occurs when criminal opportunities are closed off, resulting in a shift of crime. Reppetto (1976:168) suggests displacement may take at least five forms:

In the case of 'temporal' displacement the offender continues the same type of crime, in the same locations, against the same targets, and using the same tactics, but at a different time of day, week or year. This might occur in response to increased policing at certain times of day.

Displacement may be 'tactical'. Other factors remain the same, but the offender changes his method of operating. For example, because more premises are fitted with alarms, a burglar switches to 'smash and grab' instead of making a full entry.

In a third form of displacement, the offender changes target. Reppetto gives the example of robberies on buses being reduced, and subway robberies increasing, after security on buses was stepped up.

As its name implies, territorial displacement occurs when crime in one area is reduced after the introduction of increased security measures, but is shifted to other, often adjacent, areas (see Allatt, 1984).

In the case of functional displacement, the offender changes the type of crime which he commits. For instance, robbers become burglars or vice versa.

Certain types of displacement may also amount to escalation. This would apply where functional displacement involves a switch to a more violent type of crime. Another example would be a robber adopting more extreme tactics to overcome target hardening techniques used to protect cash in transit.

10.14 Displacement as an obstacle to crime prevention

Reppetto (1976:170) suggests that those who oppose crime prevention programmes on the grounds of displacement make two basic assumptions:

The first assumption is that the offender population is totally deterministic and therefore inelastic. A particular offender is obliged to carry out a given number of offences over a certain period, so the frequency of offending will not be altered by closing off some opportunities (note also Cornish and Clarke, 1986). To counter this notion, a parallel is sometimes drawn between crime and suicide, an act which is often thought to result from deep-seated motivation (Hough *et al*, 1980). Studies by Hassall and Trethowan (1972) and Brown (1979) suggest that changing domestic gas supplies from town gas to the less toxic natural gas brought about substantial reductions in suicide in this country. These reductions were not cancelled out by large-scale displacement to other methods of suicide. Although largely agreeing with these findings, a more recent discussion finds that displacement to other means of committing suicide may have occurred in other countries after a similar change was introduced (Clarke and Mayhew, 1989).

Reppetto refers to several studies which have noted that rather than seeking opportunities because of a pre-existing motivation to offend, some offenders, especially very young ones, act in response to presented opportunities. He states that many of the burglars interviewed in his own examination of residential crime in Boston (USA) could be classified as 'opportunistic' (1974:11).

The second assumption described by Reppetto is that offenders enjoy total mobility in relation to type of crime, time of commission, tactics, target and area. He submits that, in reality, offender mobility will be limited by several factors, of which the main ones will be personality, age, and the structure of the crime (1976:171).

Put simply, an offender's personality may limit his functional mobility on the round-peg-in-a-round-hole principle. Gibbons and Garrity (1962) suggest offence behaviour is closely linked to an offender's attitudes. This was partly borne out in Reppetto's interviews with convicted burglars. Many indicated that they preferred burglary (of unoccupied premises) because they wished to avoid confrontation (1976:172; Conklin, 1981). Reppetto points out that the level of commitment to a particular type of crime will vary between individuals, and that personality may also influence the choice of targets and tactics.

According to Reppetto, younger offenders tend to be more restricted functionally, and in terms of tactics, because they have fewer skills and resources. Attendance at school, or parental curfews may place temporal limits on youngsters' opportunities for crime. Young offenders are more territorially bound than older ones, partly due to lack of transport, but also because they have little information about targets outside their immediate neighbourhoods (1976:173).

In this area of discussion, one of the concerns of environmental criminology is highly valid, namely, interest in the distances which different offenders travel to reach targets. Rhodes and Conly use the term 'criminal commute', choosing that expression deliberately because of a perceived similarity with ordinary commuters travelling to work. They suggest criminals become aware of environmental cues in the same way as non-criminals, in the course of moving about an area between home and work, places of recreation and so on. Offenders construct 'cognate maps' which are used in choosing locations for crimes (1981:168).

For domestic burglaries, the average crime trip is short, and this crime has been said to take on 'an almost claustrophobically local aspect' (Forrester *et al*, 1988:2).

A further limit will be imposed on offender mobility by the type of crime committed. Here, 'type' implies finer distinctions than merely theft or burglary or robbery. For instance, assuming premises are at greater risk of burglary when they are unoccupied, a burglar's preferred hours of operating are likely to differ according to whether he attacks residential properties or commercial premises.

Displacement is a vital issue so far as situational strategies are concerned, since ultimately their value depends on their capacity to avoid substantial displacement (Reppetto, 1976:167).

Nevertheless, it has to be admitted that a certain amount of displacement is probably inevitable in any programme based on the reduction of opportunities for crime, since not all opportunities can be closed off. A large number of potential targets will frequently be available and general levels of security are often low (Reppetto, 1974:71; Hough *et al*, 1980:11).

It has been argued that if crime prevention activity leads to displacement which is less in quantity or effect than the reduction achieved, there has been a net crime reduction (National Crime Prevention Institute, 1986:186). Elsewhere, displacement is described as 'not an "all or none" phenomenon' and a net reduction is viewed as a success provided the benefits gained from the reduction outweigh the social costs (Hough *et al*, 1980:12).

Several questions need to be asked. Who assesses the social costs and decides whether one effect outweighs another? Is it a success if burglars move their activities from an area where residents can afford to adopt new security measures to an area where they cannot?

Given the apparent inevitability of some displacement, it is essential that the designer of a preventive programme takes it into account and addresses the kinds of moral question raised above. Brantingham and Brantingham recommend that if programmes are going to shift crime, the movement ought to be towards less confrontational or intrusive crimes. Interestingly, they also comment that in all programmes there is a likelihood of some displacement towards non-criminal behaviour (1984:87).

10.15 Research into displacement

Unfortunately, it is unlikely that displacement is sufficiently well understood for such aims to be achieved with much sophistication. Reppetto (1974, 1976) identified displacement as an area ripe for further research, yet much more recently Cornish and Clarke (1986) said that there was still little systematic evidence about this phenomenon. This may partly be due to the fact that one of the few points about which there is broad agreement is the difficulty of identifying and measuring different types of displacement effect (Bennett, 1986, 1987; Hough *et al*, 1980; Trasler, 1986).

Perhaps Bennett (1986) and Clarke (1987) are right in submitting that the answer to explaining displacement lies in a clearer understanding of the ways in which offenders make decisions. If so, attempts to study displacement in isolation from the offender's perspective will yield little. A brief look will be taken at some of the implications of the offender-based research for the issue of displacement.

A high proportion of burglars are relatively amateurish, and use mundane methods of entry (Pope, 1977; Scarr, 1973; Winchester and Jackson, 1982). It has therefore been suggested that the reduction of opportunities need not result in substantial displacement (Waller and Okihiro, 1978).

Bennett and Wright asked a sample of burglars what they did if they were prevented from committing a particular offence. Of those who answered, 43 per cent said they would usually burgle another target on the same day. Forty-one per cent said they would not usually attempt another offence that day. The other 16 per cent suggested their actions would depend on other circumstances. Using whether or not another offence would be committed on the same day is a crude criterion for testing displacement, but if that test is adopted, 41 per cent of the burglars who responded can be treated as not having been displaced (1984:53).

Bennett and Wright admit that most of the category who claimed they would not offend on the same day if they were put off, said they would attempt another offence within days or weeks. They say it is debatable whether that should be regarded as displacement or prevention, and go on to maintain that their findings suggest the motivation to offend is not irrepressible. In any event, it is argued that causing burglars to reschedule their offending will, over time, lead to an absolute reduction in offences instead of equal displacement (1984:55).

10.16 Assumptions underlying the situational approach

Supporters of situational crime prevention appear to hold assumptions which are more or less directly opposite to those held by critics who emphasise the likelihood of displacement. More specifically, Bennett and Wright say that situational prevention is based on general assumptions about how potential offenders think. Five general assumptions are put forward:

1. The decision to offend is, to some extent, situationally determined.
2. Offenders freely choose to offend.

At first sight these two assumptions appear to contradict each other. However, this is not the case if one remembers the assertion by Bennett and Wright that the criminal event follows not one but several decisions, and also that rational choice theory does not require an offender to act with full rationality.

3. Offenders are inflexible in relation to their time of operation and the target selected.
4. The motivation to offend is not constant and irrepressible.
5. Crimes prevented will not be (totally) displaced.

As can be seen, the assumptions are partly overlapping (Bennett and Wright, 1984:30).

These assumptions are not entirely incompatible with the dispositional emphasis in many theories, Bennett and Wright point out that Ferri (1895) and Lombroso (1911) found room for a 'residual category of situational ... criminals in their categories' (1984:16). Sutherland and Cressey (1955) accepted that situational factors, such as alarms or potential witnesses, might influence the occurrence of crime, but they emphasised the importance of the individual's history to the way in which he interprets those factors.

Notwithstanding the apparent acceptance that background factors are to some extent relevant, and the fact that situational elements may sometimes be taken to include social and cultural factors as well as physical ones, much recent material has tended to focus on physical factors. Bennett and Wright say this is understandable, as discussion is closely linked to current crime prevention strategies which themselves concentrate on physical elements because they are more easily altered than social or cultural ones (1984:18). Pragmatism rises up again, and the theoretical development of the situational perspective suffers as a result.

10.17 Conclusion

Clearly, the theoretical background to the situational approach to crime prevention is far from fully developed. It has been suggested that the validity of situational crime prevention depends on the soundness of rational choice theory, on the capacity of situational measures to avoid major displacement, and on the accuracy of the assumptions which underlie the approach.

There are obvious links between each of these areas, but they have yet to be fully explored. Nee and Taylor point out the danger that: 'without a firm set of theoretical foundations ... the approach will remain endemic and patchy, and will lack coherence and credibility' (1988:114).

Further research is needed and areas ripe for study include the potential of situational measures to affect the commission of expressive crimes; whether displacement effects can be predicted and controlled; further research into offenders' thought processes; the reasons why persistent offenders continue to offend or desist from doing so; sources of initial motivation towards crime; fresh area studies to assess the interaction between different factors in physical and social environments; and ways of reducing the difficulties associated with the implementation of crime prevention programmes.

There appears to be some merit in situational techniques, and adopting a pragmatic approach is more constructive than saying 'nothing works, so let's do nothing'. However, it is submitted that the government, agencies and, indeed, society cannot afford to ignore the possible contributions of social measures and even of the criminal justice system. Having recognised the limitations of the latter in its existing form, successive governments have continued to make piecemeal adjustments rather than develop an integrated, forward-looking policy (Bottomley, 1986).

Home Office Circulars 8/84 and 44/90 both emphasised the importance of enhancing community safety through inter-agency co-operation. However, the Morgan Report, which was published in 1991, draws attention to the lack of co-ordination which still exists in many parts of the country and re-emphasies the need for each of the agencies with responsibility for community safety to co-operate fully with others in addition to delivering its own specialised contribution (Home Office, 1991).

PART THREE:
THE INSTITUTIONAL FRAMEWORK OF LAW ENFORCEMENT

11

The Criminal Justice System

11.1 Introduction

11.2 Models of the criminal justice system

11.3 The philosophy and aims of punishment

11.4 Developments in penal policy

11.1 Introduction

If a narrow view of the criminal justice system were to be adopted, we would probably identify the main participants as the police, lawyers, and the courts. These are the parties on whom this part of the book will concentrate. Nevertheless, it has been suggested that use of the term 'system' implies a degree of integration which does not exist. Baldwin and Bottomley (1978) prefer to discuss the criminal justice 'process', in order to recognise the different objectives and philosophies involved. If we were to look at the process as a whole, we would realise that a host of parties are involved, including victims, witnesses, offenders, the police, the Crown Prosecution Service, defence lawyers, the Probation Service, the courts, the Prison Service, the legislature, and the government (issuing guidelines and providing resources). Indeed, we ought to include the public, as many of the central participants claim to be reflecting public opinion in the way they act. Lack of space forces us to take a narrower view, however artificial that might be.

Clearly, the philosophies of the main participants will differ, and this will affect the way the process operates. However, without adopting simple stereotypes, it would be impossible to describe these different philosophies. It would be naïve to suggest that all police officers have the same opinion of the proper aims of criminal justice, or of the police service, or of their own roles within those larger networks. The same is true of lawyers (who might act for the prosecution one day, and for the defence on another) and of judges and all other participants in the system. Having said that, we might expect participants to be influenced by different occupational cultures and to share certain ideas with colleagues in their own professions. Variations between different professions will be considered by examining different models which have been put forward to help explain the workings of the criminal justice system.

11.2 Models of the criminal justice system

A number of writers have suggested that a criminal justice system can be viewed in terms of certain models. Each model does not represent an ideal type against which a particular system can be matched. Instead, it is a perspective for viewing a criminal justice system in order to understand its operation, functions and characteristics. Any system might resemble different models at different times. Similarly, different parties within a system might view it as resembling quite different models. The number of models offered in the literature varies between two and six.

Packer (1969) distinguished between the crime control model and the due process model. These are put forward as a framework for discussing a process, the everyday operation of which involves a constant series of adjustments between the demands of two competing value systems. Some writers have suggested the police tend to work according to a crime control model and that defence lawyers operate in line with a due process model. Chambliss and Seidman (1971) claim that the police use a crime control model for less affluent suspects, but adopt a due process model for more affluent suspects. Griffiths (1970) says Packer's models are too limited. For example, they emphasise prevention of crime, and retribution as functions of the criminal law, but ignore rehabilitation. In fact, Griffiths argues that Packer actually gives only one model, which emphasises 'struggle' between the individual and the state. Griffiths puts forward a third model, the family model, which is linked to the ideology of family life. This closely resembles the medical model, which we shall come to soon.

It is true that Packer paints a picture in which offenders struggle from start to finish. They attempt to avoid detection, deny guilt if caught, then continue to try to avoid being convicted. Based on their own empirical study, Bottoms and McClean (1976) argue that only a third of people who commit crime, actually struggle in the way described by Packer. Another third are passive respondents to the criminal justice process, and the remaining third come somewhere between the others. Bottoms and McClean also add a third model, the liberal bureaucratic model, which is said to be adhered to by humane clerks to the justices. This model emphasises smooth operation of the system. The defendant's formal rights to struggle are left open, but if he exercises them he might pay by receiving a heavier sentence. Bottoms and McClean say that to understand the system you have to use all three models at various points. They attribute the absence of struggle to an alliance between the crime control model and the liberal bureaucratic model.

McBarnet (1981) is more critical of Packer's work. She suggests the distinction between the crime control model and the due process model is a false dichotomy. A due process model is supposed to protect the rights of a suspect by requiring the police and the other parties in the process to follow the law 'in the books'. However, McBarnet argues that as this law has considerable discretion built in, it does not necessarily embody due process ideals. Due process, as practised, is said to support the crime control model. It should be borne in mind that these comments were made before the enactment of the Police and Criminal Evidence Act 1984 (PACE).

McBarnet was able to point to the fact that the conduct of the police in questioning suspects was at that time governed by the Judges Rules, which were not legally binding. At surface level, PACE and the associated codes of practice should place a far greater obligation on the police to respect the rights of suspects and to obtain evidence by fair means only. However, in 1990 a major investigation began into the activities of the former West Midlands Police Serious Crime Squad, which was disbanded amid allegations of the fabrication of evidence. In 1992, the Director of Public Prosecutions decided that none of the officers concerned would face criminal charges. Several convictions obtained on the basis of confession evidence gathered by this squad have been overturned on appeal. The interviews in which these confessions were allegedly manufactured took place after PACE was implemented.

In a book written before PACE entered the statute books, King (1981) comments on the capacity of different interest groups to thwart legal reforms by interpreting and adapting them to allow existing patterns of behaviour to continue. The same writer puts forward a well structured discussion of six models of the criminal justice process. These are:

1. The due process model.
2. The crime control model.
3. The medical model.
4. The bureaucratic model.
5. The status passage model.
6. The power model.

Each of these models has its own central function, characteristics, adherents, different factors to support its validity, and weaknesses. King has a full book in which to discuss them, but we don't. Instead the main points in relation to each model will be summarised below. The description provided by King will be supplemented to take account of other viewpoints. This will also allow each model to be covered, and in the case of readers for whom this topic is examinable, might form the basis of a revision aid. The format used differs from the table provided by King (1981:13).

The due process model

1. *Function:*
    justice.

2. *Characteristics:*
    courts act as a neutral referee;
    the defendant is given legal safeguards;
    strict adherence to formal rules;
    presumption of innocence.

3. *Adherents:*
   defence lawyers;
   researchers and observers motivated by a concern with civil liberties.

4. *Evidence to support the model's validity:*
   the existence of formal rules, such as PACE and rules of evidence.

5. *Weaknesses:*
   low awareness of relationships between participants;
   little is said about courtroom dynamics;
   consensus is assumed to exist, among participants, in relation to the objectives
      of the process;
   gaps between ideal and performance are not explained;
   broader social issues are overlooked;
   in practice, guilty pleas may be induced, eg by the prospect of a reduced
      sentence;
   the model may merge with and support the crime control model.

The crime control model

1. *Function:*
   punishment, and through that the control of crime.

2. *Characteristics:*
   implicit presumption of guilt (the police have already acted as a filter, to
      bring only the guilty before the courts);
   high conviction rate;
   support for the police;
   legal controls are largely disregarded;
   the experience is unpleasant for the defendant;
   retribution and deterrence are subsidiary functions;
   people are assumed to be responsible for their behaviour.

3. *Adherents:*
   police;
   prosecutors.

4. *Evidence to support the model's validity:*
   much police action is aimed at crime control;
   formal rules can be bent or circumvented;
   some laws expressly give powers to police and courts whilst reducing the
      rights of citizens, in order to achieve crime control (a current example
      would be police powers of stop and search under s1 of PACE).

5. *Weaknesses:*
>   low awareness of relationships between participants and of the potential for conflict;
>
>   by assuming people to be responsible for their behaviour, it ignores social or physiological pressures;
>
>   does not account for non-punitive sentences.

The medical model

1. *Function:*
>   rehabilitation/treatment.

2. *Characteristics:*
>   the court is a catalyst for the gathering of information about the defendant;
>
>   structured procedures exist for this purpose;
>
>   it is assumed that treatment is appropriate and effective;
>
>   the expertise of advisers is recognised;
>
>   the defendant is responded to as an individual;
>
>   formal rules are relaxed and decision-makers have discretion;
>
>   people may be victims of events beyond their control;
>
>   guilt and punishment are rejected as irrelevant concepts.

3. *Adherents:*
>   some probation officers.

4. *Evidence to support the model's validity:*
>   the existence of procedures for receiving social enquiry reports and medical evidence;
>
>   rehabilitative aspects of some types of sentence, eg probation.

5. *Weaknesses:*
>   absence of evidence that rehabilitation works;
>
>   courts are not really geared to the medical model;
>
>   information gathering is imprecise;
>
>   resources are insufficient for such a model to operate effectively;
>
>   often no attempt is made to apply the model in practice;
>
>   if treatment fails, the criminal justice process falls back on punishment;
>
>   the recipient may view the sentence as punishment rather than treatment;
>
>   there is an assumption that people want to be treated;
>
>   the pre-sentence experience of defendants (eg arrest and interview, the court hearing) is not consistent with the medical model;
>
>   a welfare role is imposed on an otherwise unchanged and essentially punitive structure.

The bureaucratic model

1. *Function:*
   management of crime and criminals.

2. *Characteristics:*
   the court is neutral in conflicts;
   speed and efficiency;
   formal records are important and accepted;
   economic use of resources;
   minimisation of friction and conflict;
   individuals are processed in line with standard procedures.

3. *Adherents:*
   humane clerks to the justices (per Bottoms and McClean, 1976).

4. *Evidence to support the model's validity:*
   existence of pressures to accept summary trial for offences triable either way;
   operation of plea-bargaining (Baldwin and McConville, 1977);
   concentration on obtaining admissions of guilt (Dell, 1971; King, 1981);
   regularity of contact and development of relationships between courtroom regulars;
   courts' use of special procedures which separate insiders from outsiders.

5. *Weaknesses:*
   consensus about objectives is assumed;
   clear delineation of roles and the division of labour is assumed to exist.

The status passage model

1. *Function:*
   denunciation and degradation.

2. *Characteristics:*
   publicly shames defendants and denounces their behaviour;
   gives expression of moral indignation on the public's behalf (per Garfinkel, 1956);
   reflects and reaffirms the community's values;
   emphasises ritual and ceremony;
   press have a role in communicating information about the shamed individual;
   agents (eg police) have some control over the extent to which status degradation is allowed to proceed.

3. *Adherents:*
   few participants in the criminal justice system would want to be accused of deliberately setting out to shame individual defendants. However,

magistrates and judges often attempt to denounce certain types of behaviour, and it is impossible to separate actors from their actions. Aspects of this model can be seen, to some extent, in the activities of most of the parties in the process.

4. *Evidence supporting the model's validity:*

much of the post-arrest procedure in police stations. Even without looking for ominous undertones, this can include the routine procedure of being searched and processed as a prisoner;

the formal rules and layout of courts;

special forms of address in court;

restricted participation by the defendant in court;

press coverage of criminal cases.

5. *Weaknesses:*

consensus is assumed to exist about which acts are reprehensible;

it is assumed that a defendant's reaction will be shame, rather than rationalisation of his conduct;

press coverage is not certain to follow;

in some cases, eg proceedings in juvenile courts, press coverage is prohibited.

The power model

1. *Function:*

maintenance of class domination.

2. *Characteristics:*

class values are reinforced;

the defendant is alienated and suppressed;

issues of class conflict are not dealt with openly;

there are gaps between rhetoric and reality in the operation of the process;

co-existence of formal rules with discretion and flexibility in the process allows the maintenance of a façade which hides the use of criminal justice to serve the goals of the power elite;

there are marked differences between the judges and the judged;

there are different forms of this model, most of which of which avoid being crude conspiracy theories. Rather than the law being a direct instrument of class power, the self-interest of various participants helps to advance the interests of the ruling class.

3. *Adherents:*

such a model would fit best with the viewpoints of radical theorists. It is possible, however, to find supporting evidence for certain aspects of the model without adopting a radical view.

4. *Evidence supporting the model's validity:*

the gulf between the formal hearing and the prior procedure in police stations (per King, 1981);

judges are largely drawn from a limited section of the community, and have very little in common with the majority of defendants (Griffiths, 1985; Legal Action Group Bulletin, January 1990:4);

magistrates also tend to have middle class values and to come from different backgrounds to most defendants (King, 1981);

lawyers do not truly represent their clients; instead they should be regarded as 'agent mediators' (Blumberg, 1967);

probation officers do not represent clients – they accept the system and induce conformity (Garofalo, 1978).

5. *Weaknesses:*

there are no overt signs of blatant coercion or repression of defendants;

there is little easily seen evidence of major contradictions between official claims and actual practice;

although conspiracy theory is avoided, the model still assumes consensus among participants about objectives.

It is worth emphasising again that none of the models is put forward as an accurate description of the way in which the criminal justice process operates. There are grains of truth in each. Using different models as perspectives when considering the working of the process has several advantages. It provides a framework for discussion and can identify disparities between rhetoric and practice. Models can help in the understanding of past trends, and can highlight the complexity of issues when future policies are being considered. An awareness of the different models provides an insight into the ideological positions of different writers. These models refer to the criminal justice process as a whole. The next section focuses on a particular aspect – sentencing.

11.3 The philosophy and aims of punishment

Even when there is sufficient evidence to place an offender before a court, prosecution does not automatically take place. An offender might be cautioned, or no further action might be taken for some other reason. However, the majority of detected offenders are prosecuted and most of these are found guilty. In England and Wales in 1995, more than 1.4 million people were found guilty of an offence; 300,000 of these were convicted of indictable offences (Home Office, 1996a:94). Following conviction, they all received one type of sentence or another; 106,200 received a conditional discharge. It might be argued that such a sentence is not really a punishment, whereas in the case of imprisonment and fines it is easy to equate sentencing with punishment. Wright suggests that punishment implies deliberate imposition of an unpleasant measure, 'because it is unpleasant' (1982:172). He goes on to point out that any compulsory measure might be unpleasant. For example, an offender who has to receive treatment is forced to give up some of his own time. Wright prefers to define punishment by reference to the intention of the sentencer, rather then the perception of the recipient. That interpretation would allow a discharge to be viewed as a punishment. The mere fact of being convicted and having the conviction marked in some way identifies the offender as a criminal. If there had been an intention to 'let him off', he might have been dealt with in some way other than prosecution. In any event, 75 per cent of offenders convicted in 1995 received a fine, which is more clearly a punitive measure. Rather than wallow in semantic technicalities, we should move on to consider the various aims or functions of punishment. Some writers choose to discuss 'justifications' for punishment (eg Walker, 1980). We will concentrate on five perceived functions: deterrence, rehabilitation, crime reduction, retribution and denunciation.

It should be borne in mind that the present chapter is concerned with sentencing generally. The next chapter will concentrate on imprisonment.

Deterrence

The belief that punishment for crime can deter people from offending can take two forms. Specific deterrence is concerned with punishing an individual offender in the expectation that he will not offend again. General deterrence is related to the possibility that people in general will be deterred from committing crime by the threat of punishment if they are caught. Any evaluation of the deterrent effect of sentences needs to take account of the different forms of deterrence, as the assumptions which underlie them are clearly different. Walker (1980) argues that the differences are minimal, saying that individual deterrence relies on memory, while general deterrence relies on the potential criminal's imagination. However, an individual with one or more previous convictions is likely to have been affected by more aspects of his experience of the criminal justice process than simply the unpleasant effect of the sentence. For example, contact with more experienced offenders may have convinced him that the prospects of being caught on a further occasion are not particularly great. Furthermore, having experienced police interview techniques, an offender may find it easier to avoid admitting his guilt on later occasions. A raw outsider with no criminal contacts may well lack these insights.

Two points are assumed to be essential if the availability of sanctions is to have a deterrent effect. First, the punishment must be sufficiently severe. This assumption can be tested by examining instances where levels of punishment have been altered. Calvert (1936) examined committal rates for a number of offences for which capital punishment was removed as a potential sentence, between 1820 and 1841. For several offences, fewer people were committed in the three years following the removal of the death sentence. For some offences, the committal rates increased, but overall the movement was downward. This suggests that the availability of capital punishment had no obvious deterrent effect.

In 1965, the death penalty was abolished as a punishment for murder in England and Wales. Research indicates that this change had no readily definable impact on the rate of murders (Beyleveld *et al*, 1979; Morris and Blom-Cooper, 1979). This challenges the claim by Ehrlich (1975) that in America, every execution deterred seven or eight other murders. Ehrlich relied on an econometric version of rational choice theory, and his claims have been criticised by other writers (eg Hann, 1976). It is frequently suggested that murder, particularly in a domestic context, is a crime where the offender is highly unlikely to make a rational choice before committing the act. If that is so, the potential consequences will be irrelevant, so that deterrence is unlikely. Walker (1985) suggests that a proper conclusion to draw is that the death sentence is no more effective as a deterrent than the penalty which replaced it, an indeterminate sentence of imprisonment.

Baxter and Nuttall (1975) examined rates of robberies and assaults with intent to rob in six urban areas after the well-publicised case of a Birmingham 'mugger' who was sentenced to 20 years in custody. There was no change in rates after the passing of the sentence. Reductions which occurred later might have been attributable to changes in policing and in the physical environment. There was no evidence of a general deterrent effect.

Secondly, deterrence will not work if the probability of detection is low, or is perceived as low by potential offenders. Supporters of deterrence assume that potential offenders weigh up the rewards and risks associated with crime. Research by Beyleveld (1978, 1979) suggests that the likelihood of detection is more important than the level of punishment. A large amount of research has shown that the risk of being caught red-handed by patrolling police is very low (Bottomley and Coleman, 1981; Steer, 1980). Similarly, the odds relating to capture as a result of police investigations seem to be stacked in favour of the offender. In 1995, less than a quarter of burglaries were cleared up. The detection rate varied between police force areas with 57 per cent being cleared up in Dyfed-Powys whilst only 1 in 10 were cleared up in Humberside (Home Office 1996a p34). The extent to which people believe they might be caught is probably more important than the actual risk of detection. Arguably, experienced criminals will be more aware of how low the risk is. Novices might be more open to the myth encouraged by detective fiction, that the police almost always get their man. This suggestion was partly supported by research into cannabis use among students (Waldo and Chiricos, 1972).

Casting our minds back to the discussion of displacement in Chapter 10, it is possible that any deterrent effects of sentencing might be watered down if people opt for different crimes which are perceived as less risky.

Even if punishment does deter effectively, a number of moral objections can be raised to the use of sentences for this purpose. Beyleveld (1978) suggests that the types of punishment needed to deter will vary between different people, different crimes and different circumstances. Wright (1982) points out that in order to deter crime, sentences may need to be set at a level which is entirely out of proportion with the seriousness of the offence.

When a particular offender has not been deterred, he must receive the threatened punishment. In many cases, the consequences of such punishment may be counter-productive (Wright, 1982:177). Martin and Webster (1971) suggest that conviction and punishment may push an individual into a position where he no longer stands to lose anything from further offending. His opportunities to live by legitimate means may be reduced, so that if it is accurate to portray an offender as making rational choices about offending, the individual with previous convictions is pushed towards choosing illegitimate means no matter what the consequences will be if he is caught. It has also been suggested that punishment might give rise to a desire for revenge on society (Shaw, 1922).

Wright suggests that the threat of severe punishment encourages offenders to try harder to avoid detection and conviction. This can lead to violent escapes, and to time being wasted as a result of not guilty pleas which have no chance of success. Furthermore, offenders such as child abusers who could benefit from help will be dissuaded from seeking it. As has been said, the use of punishment to deter must be based on an assumption that people choose to commit crime. It would be morally wrong to take that assumption too far and impose deterrent sentences on individuals who have little or no control over their impulses, or who break the law unwittingly. It has to be recognised, though, that the courts can deal with such offences in more appropriate ways. Deterrence remains a valid option in the case of intentional offenders (Walker, 1980).

Rehabilitation

The terms 'rehabilitation' and 'treatment' are sometimes used as if they mean the same thing. However, it is probably more useful to view treatment as a more narrow expression which refers to those occasions when an offender is subjected to procedures of a medical or psychiatric nature which are intended to change him in such a way that he is less likely to offend in the future. Rehabilitation will be treated here as a broader term, which includes treatment, but has a meaning similar to that proposed by Wright (1982). He suggests that rehabilitation involves offering an offender help to overcome problems which he faces, thereby attempting to make it easier for him to avoid future offending. This can encompass various types of assistance (provided in prison or in the course of a probation order) which are intended to help the offender to improve his social skills, his employment prospects, or his capacity to obtain welfare benefits. Rehabilitative ideals can be seen in the official terms of reference of some of those dealing with offenders after conviction. Probation officers should advise, assist and befriend clients.

The duty of the Prison Service, according to a statement of purpose issued in 1988, was to treat inmates 'with humanity and to help them lead law abiding lives in custody and after release' (Home Office, 1990:11). Nowadays there is a tendency for observers to challenge the viability of rehabilitation. Wright (1982) suggests there are five main types of criticism. Slightly modified, these are as follows:

1. Rehabilitation does not work.
2. Rehabilitation is really punishment.
3. Rehabilitation can lead to longer sentences than straightforward punishment.
4. Treatment can be degrading.
5. Rehabilitation is based on a false premise.

Rehabilitation does not work

In so far as rehabilitation is intended to curtail or reduce future offending, the acid test for its effectiveness must be whether it does so. In that sense, the test is the same as for individual deterrence. In the event that a sentenced person does not offend again, it is impossible to be certain whether he has been deterred or rehabilitated (furthermore, it may simply be the case that the original offence was a response to special circumstances which no longer exist).

A considerable number of studies have tried to assess the effectiveness of different sentences in preventing recidivism. Some have compared variations in the way a particular type of sentence is carried out, for example, different prison regimes, and different tactics of probation officers. Fortunately, these studies have been subjected to several comprehensive reviews.

Martinson (1974) examined American and British research. Many studies were found to be methodologically unsound. Martinson concluded that, except in a few cases, attempts at rehabilitation had had no appreciable effect on recidivism. Brody reviewed the use of different programmes in custodial and non-custodial settings. Some fitted our narrow definition of treatment, others involved less direct attempts at rehabilitation. Although a small number of offenders did appear to have been helped, Brody concluded that the programmes generally 'have no predictably beneficial effects' (1976:37).

Having reconsidered the studies reviewed by Martinson, Palmer (1975) argues that Martinson gave too little recognition to the positive aspects of some of the methods reviewed. Palmer found that in 48 per cent of the studies the methods adopted had been at least partly effective.

Romig (1978) reviewed more than 800 studies of juvenile justice. He found that the use of rewards in the form of approval, recreational trips and money could lead to improved behaviour. Also, programmes were more likely to succeed if the organizers had a clear idea of their objectives and of the needs of the offenders.

As has been suggested earlier in this book, the experience of conviction may encourage future offending instead of discouraging it. This is especially likely if the sentence provides an opportunity to learn from other offenders. The study by West and Farrington (1977) seems to confirm this idea.

Obviously, attempts to evaluate the effectiveness of sentences in reducing re-offending are fraught with difficulties. The fact that someone is not reconvicted does not mean he has stopped offending. He might simply be better at not getting caught. Another problem is that although we can see what happens to an offender after he has been through a programme with rehabilitative elements, we cannot predict what would have happened if his sentence had contained no such elements.

The Morison Committee (Home Office, 1962) suggested that reconviction was a misleading criterion for measuring the effectiveness of a rehabilitative sentence (they were concerned with probation). Whether or not a probationer was reconvicted did not accurately assess the extent to which he had adjusted to society and learned to cope with difficulties. An offence might be no more than a temporary relapse. If the probationer had avoided offending in situations where previously he would have committed an offence, that was a mark of success. Unfortunately, the Committee did not suggest the criteria by which successful social adjustment can be measured. Elsewhere, attempts have been made to examine the social problems which offenders experience after completing their sentence.

Bottoms and McClintock (1973) constructed a social problem score for ex-Borstal trainees and compared the scores they received in the year following their release against the numbers reconvicted. Only 18 per cent of those with the lowest scores were reconvicted, whereas 82 per cent of those with the highest scores were reconvicted. In practice, those who had made the poorest social adjustment after their release were most likely to become recidivists. Walker (1985) suggests that whilst it might be valid for the criminal justice process to help people adjust socially, quite apart from attempting to prevent further offending, measurements of the effectiveness of sentencing should concentrate on the avoidance of further offences. Any other criteria should be additions, not substitutes.

In a recently published Home Office study, reconviction rates were compared for offenders who had received one of four different types of sentence (Lloyd et al, 1994). The sentences included were probation, probation with an attendance order, community service orders and imprisonment. Of the offenders sentenced to the first three types of punishment, the percentages reconvicted within two years of being sentenced were 43, 63 and 49 respectively. Fifty-four per cent of prisoners were reconvicted within two years of being released. The research suggested that the two factors most closely associated with reconviction were age and criminal history. Gender, previous imprisonment as a young offender and the type of offence were also relevant. Thus younger and male offenders were more likely to be reconvicted than older and female offenders. The variations in reconviction rates for the different types of sentence might be explained by the ages and histories of the offenders, factors which in themselves would have influenced the original penalty.

Rehabilitation is really punishment

As was suggested earlier, from the offender's viewpoint any type of sentence might be seen as a punishment, even if the sentencer's intentions were in some other direction. A requirement to undergo psychiatric treatment, to comply with a probation order or to perform community service might be intended to benefit the offender, but it inevitably restricts his liberty at the same time. This seems to be unjustified if the attempt at rehabilitation does not work. If the criminal justice process is really punishing people, it ought to own up, instead of hiding behind a mask of benevolence.

Rehabilitation can lead to longer sentences than straightforward punishment

It is obvious that any sentence which emphasises treatment or training will need to be sufficiently long to allow its rehabilitative objectives to be achieved. Wright (1982) suggests that in the 1960s, judges were persuaded to pass longer sentences so that treatment or training could be provided. In *R v Turner* (1967) 51 Cr App R 72, the Court of Appeal showed that this practice was acceptable. Walker (1980) argues that in Britain the rehabilitative ideal cannot be blamed for producing indeterminate or semi-determinate sentences. As he points out, for the ordinary prisoner, remission is not linked to his apparent response to treatment. In the case of offenders required to be detained in mental hospitals by virtue of s37 of the Mental Health Act 1983, medical experts have far more power to decide when (or if) a person should be released. Once again, if treatment and training do not work, sentences cannot be justified on rehabilitative grounds. If their true purpose is punishment or containment, that should be made clear.

Treatment can be degrading

A variety of sentences may involve the offender receiving some sort of treatment which might benefit him, but which might also cause discomfort or physical injury. For example, even as part of non–custodial sentences, offenders may take part in group counselling sessions. Even where these are run by trained staff, there is a possibility of uncovering problems which are not subsequently dealt with. Participation in such sessions might be voluntary, but offenders may well feel pressure to comply in the hope of completing their sentences earlier.

Incarcerated offenders might be subjected to more severe forms of treatment, including the administering of drugs, or hormone therapy for sex offenders. The Butler Committee (Home Office, 1975) recommended that treatment should not be imposed without an offender's consent unless it was necessary to save his life, or was needed to prevent deterioration, or if it was the minimum interference needed to prevent immediate violent behaviour. If an offender was incapable of appreciating the nature of the treatment, it could be administered without consent. In the case of irreversible procedures, a second medical opinion had to be obtained. Once again, it is hard to accept that someone in custody is totally free to choose whether or not to consent to treatment.

A former medical adviser to the Chief Inspector of Prisons wrote an article in the *Lancet* after he had resigned. He described the importance of prison medical staff avoiding the danger of acting as a 'rubber stamp' for the management and said that 'medical management "for his own protection" of a prisoner may in reality involve intimidatingly severe additional deprivation' (Lee, 1983). The Chief Inspector's report for 1988 makes no reference to such treatment, but made some findings which gave cause for concern. For example, some prison pharmacies were found to have stocks of items which were dangerous but had no therapeutic value, and other substances which might be carcinogenic (Home Office, 1989a: para 2.66).

Rehabilitation is based on a false premise

Certain types of treatment address individual characteristics of offenders. This seems to be justified if their criminality is linked to those characteristics. However, as we have seen, biological and psychiatric explanations are of little value in accounting for the behaviour of most criminals.

Instead, the majority of theories nowadays attempt to explain crime by reference to social factors. In so far as crime is a result of the way an individual interacts with his environment, it may be valid to help him to change so that his future interactions have more favourable outcomes. For example, he might be helped to improve his social skills or level of education, or given vocational training, so that his access to legitimate opportunities is enhanced. However, all of these efforts will be virtually ineffective if the society to which the individual returns is left intact. If he returns to a setting where housing is inadequate, leisure opportunities are limited, and where there are no jobs, then his new skills are worthless. In short, rehabilitation will not occur if it is society, rather than individuals, which requires treatment.

Crime reduction

Crime reduction overlaps with several other aims of sentencing. For example, if different penalties can reduce crime, they might do so in a variety of ways:

1. Deterrence (specific or general).
2. Rehabilitation of offenders.
3. Incapacitation of offenders so that they are disbarred (at least temporarily) from offending against the public at large. It should not be forgotten that a number of assaults and other crimes occur inside prisons.
4. Education of the public so that they are more likely to condemn law breaking behaviour by others, or to have a higher regard for the criminal law themselves. There is an element of such an objective in the following words of Lord Justice Lawton in *R* v *Sargeant* (1974) 60 Cr App R 74, at 77:

'... society, through the courts, must show its abhorrence of particular types of crime ... The courts do not have to reflect public opinion ... Perhaps the main duty of the court is to lead public opinion'.

Denunciation of criminal conduct will be discussed in a later section. Crime reduction depends for its effectiveness on the other functions of the criminal justice process.

Retribution

Retribution rests on the notion that if a person has knowingly done wrong, he deserves to be punished. This idea is featured in the government's White Paper *Crime, Justice and Protecting the Public*, Cm 965, 1990. The government's aim, repeated several times, was to ensure that convicted criminals receive their 'just desserts'.

A principle which most retributivists seem to accept is that a person should not be punished unless he is guilty of an offence. That principle is referred to as 'retribution in distribution' (Walker, 1985). A further limitation on retributive punishment is that the punishment should fit the crime. A sentencer should take into account the seriousness of the offence, the culpability of the offender, and the degree to which punishment will affect the offender. This is recognised as virtually impossible, and a more usual approach is to make the penalty proportionate to the crime alone (eg Cross, 1975). The White Paper proposed a variety of measures to ensure that sentencing decisions are focused on the seriousness of the offence, rather than the character of the offender.

Many of these proposals were incorporated into the Criminal Justice Act 1991 (CJA 1991), the sentencing provisions of which came into force on 1 October 1992. Some of the central aspects of the Act have since been amended, but it is worth considering them, and the manner in which they were altered, in order to illustrate the continuing absence of a coherent criminal justice policy. The Act gave statutory effect to the principle that imprisonment should be reserved for those who have committed serious offences. It provided that a court would only be able to impose a custodial sentence when it was of the opinion that:

'... the offence, or the combination of the offence and one other offence associated with it, was so serious that only such a sentence can be justified (s1(2)(a) since amended).'

or

'... where the offence is a violent or sexual offence, that only such a sentence would be adequate to protect the public from serious harm (s1(2)(b) since amended).'

Section 2 is concerned with the length of custodial sentences. It states that such a sentence shall be:

'... for such a term (not exceeding the permitted maximum) as in the opinion of the court is commensurate with the seriousness of the offence, or the combination of the offence and other offences associated with it (s2(2)(a)).'

or

'... where the offence is a violent or sexual offence, for such longer term (not exceeding that maximum) as in the opinion of the court is necessary to protect the public from serious harm from the offender (s2(2)(b)).'

Case law had previously emphasised that at the time of sentencing, an offender is being punished for the instant offence, not for his previous bad record. Section 29(1) confirmed that point by providing:

'... an offence shall not be regarded as more serious ... by reason of any previous convictions of the offender or any failure of his to respond to previous sentences.'

This apparently straightforward provision is less clear when considered in conjunction with s29(2), which said:

'Where any aggravating factors of an offence are disclosed by the circumstances of other offences committed by the offender, nothing ... shall prevent the court from taking those factors into account for the purpose of forming an opinion as to the seriousness of the offence.'

Not surprisingly, the legislation created a degree of controversy among sentencers and commentators. Questions typically raised were whether sub-sections 29(1) and (2) were compatible with each other and, if they were, what offences could be considered in relation to sub-section (2)? Different viewpoints were aired in articles and correspondence in various issues of the *Justice of the Peace* in the last quarter of 1992.

On 27 and 30 November 1992, the Court of Appeal contributed to the discussion by offering guidance in reserved judgments delivered by Lord Taylor LCJ in relation to a series of cases listed together for hearing. The judgments were reported in *The Times*, 3 December 1992.

Section 6 of the Act required a court to weigh the seriousness of an offence in a similar fashion before it is able to impose a community sentence (see also section '13.8 Restrictions on the use of community sentences'). In its original form, the CJA 1991 had given legislative force to the government's then view that just desserts and protection of the public were the principal functions of sentencing. The Act was clearly intended to lead to a reduction in the use of custody. However, reacting to press and public concern about the rise in crime and the perceived inadequacy of existing penalties for dealing with persistent young offenders, the government indicated that parts of this legislation had come to be seen as soft. Amendments to the Act would form part of a broader strategy to get tough on crime. A few days before he left the post of Home Secretary, Kenneth Clarke told the Annual Conference of the Police Federation 'the use of custody will be driven by what is just and fair retribution, not by the constraints of the prison population' (*Police*, June 1993:16). This stance was reinforced by Mr Clarke's successor, Michael Howard.

The Criminal Justice Act 1993 was passed with considerable speed and several of its provisions came into effect on 16 August 1993, making significant amendments to Part I of the Criminal Justice Act 1991.

Section 66(1) of the 1993 Act substitutes a new s1(2)(a) of the 1991 Act, so that a court can pass a custodial sentence if it is of the opinion that the present offence and one or more offences associated with it are so serious that only a custodial sentence can be justified.

Section 66(4)(a) of the 1993 Act amends s6(1) of the 1991 Act enabling a court to decide whether the seriousness threshold for passing a community sentence has been crossed by considering the instant offence alongside as many associated offences as it sees fit. The amendments have dismantled the one-on-one rule provided in the 1991 Act under which a sentencing court could only combine the offence under consideration with one other associated offence when determining whether or not the seriousness threshold related to custody or a community sentence had been passed.

Section 29 of the 1991 Act has also been replaced. In assessing the seriousness of the current offence, a court can now take account of any previous convictions (other than spent ones). There is no requirement for the earlier offences to be similar to the present one. The Act does not include guidance to assist sentencers in determining which previous convictions are relevant, but the Justices Clerks' Society recommends that a court should identify the parts of an offender's record which it is taking into account and state its reasons.

Walker points out that it is very difficult to answer the question 'Why *must* offending be penalised?' (1985:109). A retributive penalty, after all, is punishing someone for something done in the past. If it also aims to change their future behaviour, its aim is rehabilitation or deterrence, not retribution.

One can put forward several grounds to support retributive punishment. One is that the penalty cancels out the offence. That particular ground is weak, and Walker (1985) describes it as 'metaphorical'. Once a crime has occurred, the clock cannot be put back. Even if a thief replaces a stolen item, he is really making reparation. The argument that a penalty makes the offender repay his debt to society is equally nebulous so far as retribution is concerned.

Two other grounds which Walker (1980) says might be suggested by moral philosophers are that punishment purges an offender's guilt by inducing suffering, and that it induces repentance and moral improvement. The first argument might apply to some offenders, but it is not true of others who will rationalise their behaviour and regard the punishment as unjust. Similarly, the second suggestion will apply only to a few offenders. In any event, it is debatable whether a sentence which is intended to benefit an offender can be viewed as retributive.

Walker (1980, 1985) suggests that the strongest (or least weak) justification for punishing offenders is that doing so satisfies a requirement that where a rule imposes a penalty for its own breach, that penalty must be imposed when the rule is broken. This seems tautologous, but it is argued that if the penalty were not imposed, that in itself would be an infringement. On this interpretation, punishment is not only proper, it is essential.

Denunciation

One justification for imposing penalties is that they denounce particular types of behaviour, and reaffirm the validity of moral attitudes opposed to that behaviour. Walker argues that denunciation may take the form of a ritual. The court hearing followed by the passing of a sentence has ceremonial functions, as do funeral services or induction ceremonies. In order to fulfil its ceremonial function, a sentence has to be sufficiently well-advertised and severe enough to satisfy the intended audience. Curiously enough, a sentencer who seeks to pass a denunciatory sentence will be relying on his audience containing a sufficient proportion of retributivists. However, a retributive sentence is expected to be proportionate to the crime. A denunciatory sentence is not limited in that way.

Another ironic feature of a denunciatory sentence is that it does not have to be complied with. The symbolic function is satisfied by the passing of the sentence provided the audience expect that it will be carried out.

Walker (1980) suggests that a sentencer may have a more limited denunciatory aim. It may be his intention to inform the offender that his behaviour is regarded as unacceptable. There is no necessity for the community to be aware of the sentence. The offender must be aware of the penalty and expect to have it carried out.

Given the number of inherent contradictions in this justification of punishment, its validity is questionable. However, the White Paper mentioned earlier suggests several times that punishment can denounce criminal behaviour and express public repugnance of it.

This section has examined the functions of, or justifications for, types of sentence which would generally be regarded as imposing punishments. The next chapter will focus on imprisonment in particular, and Chapter 13 will include consideration of reparation. However, from the discussion so far it should be obvious that the different aims of punishment are not clearly separable. The legislature, in making a particular type of sentence available, might have the intention of enabling courts to deter offenders. Sentencers, however, might pass a sentence with the intention of denouncing the offender's conduct. Furthermore, an individual sentencer might use different justifications (or have different aims) when passing different sentences. Walker (1980) suggests that this type of sentencer, who opts for an eclectic approach, is not necessarily acting illogically. This approach is valid, provided the sentencer chooses between competing justifications on objective grounds, and not merely because of emotional pressures. A further complication arises if agents elsewhere in the criminal justice process, such as prison officers or probation officers, operate with different objectives, such as retribution or rehabilitation, in mind.

11.4 Developments in penal policy

It is important to remember that the criminal justice process involves a variety of different elements. Policymakers, practitioners and academic commentators have tended to separate the concerns of victims, police, courts and other agencies, and to compartmentalise the different stages in the process. This is understandable, as each agency has its own historical background and contemporary perspective. Nevertheless, the failure to consider the process as a whole has not helped to develop an integrated policy for criminal justice.

As discussions of penal policy generally focus on the aims of sentencing, this concluding section will take a brief retrospective look at changes in the philosophy underlying the punishment of offenders. Prior to the existence of a formal criminal justice process, there was an emphasis on reparation by the offender and his family. As formal legal systems began to develop, different countries adopted different approaches. In Britain, until the early part of the nineteenth century, the policy was to exclude offenders from the community by transportation, or as a more extreme measure, by execution. After America's Declaration of Independence in 1776, that country was no longer available for use as a penal colony. The possibility of using prisons was discussed but the decision was deferred. For some years, convicts were held on prison ships or transported to Australia. By the 1830s, the need for a long-term solution was being recognised, and by the middle of the nineteenth century the first centrally administered convict prisons were built. These operated alongside more than 100 local prisons.

In 1844, Joshua Jebb was appointed Surveyor General of Prisons. At that time, it was considered by many that prisoners would undergo moral development if they were kept in conditions of separate confinement. Jebb continued the use of separate confinement, but at a reduced level. He proposed a system in which convicted prisoners would be employed on public works. This would provide them with useful instruction and moral supervision. Prisoners would move through progressive stages, determined by their conduct and effort. Incentives would take the form of improved allowances. The work would be hard and the discipline strict. However, conditions must be adequate if the system were to be humane and the prisoners to be reformed. In some respects, Jebb seems to have been ahead of his time. He even suggested that prisons could run at a profit! In spite of his apparent interest in reforming convicts, Jebb expressed doubt about the feasibility of re-introducing them to society. Prison officers were expected to provide a good example to prisoners and to help with the object of reclaiming criminals. This effort to combine punishment with reformation was short-lived. Sentences became longer, and although remission was available from 1853, its use was limited. Prison conditions, including the selection of staff, were not conducive to achieving moral improvement. There were threatened and actual outbreaks of disorder. A Royal Commission established in 1863 considered sentences to be too short to instil fear in potential criminals. The recommendations of the Carnarvon Committee in 1863, and the provisions of the Penal Servitude Act 1864 and the Prison Act 1865 indicated a change to a philosophy which favoured deterrence. Regimes were intended to be, and were, extremely punitive. In 1869, Edmund du Cane was appointed Surveyor General of Prisons. In 1877, when all of the prisons were brought under Home Office control, du Cane also became Chairman of the Prison Commission which was responsible for administering the prison system. He remained in post until 1895, and had an enormous influence on prison regimes. For him, the primary purpose of punishment was deterrence and, in particular, general deterrence.

By the beginning of the 1890s, the punitive regime of the prison system had aroused sufficient adverse opinion to prompt the establishment of the Gladstone Committee. The committee reported in 1895, and its recommendations led to a change in penal policy. Reforming the criminal was now to be a major aim of imprisonment. Over the next 50 years or so, prison conditions were made less deliberately punitive, and facilities for aftercare of prisoners were implemented. Other types of sentence, such as borstal training (1900) and probation (1907), were introduced (Harding *et al*, 1985; Radzinowicz and Hood, 1986).

As we saw earlier, the popularity of rehabilitation as an aim of sentencing has waned considerably. Wright calls rehabilitation 'The Ideal That Went Out of Fashion' (1982:192). In the White Paper which preceded the CJA 1991, the government accepted that reforming an offender is 'always best if it can be achieved' (Home Office, 1990:2.6). Whilst it suggested that certain sentences served in the community might reform offenders, the White Paper did not regard imprisonment alone as being effective for this purpose. Just desserts was proposed as the first objective of all sentences, with protection of the public, reparation, and reform of the offender coming in as possible additional aims. The sentencing provisions of the CJA 1991, in their original form, placed those objectives in a similar order of importance, but the subsequent amendments indicate that confusion persists over the purposes of sentencing.

The hurried changes introduced by the Criminal Justice Act 1993 were an indication of the government taking some action on its promises to take a harder line on crime. Reinforcing this stance, the Home Secretary used the Conservative Party Conference in October 1993 as an opportunity to announce what he called 'the most comprehensive programme of action against crime that has ever been announced by any Home Secretary' (*The Times*, 7 October 1993).

Some of these proposals were included in the Criminal Justice and Public Order Act which received the Royal Assent on 3 November 1994 and has attracted considerable controversy. Some of the Act's varied provisions are described below.

Section 1 creates a new sentence, the secure training order, for persistent offenders aged between 12 and 14. An order must last for between six months and two years. The first half will be served in a secure training centre and the second under supervision in the community. The government currently plans to establish five contracted-out secure training centres, each of which will hold up to 40 detainees.

Section 16 enables courts to impose long terms of detention on 10–17 year olds convicted of certain grave crimes. Section 17 doubles the maximum term of detention for offenders aged between 15 and 17 to two years.

Given the confusion which surrounds the desired outcomes of custodial sentences for older offenders, it is debatable whether these new powers are intended to have any benefits other than the short-term ones of temporarily taking offenders out of circulation and of giving the appearance of taking tough action against crime.

Section 26 amends the Bail Act 1976 to restrict the granting of bail. In particular, a court is given greater discretion not to grant bail to so called 'bail bandits', that is people accused or convicted of having committed an indictable offence while already on bail for a previous offence.

Sections 34 to 39 provide for a court or jury to draw inferences from the fact that the defendant did not answer questions put to him by the police or has not given evidence at his/her trial. Failure to give answers is not an offence in itself, and a person is not obliged to incriminate himself. Any inference can act only as supporting evidence. Notwithstanding the limited nature of this provision, it has been seen by some as a withdrawal of the right to silence and, therefore, as one of the most controversial parts of the Act.

Sections 96 to 100 extend the potential for further privatisation of the prison service and provide an indication that the prison population is expected to continue growing for the foreseeable future.

The overall aim of the Act was said to be to ensure more guilty people are convicted without jeopardising the rights of the innocent. One almost inevitable effect will be an increase in the prison population. It is debatable whether such an outcome reflects an intention to protect the public by putting offenders out of circulation, or to deter further offending, or simply to be seen to be doing something about law and order. Certainly, the constant changes of direction suggest the absence of any coherent attempt to formulate and implement a logical and consistent penal policy.

Recent developments

The Prime Minister, John Major, in his CPC Jubilee Lecture in January 1996 elaborated on the Conservative government's higher profile for issues involving penal policy. He announced that the government were to build five secure training centres for 12–14 year olds who persistently offend. Major also revealed that MI5, the Security Service, were to be given power to support the police in tracking down drug dealers, and identified the international drugs rings as the source of the problem.

For sentences on crimes of burglary, the Prime Minister published statistics saying 'the average sentence for a burglar on his first offence is 14.4 months. And he can expect to be released after 7.2 months'. He then explained the average sentence for burglars who have ten or more convictions, quoting a period of 16.8 months with automatic release, 'with the expectation of release after 8.4 months'. He also claimed that Britain had seen 'the largest ever drop in recorded crime over a two year period: 572,000 fewer recorded crimes, 380,000 fewer thefts, 175,000 fewer burglaries, 4,800 fewer violent crimes during 1995', which he called 'the first annual drop in violent crime for almost 50 years'.

Judicial disagreement emerged once Major made these announcements. The fierce constitutional debate which ensued covered the powers of judges to pass sentences without interference from the Executive in the form of the government of the day.

The Lord Chief Justice, Lord Taylor, attacked the government's entire criminal justice programme in a lecture at King's College, London, entitled 'Continuity and Change in the Criminal Law' delivered on 6 March 1996. He said, 'we have had more Criminal Justice Acts in the past six years than in the preceding sixty'. On penal policy, he said it had 'in four years swung from one extreme to the other and frequent swings of penal policy eat away at public confidence in the criminal law'.

Other judges, notably Lord Hailsham, Lord Donaldson, Lord Ackner and Lord Justice Rose, had spoken out in 1996 against current sentencing policy.

However, the Home Office defended the government, saying that the changes announced had 'a simple aim: to protect the public from persistent and dangerous criminals', in reference to proposed plans for longer sentences, or life imprisonment, for such a group of offenders.

The government also responded by publishing a White Paper in March 1996. It is called 'Protecting the Public' (Home Office 1996c) and it is the basis for the government's major legislative proposals on crime. The rhetoric is in terms of waging war on crime. Changes to sentencing were envisaged with emphasis on the problems caused by serious, dangerous and persistent offenders, and with the aim to provide deterrence. Offenders would serve the sentence that they received from the court, which would mean the end of automatic early release and the abolition of parole for all but life sentence prisoners. There would be some reduction in sentence for good behaviour. Automatic life sentences were suggested for a second serious sexual offences or second serious offence of violence. A third offence of domestic burglary would attract a three year minimum sentence whilst a third offence for drug-trafficking would attract at least seven years. This is only an outline of the proposals, clearly there is much additional detail to take note of. The Crime (Sentences) Bill which was introduced in the autumn of 1996 contained the above White Paper proposals. It is estimated that these changes would involve an increase in prison numbers of 10,800 by 2011–2012. Whilst these are perhaps the most important proposals the White Paper explained more generally what the government hoped for. Their ideas include a stronger local emphasis on preventing and reducing crime, with the new police authorities and their chief constables taking a clear lead. Co-ordination of activity, for example through the national drugs strategy, is suggested as a general tactic to be used in tackling crime. That more criminals should be brought to justice is another aim. The most frequent and disruptive offenders would be targeted. Greater fairness in procedures and practices would be sought in order to prevent miscarriages of justice. Fewer delays in processing cases would be part of this. There would also be more emphasis on victims of crime. Finally, there are changes in relation to sentencing-in addition to those noted earlier there are proposals for tougher and more appropriate community sentences. Many of these ideas will have to await additional legislation in the future.

12

Imprisonment

12.1 The role of imprisonment

12.2 Conditions in prison

12.3 The consequences of imprisonment

12.4 Conclusion

12.1 The role of imprisonment

Chapter 11 discussed different aims (and to a limited degree the effectiveness) of sentences, without focusing on any particular type. In a sense, imprisonment is just one type of sentence, so one could attempt to justify it in terms of all the functions already discussed. It would be pointless to rehearse all of the earlier arguments, but as imprisonment is arguably the most serious punishment that British courts can impose, there are good grounds for focusing on some of its purported aims.

The intention of this chapter is not to concentrate on the effectiveness of prison in, for example, deterring or rehabilitating offenders. In fact, it is possible to address that issue in a quite succinct manner. The test in relation to both of those aims, it was said earlier, is the same: does the sentence reduce further offending? In relation to imprisonment, the answer is usually 'No'. Prison statistics estimate that 45 per cent of males and 38 per cent of females discharged from a custodial sentence in 1992, were reconvicted within two years, Home Office (1996d). Factors such as age, the number of previous convictions and individual characteristics are regarded as being just as relevant to future offending as the type or length of sentence (Home Office, 1990b: Table 9(a)). Elsewhere, the Home Office has said 'Longer periods of custody do not produce better results than shorter ones' (1986a: para 3.2).

So far as rehabilitation is concerned, the Home Office conceded in *Crime, Justice and Protecting the Public* that nowadays no one regards imprisonment (on its own) as an effective means of reforming the majority of prisoners. It will become clear when we discuss prison conditions that prison is one of the last places where most people could be expected to change for the better. As the White Paper admits, imprisonment has to be justified in some other way or else 'it can be an expensive way of making bad people worse' (para 2.7). On the subject of expense, the government's own figures make frightening reading. On average, it costs £25,000 per year, to keep an offender in custody (Home Office, 1996e).

The White Paper argues that imprisonment can be justified in terms of public protection, denunciation and retribution. Enough was said in the previous chapter about the last two functions of punishment, so they will not be covered again. The only point that will be made is that there seems to be broad agreement in principle, that any denunciatory or retributive functions of imprisonment are complete at the time of sentencing. A person is punished by being sent to prison, he does not go to prison to carry on receiving punishment (Home Office, 1979: para 110; Maguire *et al*, 1985). In practice, it seems to be an inevitable feature of prison that punishment continues throughout the sentence.

The aims and objectives which the Home Office support in relation to the use of custody have not remained static. It is therefore necessary to take a look into the past, then return to the present in an attempt to discover the role of imprisonment. We are only concerned with its role in relation to convicted prisoners. The position of remand prisoners is outside the scope of this book. Naturally, prisoners on remand experience certain aspects of prison life in a similar (though not strictly identical) fashion to sentenced prisoners and will be affected by them.

At the end of Chapter 11, when changes in penal policy were discussed, it was seen that official attitudes about the purpose of custody had moved from retribution to deterrence to rehabilitation (often referred to as 'treatment and training'), but that the rehabilitative ideal had lost its appeal in the last 20 years or so. Sadly, those general purposes seem to have overlapped to varying degrees in different periods, and it has rarely been clear what the central functions of imprisonment were meant to be. Perhaps some of the fog could be cleared by looking at the perceived terms of reference of the Prison Service.

Rehabilitative optimism was alive and kicking as the 1960s began. According to a White Paper published in 1959, the object of prison was to send prisoners out as better people, physically and morally, than when their sentences began (Home Office, 1959: para 44). That aim was reaffirmed in Rule 1 of the Prison Rules 1964, which gave the purpose of training and treatment of convicted prisoners as encouraging them 'to lead a good and useful life'. Although the rule gives the purpose of treatment and training, it does not make its provision compulsory. The optimism was a little weaker by the end of the decade. Another White Paper, *People in Prison*, gave the overriding purpose of imprisonment as 'the protection of society' (1969: para 8). It was to do this by holding them in conditions acceptable to society. In addition, so far as possible, the Prison Service should meet the aims of Prison Rule 1. In effect, the Paper did not deny the possibility of rehabilitation, but gave it second place, and raised the idea of 'humane containment' as the first task of the prison service.

The concept of humane containment was expanded by King and Morgan (1980). They provided strong arguments for minimising the use of imprisonment, but also spelt out the need to ensure that when a custodial sentence is imposed, it is served in a humane environment. This would involve a minimum use of security. The point made was that not all prisoners need the same level of security, but in practice prisoners who represent different levels of escape risk are often placed alongside each other. Security is set to cater for the highest risk. A high degree of security carries with it a high level of intrusion into the lives of prisoners, in terms of surveillance, interception of communications, searching, and monitoring of visits. Measures for maintaining control within the prison should also be no more intrusive than necessary. A further essential element of humane containment was normalisation of prison life. This meant that as far as resources and security requirements would permit, prisoners should enjoy the same general standards of life as offenders serving their sentences in the community.

King and Morgan gave evidence to the Committee of Inquiry into the United Kingdom Prison Services (the May Committee). The May Committee were not in favour of humane containment, which they likened to placing prisoners and staff in 'human warehouses' (Home Office 1979: para 4.24). Instead, the Committee proposed that Prison Rule 1 be reworded to embody the concept of 'positive custody'. The purpose of detaining convicted prisoners would be to keep them in custody which was secure but positive. Prison authorities and staff would be responsible for creating an environment in which prisoners could respond positively to society, for allowing prisoners to preserve their self-respect, for minimising the harmful effects of removal from life outside, and for preparing inmates for discharge (para 4.26). The May Committee wanted to replace the rhetoric of 'treatment and training', but retain all the 'constructive things' done in its name (para 4.27). As the Committee recognised that a lack of 'real objectives' could lead to the routine brutalization of everyone involved in the prison system (para 4.28), it is particularly unfortunate that the alternative suggested by them was loosely worded, probably unattainable, and impossible to evaluate. Their own concept of positive custody has been described as 'zookeeping' (Fitzgerald and Sim, 1982:82).

What seems to have happened since is that the Home Office has set the Prison Service objectives which are more realistic in relation to existing prison conditions and the resources available (Stern, 1987). Inevitably they are less optimistic than previously. In 1988, the duty of the Prison Service was described as to treat prisoners 'with humanity and to help them lead law abiding lives in custody and after release' (Home Office 1990: para 3.2). The spectre of rehabilitation refuses to go away, but is growing ever more faint.

Given that protection of the public is one of the major justifications claimed for imprisonment, we should take a brief look at the capacity of prison to achieve that aim by incapacitating offenders. It seems obvious that taking an offender out of circulation will prevent him from committing crimes against members of the public. However, the situation is not that simple. The experience of prison may be such that the offender is more likely to re-offend after release, and perhaps to commit more serious crimes. If that is so, crimes are not prevented, but merely deferred. In any event, some prisoners continue to commit offences, including serious assaults and homicides, while in custody. Are we to say these crimes do not count, because they occur behind closed doors, with staff or fellow inmates as victims? If we go beyond the effect of incapacitating individual offenders, to consider the effectiveness of imprisonment in reducing crime, the problem is even more complex. It is impossible to say how many unsolved crimes are committed by offenders who are never caught. They will not be affected by the imprisonment of less elusive offenders. Brody and Tarling (1980) have calculated that recorded crime rates would not be substantially affected if fewer offenders were sent to prison. A similar conclusion is reached in the Home Office Handbook, *The Sentence of the Court*, (1986a: para 3.5). This latter point is recognised in the 1990 White Paper, which proposes a reduction in the use of imprisonment for less serious offences.

The discussion so far shows that, although different aims have occupied centre stage at different times, there has always been confusion about the proper role of custodial sentences. Prison officers and management can hardly fulfil their roles if it is not clear what they are. During the 1970s and early 1980s there were numerous disputes involving prison officers, and many demonstrations by prisoners (Rutherford, 1986; King and Morgan, 1980; Home Office, 1984). The tensions which led to these can be partly attributed to internal conflicts about roles, attitudes and training needs (Harding and Koffman, 1988:151).

In an article published in March 1990, Crawford predicted that unless the Home Office addressed the problems facing the prison system 'it may find too late that it has been constructing not prisons but time bombs'. He was soon proved to be right, by a series of disturbances during April 1990, the most notable of which was the seizure of Strangeways, which took 25 days to bring to an end. Between April 1991 and March 1992 there were 18 rooftop protests and 22 hostage-taking incidents (Home Office, 1992).

The sections that follow examine conditions in prison, and the consequences of imprisonment.

Recent developments

The Home Secretary presented the 'Prison Statistics for England and Wales 1994' to Parliament in February 1996. The average population in custody (including those in police cells) during 1994 was 48,800. This figure represents an increase of 4,200 on the 1993 figure and was the highest level since 1988. The Home Office comments that the higher prison population in 1994 continues the trend started in 1993, and followed a steep fall during 1992. The statistics show a rise in the use of custody for both those on remand and those to be sentenced and reflects, in part, implementation of the Criminal Justice Act 1993. A report by the Home Office on the prison population noted an average population in custody in 1995 of 51,000 (Home Office 1996f).

The Criminal Justice Act 1993
The 1993 Act modified aspects of the Criminal Justice Act 1991. With the increase in custodial sentences, the proportion of Crown Court defendants sentenced to custody rose from 44 per cent in the first quarter of 1993, to 52 per cent in the final quarter, compared with 45 per cent in 1992 before the 1991 Act came into operation. The 'Prison Statistics for 1993' concludes that 'the rise partly reflected fewer but more serious cases committed to the Crown Court'. However, the proportion of magistrates' courts' defendants sentenced to custody for an indictable offence rose during 1993, from 4 per cent in the first quarter to 7 per cent in the final quarter, compared with 5 per cent in 1992 before the 1991 Act came into effect. The Criminal Statistics for 1995 note that the figure is now up to 9 per cent (Home Office 1996a p145).

12.2 Conditions in prison

The absence of clarity about the role of imprisonment is matched by a lack of uniformity in prison standards. The 1988 report of Her Majesty's Chief Inspector of Prisons states: 'The quality of life for an inmate was often random, haphazard and dependent on accidents of geography and allocation' (para 2.01). According to the same report, prisoners on whom fate smiled might end up in a prison which offered a reasonable quality of life. In 1983, the not so lucky might have found themselves somewhere like Wormwood Scrubs, which was described by its Governor as 'a penal dustbin full of overcrowded cattle pens' (Gostin and Staunton, 1985).

Accepting that conditions do vary between establishments, the quality of life of prisoners in many British prisons is poor and, in some cases, appalling. Regimes and general conditions are comprised of many different aspects. Not all of them can be covered here, but the following important topics will be discussed:

1. Overcrowding and physical conditions.
2. Access to meaningful activities.
3. The side-effects of maintaining security and control.
4. Contact with the outside world.
5. Discipline, grievance procedures and prisoners' rights.

Overcrowding and physical conditions

There are marked variations in conditions among the different establishments in the British prison system. Overcrowding is a problem. Over 28 per cent of prisoners are remand prisoners, most of whom were held in remand centres or local prisons, which generally have the worst overcrowding. Prisoners are obliged to share cells which were built for one inmate.

The 1988 inspection programme showed that the consequences of overcrowding are often exacerbated by other problems, such as poor sanitation, prisoners being confined to their cells for long periods, and bullying. Poor maintenance meant that substandard conditions, such as leaking roofs and shabby timber accommodation, had to be endured for years in some establishments (para 2.08). Prison food was usually adequate, although it was often prepared in 'disgraceful conditions' (para 2.11). Many inmates did not have sufficient access to regular baths or clean clothing (para 2.14). Stern describes one prison which had problems with cockroaches, and filthy, flooded toilets (1987:97). 1966 did, however, see sufficient provision of 24 hour access to toilet facilities so as to remove the practice of slopping out which had caused much concern in the past.

Access to meaningful activities

Most official reports regard opportunities for employment, education or leisure facilities as important features of a prison regime. Yet, very often, these facilities are found to be inadequate or non-existent. Prison workshops are not restricted to the sewing of mailbags, but there is little work for prisoners and most of that which is available is tedious (Wright, 1982:38). The Chief Inspector's report for 1988 shows that a few establishments offered good quality vocational training, and some provided interesting work which produced useful goods. In many others, work was mundane and undemanding (para 2.28). Even the better workshops were often forced to close because of staff shortages (para 2.29). Evidence of matching prisoners to jobs on the basis of suitability was mixed (para 2.30). The prison population includes people with useful skills, which they will never have an opportunity to use (Home Office Research Bulletin, 1978). Would it not make sense for the Home Office to subsidise its costs by obtaining more ambitious contracts with outside concerns, thus allowing prisoners to maintain their skills and self-esteem, and the Prison Department to reap the financial benefits?

The picture in relation to education in prisons is not much brighter. Staff in prison education departments have been complimented for being energetic and flexible, but accommodation and facilities are often poor. There are sometimes waiting lists for classes because there are too few classrooms. Some establishments are affected by staff shortages (Home Office, 1989a: paras 2.32–2.34).

Access to sports facilities is another feature which contributes to the quality of a prison regime. In the establishments which were inspected in 1988, facilities were generally good. In fact, many prisons were better equipped than the surrounding community. The Chief Inspector was impressed by the dedication of the PE staff. In spite of shortages of discipline staff, varied programmes were frequently offered. Furthermore, in some cases there were opportunities to maintain contact with the community by playing sports against outside teams (paras 2.38 – 2.41). Of course, not all prisoners will want, or be fit enough, to take part in strenuous exercise. Some would benefit from nothing more energetic than a walk, or the opportunity to talk to other prisoners. In practice, staff shortages can sometimes prevent prisoners from enjoying 'association' with fellow inmates or from taking the one hour a day exercise called for by Prison Rule 27. Prisoners in local prisons are more likely to be affected, and might spend 23 hours a day in their cells (Wright, 1982:44). There are examples, though, of staff doing their best to allow prisoners out of their cells for as long as possible (Home Office, 1989a: para 2.23). The findings of subsequent inspection programmes are not much more encouraging.

The side-effects of maintaining security and control

Security and control are central functions of prisons, and are analytically distinct from each other. Put simply, security relates to keeping prisoners in an establishment. Control concerns the maintenance of orderly behaviour within the prison. Although they are separate, maintenance of each function can affect the other. For example, restrictions imposed in the name of security may lead to frustration for inmates. The demands of both functions inevitably affect prison regimes (Home Office, 1985).

Since the publication of the Mountbatten Report in 1966, the classification of prisoners has rested almost entirely on security risks. Prisoners are put into four categories, A to D. Category A prisoners are those whose escape would be highly dangerous to the public, the police or the state, and who must be kept in conditions of maximum security (even if the prospect of their escaping is unlikely). Category B prisoners do not need such high security, but their escape must be made very difficult. Prisoners in category C lack the resources to make a determined attempt at escape, but cannot be trusted in open conditions. Category D prisoners can be trusted in open conditions. Lord Mountbatten also proposed that Category A prisoners should be held in a single, purpose-built maximum security prison (Home Office, 1966). That proposal was not accepted, and in the light of the Radzinowicz Report, a system of dispersal prisons was introduced to hold long-term prisoners (Home Office, 1968). It was felt that dispersal of high-security risk prisoners among those in lower-risk categories would neutralise the notoriety of the former. Of course, it can also involve placing prisoners in a more secure situation than is necessary. Security in the dispersal systems was meant to rely on achieving a very secure perimeter, so that a civilised and relaxed regime could be maintained within. In practice, this has been impossible to achieve.

The Control Review Committee observed that long-term prisons will always contain men who are aggressive, manipulative and hostile to authority. In establishments where inmates are allowed to associate relatively freely, there will be a constant danger of disruption (Home Office, 1984: para 41). Management are tempted to tighten the regime for control reasons and this inevitably leads to further frustration.

As was said earlier, during the 1970s and early 1980s there were numerous disturbances in British prisons. In the dispersal system, in particular, one of the official reactions was for security based measures to encroach deeper inside the walls. Alleged examples include greater restrictions on internal movement, more frequent searches, reduced association time, and a more pervasive use of electronic locking procedures (King and Morgan, 1980; Stern, 1987).

Problems of balancing security considerations against the demands of control, whilst maintaining a civilised regime, are not confined to the dispersal system. The same demands and their side effects also affect local and training prisons. The paragraphs which follow are all connected, in one way or another, to security and control.

Contact with the outside world

It would seem sensible to encourage prisoners to maintain contact with their families and friends, not least because this might ease their return to normal life. That notion is accepted in Prison Standing Orders (Stern, 1987:102). The two major ways of keeping in touch are letters and visits. There are restrictions in relation to both, which can partly be justified on security grounds. The frequency of letter writing is controlled. The Prison Service will pay the postage on one letter per week and one further letter can be sent at the prisoner's expense. The authorities may allow further letters to be sent on welfare grounds. Prison notepaper must normally be used (Stern, 1987). Outgoing and incoming letters have traditionally been censored. It is understandable that letters cannot contain anything which would threaten security, but prisoners and people writing to them may well feel constrained about what they can say about purely personal matters.

Visits are also subject to restrictions, some administrative, others of a geographical origin. The basic entitlement in this country is for one visit, lasting half an hour, every 28 days. Facilities for visits vary between prisons, and according to the security risk associated with the prisoner. Some prisoners will meet visitors at individual tables, some across long, communal tables, and others might be separated from visitors by glass or a grille. Visits take place within the sight and, in a few cases the hearing, of prison staff. Sometimes, prisoners' families will be unable to visit them regularly (if at all) because of the expense and difficulty of travelling. Martin and Webster (1971) found that only a third of prisoners were held, for most of a sentence, within 30 miles of home. In any event, prisoners were often moved between establishments. Obstacles to contact can only serve to increase a prisoner's isolation during the sentence, and probably during the period immediately after his release.

Discipline, grievance procedures and prisoners' rights

Rules 47 to 56 of the Prison Rules 1964, as amended, describe offences against prison discipline; state that a prisoner charged with an offence shall be able to prepare a defence; outline the adjudication (hearing) procedure; and list the punishments available. Offences range from lateness for work, or idleness, to serious assaults. Punishments include forfeiture of privileges, cellular confinement and loss of remission. Uglow (1995) p293 notes that in 1991 85,648 offences against discipline were proved. Until 31 March 1992, most charges were dealt with by Governors, but the more serious ones had to be referred to Boards of Visitors. The Boards no longer have any disciplinary function. A Governor is able to delay a prisoner's early release by imposing up to 28 additional days. Now that Boards of Visitors no longer have any disciplinary functions, the Home Office has issued Governors with guidelines for referring certain criminal offences to the police.

According to the Chief Inspector of Prisons, the power to adjudicate in disciplinary matters and to punish people by further restricting their liberty or removing privileges ought to be 'carefully and judiciously exercised'. However, the inspections carried out in 1988 revealed that appropriate standards of justice were not always being applied in Governors' adjudications. The physical setting for adjudications and the demeanour of escorting officers were frequently oppressive. Sometimes the wrong charges were laid, and punishments were imposed which seemed excessive. One case was found where the punishment exceeded the permitted maximum. Records of hearings were often so poor that it would have been difficult for anyone examining them later to understand what had happened. Some of the omissions represented 'serious infringements of inmates' rights', but there were some establishments where the adjudication process was fair and objective (Home Office, 1989a: paras 2.44–2.46).

Prison Officers, as well as prisoners, would presumably agree with the comment of the Prior Committee that the prison discipline system must be 'swift, fair and conclusive' (Home Office, 1985a). Indeed, in its evidence to that Committee, the Prison Officers Association feared that opening the system to excessive scrutiny could lead to overt and formal disciplinary measures being supplemented by administrative sanctions, such as segregation, relocation, and adverse parole reviews.

Improper use of disciplinary measures or of unofficial sanctions, and undue interference with a prisoner's liberty within the prison is likely to breed resentment and, in any event, such actions appear to be wrong in themselves. It follows that prisoners should be able to use effective procedures for redressing their grievances. In the first instance, a prisoner with a complaint may apply for an interview with the Governor, the Board of Visitors, or a Regional Director. The Chief Inspector of Prisons found that in most of the prisons inspected during 1988, grievance procedures were sensibly organised and clearly understood. Generally, prisoners who wished to speak to the Governor were not prevented from doing so, but many applications were intercepted at lower levels and dealt with by other staff. A prisoner can also send a petition to the Home Secretary. It would not be surprising to find some prisoners being reluctant to regard any of the parties mentioned here as sufficiently independent of the system about which they wish to complain. This type of concern might be particularly acute in the case of a prisoner aggrieved at the conduct of a prison officer. Prison Rule 47(12) creates an offence of making a 'false and malicious allegation against an officer'. In addition to discouraging frivolous complaints, this rule might have the same effect in relation to legitimate ones.

Any difficulties might be lessened if prisoners were able freely to take their grievances outside the prison walls to lawyers, MPs and the courts. Until quite recently, Home Office restrictions and the attitude of the courts had the combined effect of allowing the prison authorities to wash their dirty linen in private. In *Becker* v *Home Office* [1972] 2 QB 407, Lord Denning said: 'If the courts were to entertain actions from disgruntled prisoners, the Governor's life would be made intolerable. The discipline of the prison would be undermined'. Ten years later, Lord Wilberforce pointed out that 'a convicted prisoner ... retains all civil rights which are not taken away expressly or by necessary implication' (*Raymond* v *Honey* [1982] 1 All ER 756).

An example of a right expressly taken away is the capacity to vote (s3 of the Representation of the People Act, 1983). The question of which rights are removed by necessary implication is not so easy to answer (Walker, 1985).

Prisoners are now allowed to contact their own lawyers if they wish to commence civil proceedings. This was not always the case, and it took an action before the European Court of Human Rights to clarify the position (*Golder* v *United Kingdom* [1975] 1 EHRR 524). Golder had wanted to consult a solicitor about bringing an action against a prison officer for defamation and was prevented from doing so. The court held that there had been breaches of Articles 6 and 8 of the European Convention on Human Rights.

The circumstances leading to the decision of the European Commission in *Silver and Others* v *United Kingdom* [1980] 3 EHRR 475, were that the prison authorities had stopped 58 letters sent out by prisoners to various parties, including lawyers and MPs. The Commission found that there had been a breach of Article 8 which upholds freedom of correspondence, in the absence of grounds such as national security or prevention of crime or disorder. One of the British government's arguments was that the Prison Department operated a 'prior ventilation rule'. Prisoners had to exhaust internal procedures before they could complain to someone outside the prison. The Commission did not accept that as a defence. The so-called rule was part of unpublished standing orders, not of published prison rules. The government's needs would have been equally well served by a 'simultaneous ventilation rule', that is, a requirement that internal and external complaints were to be made at the same time. The blocking of letters to MPs and lawyers was in breach of the Convention.

The standing orders relating to correspondence were re-written in the light of *Silver* and published in 1981. In 1984, the Queens Bench Divisional Court held that the simultaneous ventilation rule should not apply when a prisoner was writing to his lawyer (*R* v *Secretary of State for the Home Department, ex parte Anderson* [1984] 1 All ER 920).

In the *Silver* case, the government also tried to justify blocking letters from prisoners to their wives on the basis that this was necessary to prevent disorder. The letters had contained complaints about the way prisoners were being treated. Again, the Commission considered there had been a breach of Article 8 of the European Convention.

Even before these developments had taken place, there were examples of prisoners bringing successful actions against the prison authorities. Following a riot at Hull Prison in 1976, 185 prisoners were charged with discipline offences. Several received severe punishments, including the loss in one case of 720 days of remission. Seven prisoners tried to have the decisions overturned, claiming that the Boards of Visitors had not given them the benefit of natural justice. The Divisional Court ruled against the prisoners, stating that the prison discipline system had to operate expediently. On appeal, the Court of Appeal decided in favour of the prisoners. Boards of Visitors were acting in a judicial capacity and had to comply with principles of natural justice (*R* v *Hull Prison Board of Visitors, ex parte St Germain* [1979] 2 WLR 42).

The disturbances which took place in Strangeways and five other establishments in April 1990 confirmed the potential for disorder which exists inside British jails and, for a time at least, forced the policy makers to pay serious attention to the subject of prison conditions. Lord Justice Woolf was appointed to head an inquiry into the disturbances and has produced a comprehensive report running to almost 600 pages (Home Office, 1991a).

Understandably, the philosophy behind the Woolf report continues to recognise the importance of maintaining security and control, but it emphasises that these must be balanced with justice. In this context, 'justice' means treating prisoners with fairness and humanity. Several of the recommendations address ways of achieving this type of justice. For example, each prisoner should know exactly what is expected of him and what he can expect from the prison. These expectations should be set out in a form of compact, to be reviewed during the sentence. When decisions are made which have a materially adverse effect on prisoners, they should be given the reason behind those decisions. Grievance procedures should be made more effective, with most complaints being dealt with by the governor. To deal with complaints which cannot be satisfactorily resolved, prisoners should ultimately have access to an independent, legally qualified adjudicator. The report calls for improvements to be made in several other areas, for example, the quality of buildings; overcrowding; ties with prisoners' families and the community; work and education; and the recruitment and training of staff. It is also suggested that methods of dealing with disturbances must be improved.

As soon as the Woolf Report was published, the Home Secretary announced the following improvements: reduction of censorship; an increase in family visits (including provision of financial assistance where necessary); installation of more telephones for use by prisoners; and the ending of 'slopping out'. In September 1991 the Home Office published a White Paper, *Custody, Care and Justice: The Way Ahead for the Prison Service in England and Wales* (Home Office, 1991b). In it, the government accepts one of the central propositions in the Woolf Report that security and control must be kept in balance with justice and humanity. The White Paper recognises that a better and more stable prison system requires a coherent and consistent strategy for the Prison Service. It reaffirms the following statement of purpose, first issued in 1988:

'Her Majesty's Prison Service serves the public by keeping in custody those committed by the courts. Our duty is to look after them with humanity and to help them to lead law-abiding and useful lives in custody and after release' (paragraph 1.1).

The paper identifies the government's key priorities as being to: improve necessary security conditions; improve co-operation with other agencies; increase delegation of responsibility and accountability within the service; improve the quality of work for staff; recognise the status and particular requirements of unconvicted prisoners; provide a code of standards for activities and conditions in prisons; improve relationships with prisoners, including the provision of a statement of facilities and sentence planning for each prisoner; provide access to sanitation for all prisoners at all times; end overcrowding; divide larger wings into more manageable units wherever possible; and develop community prisons serving prisoners within given areas.

The remainder of the paper contains both firm proposals for action and suggestions for discussion. It is encouraging that the Home Office has recognised the need to develop a humane system of imprisonment, but it comes as no surprise that the implementation period extends into the next century and that privatisation features in the government's plans. It is intended that some prisons and secure training centres will be built and operated by the private sector. However, the White Paper expressly states 'Not everything can be implemented at once. Not everything can be afforded immediately' (Home Office, 1991b:3).

The overview of prison conditions in this section has shown that improvements are long overdue. Some prisoners live in reasonable accommodation, perform useful work and enjoy meaningful activities. Many others live in cramped surroundings and spend almost all of their time in a cell. It is perfectly reasonable to take the view that prisoners cannot expect to lead a luxurious lifestyle. However, if people are placed in conditions which do not meet humane standards, we should not be too surprised if they are hostile to society on their release. Furthermore, it surely cannot be acceptable that two prisoners with similar backgrounds, given identical sentences for identical crimes, can serve their time in widely different conditions merely because they end up in different prisons.

12.3 The consequences of imprisonment

It was seen earlier that the positive effects of imprisonment are limited. Having examined the types of conditions which exist in prisons, this is hardly surprising. The main purpose of this section is to look at some of the unintended effects of imprisonment which might have a negative influence on an offender's lifestyle after his release. Before we proceed we should note Walker's observation that any effects of imprisonment will not necessarily be permanent (1985:159). Prison, after all, is a temporary experience (although its length varies), whereas the community into which a prisoner is discharged will surround him permanently, unless he escapes from it, perhaps by going back into prison. Examples of possible unintended effects of imprisonment are:

1. Impairment of physical health.
2. Impairment of mental health.
3. Providing a criminal education.
4. Damaging ties with the outside world.
5. Reducing employment prospects.

Impairment of physical health

There is almost no research into the likelihood of the physical health of inmates being impaired by their experience of prison conditions but risks might be expected to exist, given the findings of the Inspectorate about poor sanitation (Walker, 1985). A comparative study carried out in Tennessee, USA, found a higher rate of recorded acute disorders among male prisoners than among paroled offenders, probationers or similar age males in the general population (Jones, 1976). Walker points out that the higher rates might be partly explained by the advantages which accrue to prisoners who report sick combined with the relative ease of doing so. He also suggests that some prisoners who are ill at the time of admission may benefit by obtaining health care which they would not have sought in the outside world. Even after attention has been sought, there might still be problems, because in his report for 1990–91, the Chief Inspector of Prisons concluded that 'the standard of medical care afforded to prisoners falls far short of that provided in the community' (Home Office, 1991(c):4.54).

The previous chapter touched on the possibility that certain types of treatment administered in prison might harm prisoners rather than help them. Prisoners are exposed to physical injury as a result of assaults by other inmates or, more rarely, by prison staff. Between April 1992 and March 1993, 2,061 assaults on prisoners were recorded. Bringing about a reduction in assaults has been identified as a specific target for the Prison Service (Home Office, 1993a:8). As unreported offences are not included, the true extent of inter-prisoner violence is not known. Suicides, attempts and cases of self-mutilation occur among prisoners. Between April 1992 and March 1993, 43 prisoners took their own lives (Home Office, 1993a:para 82). A Circular Instruction dealing with suicide prevention was distributed in 1987 but, in 1991, the Inspectorate found marked variations between the ways in which monitoring groups operated in different prisons. There were very few prisons in which self-inflicted injury was taken seriously (Home Office 1991c:4.19). During 1992 the Prison Service published its own guide to suicide prevention and Suicide Awareness Teams have been set up in all establishments. During 1993–94, pilot schemes for training staff in recognising prisoners at risk were being expanded to cover all penal establishments (Home Office, 1993a:15). The figure for 1994–1995 was lower, with 33 prisoners taking their own lives (Home Office 1996e).

A more recent phenomenon is the danger presented by HIV. Although the extent of homosexual activity in male prisons is not known, it undoubtedly occurs. As such activity is illegal, the Home Office has expressed reluctance about issuing free condoms because to do so could be seen as condoning unlawful behaviour (*The Times*, 11 March 1988; Trace, 1990). Condoms are issued to inmates in some jurisdictions in the United States, but in most administrations, the same view is taken as in Britain (Hammett, 1988). It appears that a greater risk of the spread of HIV is presented by the intravenous injection of drugs. Quite understandably, the authorities try to prevent drugs from being brought into prisons, and they do not supply prisoners with syringes. As a result, the needles which are smuggled in tend to be shared, so that there is a high risk of spreading HIV (Trace, 1990; Blumberg, 1989). The Prison Service has established an AIDS Advisory Committee to update its policy on HIV prevention. Interestingly, although Gomme (1992) argues in favour of a much clearer strategy, she does not support the issuing of condoms or the introduction of a needle exchange scheme.

Impairment of mental health

The prison population contains people suffering from mental disorders, such as schizophrenia and psychopathy, and from depression. In the majority of cases, these conditions will have existed prior to admission and will not have been caused by prison life. However, in the absence of proper medical care these conditions are unlikely to improve in prison, and may even be made worse. The Chief Inspector's 1991 report suggests that although more prisoners who could benefit from treatment in psychiatric units are being diverted to the National Health Service, too many are still being imprisoned. Staffing levels and inadequate facilities make it difficult for prison personnel to provide mentally ill prisoners with the same standard of care as can be given in NHS hospitals (Home Office, 1991c:4.24–4.29).

Another argument is that prison leads to institutionalization for longer term prisoners. Cohen and Taylor's *Psychological Survival* provides an interesting account of the possible effects of custody on the mental well-being of long-term prisoners, but does not provide concrete proof that psychological damage occurs. Sapsford (1978) studied 60 lifers and found that as their sentences progressed, they became less able to make independent decisions, and more attached to prison routine.

The government's 1990 White Paper suggests that imprisonment is likely to reduce an offender's self-reliance and feeling of responsibility (para 3.1). Even if it cannot be said that prison life damages mental health, it seems inevitable that its demoralising aspects will deny the individuality of prisoners and impair their self-image. Career plans for prisoners have been suggested as a means of countering this and are being introduced.

Providing a criminal education

It is often claimed that prison acts as a school for crime. Prisoners living cheek by jowl with each other are likely to spend some time discussing crime and swapping ideas about criminal techniques and ways of evading capture in future (Stern, 1987). In addition to learning different tactics, it is possible that offenders' attitudes change during a sentence, to become more favourable to criminal behaviour. Walker (1985) argues that in the case of short sentences, only a minority of offenders who had previously been quite law-abiding would be affected in this way. There will be some offenders whose usual contacts in the outside world participate in criminal acts, so it is unlikely that their own conduct will be influenced any differently by meeting similar associates in custody. There is evidence in relation to male offenders that the more time a person has spent in prison, the more likely he is to be reconvicted (Nuttall *et al*, 1977). Whether this is due to learning in the school of crime or to other factors is not clear.

Damaging ties with the outside world

Any interruption of normal contact will usually be unpleasant for a prisoner and his family during the currency of a sentence (although, if there has been domestic violence or child abuse, imprisonment may provide a temporary respite for the family). The consequences are more serious if permanent breaks occur. A study by Morris (1965) indicated that the marriages of first-time prisoners were not likely to break up. This was less true of recidivists and long-term prisoners.

Reducing employment prospects

Notwithstanding the assistance of the Probation Service and organisations such as the National Association for the Care and Resettlement of Offenders, it is often more difficult for offenders to obtain employment after their release from prison than it was before they went in. Opportunities for vocational training in prison are limited. More seriously though, whether a former prisoner has gained new skills or not, employers are unlikely to want to take him on. Schwartz and Skolnick (1962) conducted an experiment in which job applications were sent to 100 employers. Twenty-five showed the applicant to have a conviction for assault; 25 mentioned an acquittal on an assault charge; 25 indicated an acquittal certified by a letter from a judge; and the remaining 25 applications did not mention criminal proceedings. The researchers counted the number of employers who said they would consider the applicant. The figures were, respectively: 1; 3; 6; 9. They suggest that even an acquittal has a stigmatising effect for employment purposes, but that a conviction is regarded more seriously. Presumably, receipt of a prison sentence would be more damning still. The inability to obtain legitimate employment must surely make it more difficult for an ex-prisoner to go straight, particularly when that might also mean abandoning criminal friends and the excitement associated with some forms of crime.

12.4 Conclusion

This chapter shows that imprisonment is frequently ineffective as a means of satisfying the major aims of punishment. In fact, it appears to be worse than other types of sentence in that respect. What is more, imprisonment is expensive and can lead to consequences which it is hard to justify in a humane society.

13

Early Release, Suspended Sentences and Community Penalties

13.1 Changes in the legal framework

13.2 The background to early release

13.3 The current system for the early release of prisoners

13.4 The effectiveness of early release

13.5 Alternatives to imprisonment

13.6 The suspended sentence

13.7 Community orders

13.8 Restrictions on the use of community sentences

13.9 The community service order

13.10 Breach of community sentences

13.11 Reparation

13.1 Changes in the legal framework

This chapter deals both with the mechanisms by which offenders sentenced to imprisonment can be released before they have served their full sentences, and with some of the sentences which courts can impose for offences which they do not consider to be serious enough to warrant a custodial sentence. Provisions of the Criminal Justice Act 1991, which came into force on 10 October 1992, made substantial alterations to the law in each of those areas.

13.2 The background to early release

Before the law was changed in 1992, in the normal course of events, a prisoner serving a determinate sentence was released after serving two-thirds of the original term. The full sentence was reduced by remission of up to a third, provided no days had been forfeited for breaches of prison discipline. Remission had its origins in the days of transportation, when transportees were allowed a ticket of leave after serving part of the original period of removal, provided their behaviour had been good. This entitled them to a certain amount of freedom within the penal colony until the end of the transportation period. As transportation was phased out, a system of early release was introduced for convicts serving a sentence of penal servitude. When a prisoner left custody on remission he was not subject to any special supervision – his sentence was complete. Remission was abolished by the CJA in 1991.

The parole system also had its roots in the same traditions, but in its mode of operation it was a new concept so far as the British criminal justice process was concerned. Parole differed from remission in various ways. For example, the prisoner was released under a licence which imposed conditions, and which remained in force until the time when he would have been released without parole. If the conditions of the licence were broken, or if he re-offended while it was still current, the parolee was liable to be recalled to prison.

Since early this century, people sentenced to borstal training or preventive detention could be released on licence. However, the first real call for a comprehensive system of parole came in 1964, when a Labour Party Study Group, chaired by Lord Longford, published its report, *Crime – A Challenge To Us All*. In 1965, a White Paper entitled *The Adult Offender* described the advantages of releasing some prisoners before they became eligible for release on remission. This suggested that prisoners, particularly those serving long sentences, reached a peak of rehabilitation but then began to deteriorate. Some could benefit from early release under supervision. The White Paper envisaged that a prisoner's date of release would be linked to his response to training whilst in prison, and to expectations about his behaviour after release. Given the grave reservations expressed in previous chapters about the capacity of prison to rehabilitate people, the White Paper appears to have linked parole to a misguided concept. Adopting a more cynical viewpoint, one might point to comments in the White Paper that arrangements for parole would provide a strong incentive to reform, thereby assisting the task of prison administration. In other words, prisoners would respond to training if to do so meant an earlier release date. The prison authorities would benefit from having a prison population which was both smaller and better behaved.

The White Paper also suggested that the proposed parole scheme would apply to all prisoners serving a determinate sentence of 12 months or more. A prisoner would become eligible to be considered for parole after serving one-third of his sentence, or 12 months in custody after sentence, whichever was the longer. Most of the White Paper's proposals were incorporated in the Criminal Justice Act 1967, and the parole scheme operated from April 1968. A number of modifications were subsequently made. For example, in June 1984 the Home Secretary used powers under the Criminal Justice Act 1982 to reduce the minimum qualifying period for parole from 12 months to 6 months (time served in custody after sentence). One effect of this was to alter the anomalous situation where prisoners sentenced to short terms seemed to be treated less favourably than those serving longer sentences. Prior to the change, prisoners sentenced to any term between 18 and 36 months could be released at about the same time. After the change, the same criticism could be levelled in respect of prisoners sentenced to between 9 and 18 months. In 1985, the Lord Chief Justice notified the Home Secretary of judges' disquiet about the way parole affected sentences of less than two years (Home Office, 1988a: para 35). In addition, the reduction in the minimum qualifying period meant that far more short-term prisoners were considered for parole. In 1983 the number of prisoners serving less than two years who were considered for parole was 265, but in 1986 it was 10,603. The change also shortened the average period which parolees spent on licence after release, from 8 months in 1983 to 5.5 months by 1987 (Home Office, 1988a: paras 39–40).

During 1987 the Carlisle Committee began a wide-ranging review of the parole system. Its report contained numerous proposals for change (Home Office, 1988a). Many of these were adopted in the CJA 1991. Others were rejected. To a large extent, the government's choice between different proposals was influenced by its own emphasis on just desserts and protection of the public. The CJA 1991 introduced a new scheme for the early release of prisoners serving determinate sentences.

13.3 The current system for the early release of prisoners

The system for granting parole which operated prior to October 1992 will not be examined. The current scheme involves the automatic early release of prisoners serving less than four years (short-term prisoners) and discretionary early release of inmates serving four years or more (long-term prisoners). Estimates suggest that only 4,200 cases will need to be considered for discretionary release each year under the new system, compared with 23,000 cases per year before the changes were implemented. The following aspects of the new system will be covered below:

1. The three types of early release.
2. Discretionary life sentence prisoners.
3. Openness in decision making.
4. Young offenders.
5. Breach of licence.
6. Compassionate release.

It should be noted that whilst this is a new system, it may be abolished in the near future. This issue is returned to at the end of section 13.4 below.

The three types of early release

The CJA 1991 introduced three main routes to early release: automatic unconditional release; automatic conditional release; and discretionary conditional release.

Automatic unconditional release (s33(1)(a))

A prisoner aged 18 and over who is serving less than 12 months is released automatically after serving half of his sentence. He is not subject to supervision after being released, but if he is convicted of a further imprisonable offence committed before the end of the original full sentence, the court dealing with the new offence can direct that all or part of the balance of the first sentence must be served.

Automatic conditional release (s33(1)(b))

A prisoner serving a sentence of one year to less than four years is released automatically on licence at the half-way point of his sentence. For both types of automatic release, the release date can be put back if the Governor has imposed additional days because of breaches of discipline.

Compulsory supervision after release expires when the 75 per cent point of the sentence has been reached. In the case of some sex offenders, s44 allows a judge to order, at the time of passing sentence, that supervision will continue until the end of the sentence.

Prisoners remain at risk of being ordered to serve all or part of the outstanding portion of the sentence if they are convicted of a further imprisonable offence committed before the end of the original term.

Governors sign prisoners' licences on behalf of the Home Secretary. Most prisoners are subject to standard conditions, but a Governor may take account of the recommendations of the supervising officer and impose additional conditions.

Discretionary conditional release (s35(1))

A prisoner serving four years or more becomes eligible to be considered for early release after serving half of his sentence. Every case must be considered by the Parole Board which was made an incorporated body in 1996.

Section 32(6) enables the Secretary of State to direct the Parole Board as to the matters it will take into account when making a recommendation. In particular, these are based on the need to protect the public from serious harm, the prevention of further offending and the desirability of rehabilitating the offender. The Home Secretary formally retains responsibility for making parole decisions but delegates that responsibility to the Parole Board in respect of prisoners sentenced to less than seven years.

Even if a long-term prisoner has been refused discretionary early release on licence, he is automatically entitled to be released on licence after serving two-thirds of his sentence. Every long-term prisoner is under supervision after his release until the 75 per cent point of his sentence has been reached. As with short-term prisoners, the sentencing judge can order that certain types of sex offender will be supervised until the end of the sentence.

Long-term prisoners are subject to the same 'at risk' provisions as short-term prisoners if they commit further offences before the end of the original prison term.

Discretionary life sentence prisoners

The CJA 1991 also changed the early release procedures for prisoners serving discretionary life sentences, that is, those sentenced to life for an offence other than murder. The sentencing court specifies a period, commensurate with the seriousness of the offence, after which the prisoner should be eligible for early release under the new procedure. This period is likely to be between a half and two-thirds of the determinate sentence that the court would have imposed if it had not passed a life sentence. Once that period has been served, the prisoner is able to require the Secretary of State to refer his case to the Parole Board and the Board is empowered to direct the Secretary of State to release the prisoner on licence if it is satisfied that continued imprisonment is no longer necessary to protect the public.

Openness in decision making

As was suggested in *Crime, Justice and Protecting the Public*, the Home Secretary has expressed a commitment to allow prisoners access to the information on which decisions about conditional early release are based and to give reasons for those decisions.

Young offenders

Any offender under the age of 22 years who is released early from a custodial sentence receives a minimum of three months compulsory supervision, no matter which of the three routes to release has been followed (s65).

Breach of licence

Section 38(1) makes failure to comply with a condition of a licence an offence, in the case of short-term offenders only. Breaches are dealt with by a magistrates' court which is able to impose a fine of up to £1,000 and/or order a return to custody for the balance of the licence period or for six months, whichever is the shorter. A breach of licence by a long-term or life sentence prisoner is dealt with by the Parole Board.

Compassionate release

The Secretary of State is empowered to release a prisoner on licence on compassionate grounds before the half-way point of a sentence has been reached (s36). Unless it is impracticable to do so, the Secretary of State consults the Parole Board before releasing a long-term or life sentence prisoner under this provision.

The changes introduced by the CJA 1991 are intended to make the arrangements for the early release of prisoners more consistent and fairer. They have to be considered as part of a broader package which seeks to reserve the use of imprisonment for serious offences and to reduce the prison population by changes made at the sentencing stage as well as subsequently.

13.4 The effectiveness of early release

Part of the justification for releasing prisoners before the end of a sentence lies in the notion that there is an optimum time for release, and an implied aim is therefore to release them while their rehabilitation is at a peak. A proper test of the efficiency of early release ought to assess the extent to which that aim is achieved. Unfortunately, such an assessment is impossible. It would require us to compare the known against the unknown. Although it is possible to discover whether a particular parolee does or does not re-offend during a certain period, it is impossible to say how he would have behaved if he had been released early, but without supervision. Similarly, we can't say what he would have done if early release had been refused. Up to now there has been no experimental research in Britain, using similar risk prisoners, some of whom are released early and others who are not.

Less ambitious methods have to be adopted, such as asking how many prisoners released early re-offend before the date on which the sentence would ordinarily have ended. Until the current system has run for some time it will be necessary to use data concerned with parole. Much of the available information is dated. In 1988, 27 per cent of parolees recalled to prison during the licence period were recalled because of a further conviction (Home Office, 1989c). A Home Office study suggests that a more accurate level of re-offending during the licence period is 19 per cent (Ditchfield, 1989). Arguably, this is more of a test of the effectiveness of short-term supervision.

Some research has looked at re-offending in the slightly longer term, and has compared the reconviction records of parolees against those of prisoners released without parole. The *Review of Parole in England and Wales* (Home Office, 1981) includes the following table which compares reconviction rates for the two types of ex-prisoner. The follow up period was three years.

Table 4: *Three-year reconviction percentages of adult males discharged from prison sentences in 1973*

Sentence length	19 – 48 months			49 months – 10 years		
	High risk	Medium risk	Low risk	High risk	Medium risk	Low risk
Released on parole	84%	49%	25%	63%	40%	23%
Not on parole	77%	66%	30%	71%	62%	34%
Numbers	170	148	128	101	103	109

(Source: Home Office, 1981: Table 14A.)

In five out of six categories, the parolees had lower reconviction rates. It was only in the high-risk/medium-sentence category that the parolees fared worse. As Walker suggests, the difference in that category might be affected by low clear up rates for the types of offence in which such offenders are likely to be involved (1985:205). In a study by Morris and Beverly, criminal records were checked for a sample of ex-prisoners, including 100 who were on parole and 113 who were not. In the 12 months after release, 12 per cent of the parolees were reconvicted, compared with 25 per cent of the non-parolees (1975:145).

Both sets of figures suggest that conditional release is followed by a lower rate of reconviction than unconditional release. It is not clear whether this is due to the influence of supervision, or the threat of recall to prison. The fact that parole is given to prisoners who represent a better risk might have an effect on the apparent differences in re-offending. Furthermore, in the case of non-parolees it is feasible that the refusal of parole might have increased their commitment to crime.

As the Carlisle Committee pointed out, it can be argued that parole is as much concerned with reducing the number of people in prison as it is with rehabilitating offenders. If we accept the achievement of such a reduction as an objective of parole, then it has been effective. During 1989, the average number of offenders on parole was 6,600 (Home Office, 1991d). Obviously, a vast amount of money was being saved. The Crime (Sentences) Bill which was introduced in the autumn of 1996 may bring major changes as it proposes the abolition of early release and the restriction of parole to life sentence prisoners.

13.5 Alternatives to imprisonment

During the 1960s it became necessary to search for alternatives to imprisonment because prisons were becoming increasingly overcrowded. However, as Harding and Koffman (1988) point out, any measures designed to reduce the use of imprisonment would need to satisfy criteria other than straightforward expediency. For example, the alternatives would need to combine some form of deterrent effect with economy. Hood (1974) suggests that during the same period probation was losing popularity as an alternative because it was viewed in some quarters as a soft option. The same author argues that the subsequent introduction of two alternatives, namely, suspended sentences and community service orders, was not founded on any systematic analysis of crime or the effects of punishment. He also suggests that some would argue there is no coherent body of criminological knowledge on which to base changes in sentencing laws, so that the only way to proceed is by trial and error, followed by evaluation. In *Crime, Justice and Protecting the Public*, the government asserts that because no other penalty can restrict a person's liberty in the same way as a custodial sentence, there are no such things as alternatives to imprisonment, merely other ways of punishing. This viewpoint is now recognised in the CJA 1991.

13.6 The suspended sentence

The fully suspended sentence was first introduced by the Criminal Justice Act 1967, but the relevant powers are now provided by ss22 to 27 of the Powers of Criminal Courts Act 1973. When a court sentences an offender to not more than two years imprisonment, it can order that the sentence will not take effect unless the offender commits a further offence, which is punishable by imprisonment, during a period specified by the court. The period of suspension must be between one and two years. A court cannot impose a suspended sentence unless it is satisfied that a sentence of imprisonment would have been appropriate if the power to suspend such a sentence had not been available.

From 1 October 1992, s5(1) of the CJA 1991 amended s22 of the Powers of Criminal Courts Act 1973 by adding a requirement that the court must also be of the opinion that the passing of a suspended sentence can be justified by the exceptional circumstances of the case. The Act does not provide any guidance about what might constitute such exceptional circumstances. In *R* v *Okininan* [1993] Crim LR 146, the Lord Chief Justice pointed out that the meaning of 'exceptional circumstances' will depend on the facts of each case. A further amendment requires the court to consider whether the circumstances are such as to warrant the imposition of a fine or the making of a compensation order in addition to passing a suspended sentence. This requirement was added so that neither offenders nor the public would view the passing of a suspended sentence as being 'let off' (Home Office, 1990: para 3.22).

A suspended sentence is not automatically activated if the offender is convicted of another imprisonable offence. The court by which he is convicted must order that the suspended sentence will take effect, with the original term unaltered, unless it is of the opinion that it would be unjust to do so. If the court is of that opinion, it has three further options. It may bring the sentence into effect but reduce the term of imprisonment. It can vary the original order so that the period of suspension begins again, with a maximum limit of two years from the date of the variation. Alternatively, the court can make no order at all in relation to the suspended sentence. When a court activates a suspended sentence, it can make that sentence concurrent with, or consecutive to, any sentence of imprisonment which it imposes for the new offence.

The suspended sentence has tended to be well used by courts. The Carlisle Committee point out that the proportion of offenders receiving fully suspended sentences remained fairly constant between 1973 and 1987 at about 11 per cent. Over the same period the proportion sentenced to immediate imprisonment varied between 12.5 per cent and 18 per cent (para 484). In 1992, 22,000 fully suspended sentences were imposed compared with 42,300 sentences involving immediate custody (Home Office, 1993: Table 7.1). One possible effect of s5(1) of the CJA 1991 was that courts would be discouraged from imposing suspended sentences. The figures for 1995 suggest that this has not happened with 32,000 suspended sentences and over 60,000 sentences involving immediate custody (Home Office 1996a p144).

Notwithstanding the frequent use of suspended sentences, a number of criticisms can be levelled at this particular penalty. By looking at the background to its introduction, it becomes obvious that the purpose of the suspended sentence is not clear.

Bottoms (1981), in a review of the operation of suspended sentences, describes the views of advocates of the suspended sentence during the 20 years or so before it was introduced. Its supporters put forward two main arguments. One was that, compared with non-custodial orders, such as probation, the suspended sentence was a more effective deterrent for individual offenders. This was said to be so because an offender knew in advance what the consequences of re-offending would be. The other argument was that a suspended sentence could mark the gravity of an offence, but avoid actually sending an offender to prison. Whereas the first argument sees a suspended sentence as an alternative to non-custodial measures, the second clearly views it as an alternative to imprisonment. Bottoms claims the two arguments can stand side by side, as they can apply to different types of offender.

When the suspended sentence was first introduced, the legislation did not require courts to be satisfied that imprisonment was an appropriate punishment before imposing a suspended sentence. For a short time, sentencers were unsure about what was expected and it became necessary for the Court of Appeal to offer guidance. In *R v O'Keefe* [1969] 1 All ER 426, Lord Parker, CJ, was of the opinion that suspended sentences were often used by lower courts as 'a soft option, when the court is not quite certain what to do' (at 427). It was also observed that there were cases where such a sentence had been imposed when a probation order was appropriate. The Court of Appeal outlined the proper procedure. Before a court could impose a suspended sentence it had first to eliminate other possible (non-custodial) orders, then to say to itself that this was a case for imprisonment, before finally asking whether immediate imprisonment was necessary or if a suspended sentence could be given. A change of policy in relation to young offenders suggests that courts have continued to use suspended sentences when non-custodial sentences were probably more appropriate. Since May 1983, it has not been possible to give a suspended sentence to offenders under 21. In 1982, 6 per cent of offenders aged 17 to 20 were given suspended sentences, and 16.9 per cent were given immediate custody. In 1984, although there were obviously no suspended sentences, the proportion sentenced to immediate custody had only increased to 18.5 per cent. Thus the major shift had been towards non-custodial measures (Home Office, 1988a: para 487).

The requirement on a court to be satisfied that imprisonment is the appropriate sentence, before considering a suspended sentence, is now confirmed in s22(2) of the Powers of Criminal Courts Act 1973. It has been suggested that courts did not always follow the Court of Appeal's guidance and that suspended sentences continued to be imposed on offenders who would not ordinarily have been imprisoned (Sparks, 1971; Oatham and Simon, 1972).

A second criticism of suspended sentences is that rather than reducing the prison population, they may actually have increased it (Bottoms, 1981). It should be no surprise that some people receiving suspended sentences end up in prison anyway, because they re-offend. In 1995, 7,000 offenders breached a suspended sentence – this figure represented 22 per cent of the offenders receiving such a sentence; 5,000 of them were imprisoned because of the breach (Home Office, 1996: Table 7.25).

In so far as the suspended sentence seems to rest partly on the notion of giving offenders a last chance to avoid imprisonment, it is quite logical to assume that such sentences should rarely be given to offenders who have previously served time in prison. If recidivists in this category have not been deterred by actual imprisonment, it is hard to see why a suspended sentence should discourage them from further offending. Furthermore, as prison did not have any reformative or deterrent effect for them, perhaps some form of explicitly non-custodial sentence would be more appropriate anyway. Soothill (1972) followed a group of 392 men released after serving sentences of less than 12 months; 206 of the men were reconvicted during the first year after release, and 70 of these (34 per cent) were given suspended sentences. In a later article, Soothill (1981) postulates that in imposing suspended sentences on ex-prisoners who re-offend soon after their release, courts are more concerned with doing something to manage the 'stage-army of deviants' who appear before them than with analysing the logic of the procedure involved. Using a suspended sentence allows them to avoid adding to the prison population (at least in the short term) while still appearing to deal with crime in a serious manner. Soothill suggests that a suspended sentence might be appropriate for the ex-prisoner who has been out of prison for some time before re-offending. The granting of a 'second chance' in this manner might also be appropriate in the case of the recently released recidivist whose circumstances have genuinely changed since his latest offence, so that he now has a better chance of avoiding crime. Well-worn courtroom incantations such as 'My client informs me that he begins new employment next week' are no doubt sometimes based on fact. In cases such as these, the prospects of going straight might be enhanced by a sentence involving supervision.

Two of the major bodies interested in penal reform have varying views on the value of the suspended sentence. In their submission to the Carlisle Committee, the Howard League said that fully suspended sentences continued to have a useful role, whereas the Prison Reform Trust described suspension of sentences as an experiment which had failed (para 489). The Carlisle Committee declined to make any recommendation about fully suspended sentences. Partly suspended sentences were abolished by the CJA 1991.

13.7 Community orders

By reserving custodial sentences for the most serious offences, the CJA 1991 makes it clear that different types of sentence can no longer be viewed as alternatives to imprisonment. The Act describes six types of community order as follows: curfew order; attendance centre order; probation order; supervision order; community service order; and combination order. The community service order will be dealt with in more depth below. For the first time, a probation order is a sentence of the court, rather than an order made instead of imposing a sentence. It is worth noting that the curfew order and the combination order are new. A combination order can be imposed on an offender aged 16 or over who is convicted of an imprisonable offence and involves combining a probation order with a community service order. The Act describes a community sentence as being a sentence which includes one or more community orders.

13.8 Restrictions on the use of community sentences

Section 6(1) of the CJA 1991 provides that a court shall not pass a community sentence on an offender unless it is of the opinion that the offence, or that offence in combination with another associated with it, was serious enough to warrant such a sentence. If the court does not form that opinion, it can only bind the offender over or impose an absolute or conditional discharge or a financial penalty.

Section 6(2) states that when a court passes a community sentence the order or orders shall be such as to be, in the opinion of the court, the most suitable for the offender. Furthermore, any restrictions on liberty created by the order or orders must be commensurate with the seriousness of the offence or that offence and others associated with it.

13.9 The community service order

A court can impose a community service order (CSO) on an offender aged 16 or older, who has been convicted of an offence for which an adult could be sentenced to imprisonment. Such an order requires the offender to perform unpaid work for the community. The minimum amount of work which can be imposed is 40 hours and the maximum 240 hours. The order must be completed within 12 months.

A CSO can only be made after the court has considered a social enquiry report on the offender. The offender must consent to the order being made. If he does not consent, a different sentence will be imposed, but the offender is not informed of the nature of the alternative before he makes his decision.

The order is carried out under the direction of a supervisor provided by the Probation Service or a local voluntary or public body. Types of work vary, and can include such tasks as clearing waste ground, decorating community buildings and helping elderly or disabled people.

In April 1989, the government introduced national standards which outlined the types of work to be performed, the way in which hours worked are to calculated, and the action to be taken when an offender fails to meet the requirements of the order. The standards require that an offender must be taken back to court if he fails to turn up for work on two occasions without good reason (Home Office, 1990a).

The legislation governing CSOs is set out in ss14–17 of the Powers of Criminal Courts Act 1973, as amended by s10 CJA 1991. The introduction of this sentence was recommended in 1970 by the Advisory Council on the Penal System, usually referred to as the Wootton Committee. In 1973, CSOs were piloted in six areas and in 1975 they were introduced on a national basis.

Harding and Koffman (1995) suggest that there is considerable doubt about the underlying philosophy of the CSO. This is not surprising, as the Wootton Committee itself suggested that this sentence could appeal to supporters of different penal philosophies. To some it would be a cheaper, constructive alternative to a short prison sentence. Others would recognise its emphasis on making reparation to the community. Some would welcome the potential for bringing offenders into contact with needy members of the community, while others still would consider that a community service order could broaden opportunities for making the punishment fit the crime. For the Committee the greatest attraction of the CSO was the potential for changing an offender's outlook through personal service to the community (Home Office, 1970: paras 33–34).

Young (1979) points out that although the Wootton Committee asserted that the CSO could achieve punishment, reparation and reintegration, it made no attempt to analyse the capacity of a single sentence to serve such a variety of penal objectives.

Hood (1974) also questions the claims made by the Wootton Committee. In particular, Hood argues that the Committee failed to tie its proposals to any analysis of criminological knowledge. Contemporary sociological theory did not support the notion that an offender would be positively influenced through wholesome contact with the volunteer workers, whom he might work alongside on community projects. Nor was it clear why an offender who was himself deprived should be helped by contact with other members of the community who needed help and support.

Hood raises the possibility that the central problem which the Committee had to solve was to suggest a new sentence which could reduce prison overcrowding but still be acceptable to the courts. He suggests that before it went on to propose a new type of sentence, the Committee should have evaluated the use of existing non-custodial sentences such as probation, and considered the possibility of making improvements to them.

Willis (1977) highlights points in the Wootton Committee's report where the CSO is identified as an alternative to short prison sentences, and others where it is offered as an alternative to established non-custodial measures. Like Harding and Koffman, Willis submits that the Wootton Committee's failure to clarify the place of this order within the then existing framework of sentencing has contributed to subsequent confusion about its use.

Calculating the number of hours of work to be performed under a CSO on a tariff basis would enable a court to inform the offender, the police, and any later court (in the case of a breach) of how seriously it views a particular crime. On the other hand, the use of a tariff would seem to emphasise the punitive aspects of a CSO, rather than its capacity for rehabilitation. CSOs are said to be punitive in so far as they deprive people of their liberty during their leisure time. Harding and Koffman even liken the CSO to a 'fine' on time (1988:219).

Notwithstanding the enduring ambiguity about its proper role, the CSO continues to be widely used by sentencers. During 1995, 48,300 CSOs were imposed. This sentence was used for 10 per cent of offenders sentenced for indictable offences. The proportion of orders breached during 1995 was 26 per cent (Home Office, 1995: p185). The CSO is also a comparatively cheap sentence. Using figures produced in 1990, a CSO of 100 hours which was successfully completed cost less than £450, compared with £1,000 a year to supervise someone on probation, or £304 a week to keep an offender in custody (Home Office, 1990: para 9.2). According to Harding and Koffman, even critics regard the CSO as a 'worthwhile development built on shaky philosophical foundations' (1995: 220). Wright describes it as 'one of the most constructive innovations ever made in penal theory and practice' (1982:98).

13.10 Breach of community sentences

Schedule 2 to the CJA 1991 provides that when an offender has failed to comply with the requirements of a probation order, community service order, curfew order or combination order, a court can fine the offender or make a community service order of not more than 60 hours or revoke the existing order and pass any sentence which it could have imposed for the original offence. This would include passing a custodial sentence, in which case the court is entitled to assume that an offender who has wilfully and persistently failed to comply with the requirements of the earlier sentence, has refused to give his consent to a community sentence which has been proposed by the court.

The commission of a further offence during the period of a community sentence is not in itself a breach of the order, but the court dealing with the new offence can revoke the order and substitute a new penalty which takes account of the new offence and of the outstanding portion of the existing order.

If a young offender has failed to comply with the requirements of an attendance centre order, a court may fine him and allow the order to continue. Alternatively, the court can revoke the order and impose any penalty open to it at the time of sentencing for the original offence. The court must take into account the extent to which the offender has complied with the requirements of the order.

A breach of the requirements of a supervision order can be dealt with by way of a fine or by the imposition of an attendance centre order.

13.11 Reparation

This part of the book has considered different functions of sentencing offenders, including retribution, deterrence and rehabilitation. Almost exclusively, the sentences discussed are intended to serve the aims of society or to affect the offender. The victim is frequently ignored. Indeed, it is a feature of a developed criminal justice process that once proceedings are commenced, the needs of the system are paramount and the victim is relegated to a minor role. Arthur *et al* (1979) have suggested that justice would be better served if we concentrated on meeting the needs of victims, society and the offender instead of the meting out of punishment. Their particular claims were made from an idealistic perspective which is probably too ambitious to be realised in the foreseeable future. However, different methods already exist to achieve reparation.

What is reparation? In proposing an alternative approach to dealing with crime, Wright discusses the process of 'making amends' (1982: Chapter 10). He uses that term to cover different methods by which an offender can make up for his transgression. Wright defines reparation narrowly, to cover occasions when an offender contributes money or services to the community or the state. I prefer a broader definition in which reparation means 'making amends' and includes any process by which an offender compensates a victim or recognises the consequences of his action and attempts to make up for what he has done. Although the victim can never be put back into the position he was in before an offence, it must surely be to his benefit both to receive compensation and to feel his needs are recognised. Offenders are not allowed to escape scot free, but some may recognise that making reparation is not intended as a punitive exercise. A few may even reflect on the experience and benefit from atoning for their wrongdoing.

Within this broader definition, reparation may take one of four forms: individual reparation, reparation to the community, restitution and compensation.

Individual reparation

Instead of, or as well as, paying monetary compensation, the offender performs some service for his victim, perhaps by repairing damage he has caused. This will often be coupled with a personal meeting and an apology. During the mid 1980s, four experimental schemes of this type were funded by the Home Office (Marshall and Walpole, 1985). It appeared that victims felt they were under pressure to co-operate. Also, there was confusion over who was meant to benefit – the victim or the offender (why not both?). The government does not intend to introduce reparation as an order available to the courts. It takes the view that reparation might be arranged informally, and in addition to any sentence imposed on the offender (Home Office, 1990: para 4.26).

Reparation to the community

Although the Community Service Order is at least partly punitive, it can also be regarded as a way of enabling an offender to make amends to the community. Such an interpretation is especially valid in relation to offences where there are no individual victims.

Restitution

When property is recovered from a convicted thief or handler, the court can order that he return it to the victim (s28 of the Powers of Criminal Courts Act 1973).

Compensation

Given the common sense recognition that once an offence has been committed it is impossible to fully restore the *status quo ante*, a realistic alternative (in cases where restitution is not possible) is to order the offender to pay compensation to the victim.

Courts were given the power to make a compensation order by the Criminal Justice Act 1972, and the relevant provisions are now contained in ss35–38 of the Powers of Criminal Courts Act 1973, as amended. Originally, a court could only make a compensation order in addition to imposing some other penalty. However, an amendment was added by s67 of the Criminal Justice Act 1982, so that a court can make an order for compensation instead of or in addition to another penalty. A further amendment was made by s104 of the Criminal Justice Act 1988, so that a court which has the power to make a compensation order must record its reasons if it chooses not to do so.

In *R* v *Inwood* (1974) 60 Cr App R 70, Lord Scarman pointed out that a compensation order ought not to be made where there was real doubt about the ability of the offender to pay. Futhermore, when such an order is made alongside the imposition of a prison sentence, the long-term effect might be to force the offender back into crime after his release.

In *R* v *Maynard* [1983] Crim LR 821, the Court of Appeal made it clear that the amount of compensation should correspond with the loss to the victim, and not be inflated in order to provide extra punishment by depriving the offender of any profit made. If such action was considered necessary, the use of a fine would be appropriate.

Harding and Koffman argue that because a court can now make a compensation order without imposing any other sentence, the law is confusing compensation with punishment by suggesting that compensation is the 'penalty' for an offence (1995:344). Technically speaking, they are correct, but from another point of view the law is simply recognising that in some cases the notion of a penalty is not appropriate. Instead, the needs of both offender and victim are better met by an award of compensation. Section 35(4A) of the Powers of Criminal Courts Act 1973 requires a court to give precedence to compensation in a case where it considers both a fine and compensation to be appropriate but the offender does not have sufficient means to pay both in full. This allows the proposed fine to be reduced so that the offender can afford to pay compensation to the victim.

During 1995, compensation orders were made against 95,000 offenders. In the magistrates' courts, in 6.6 per cent of those cases, a compensation order was the sole or main penalty. The average amount was £168 in magistrates' courts and £1,663 in the Crown Court (Home Office, 1996a: p181).

14

Police Organisation, the Decision to Prosecute, and Cautioning of Offenders

14.1 The organisation of police forces in England and Wales

1996 saw the arrival of a new Police Act 1996 most of which came into force in August of that year. It consolidates (principally) the Police Act 1964, Parts I and IX Police and Criminal Evidence Act 1984 and Chapter 1 Police and Magistrates' Courts Act 1994. It deals with matters such as the organisation of police forces, Chief Constables, Police Authorities, the role of the Secretary of State, Police Representative Institutions, Police Complaints Authority, and disciplinary and other proceedings. Further legislation is planned, including proposals for the establishment of a National Crime Squad for England and Wales. The Home Secretary, Mr Howard, made it clear that this would not be a British version of the FBI. It also proposes to put the National Criminal Intelligence Service (NCIS) on a UK-wide statutory footing; to put the authorisation of intrusive surveillance operations by the police and customs on a statutory basis; to enable a Criminal Records Agency to supply information on criminal records to individuals and to registered bodies; and to put the Police Information Technology Organisation (PITO) on an independent statutory footing. The National Crime Squad, NCIS and the authorisation of intrusive surveillance operations are part of a package of measures to assist the police and other law enforcement agencies in tackling serious and organised crime. Two independent statutory bodies similar in nature to police authorities would be created to maintain the National Crime Squad and NCIS.

There are currently 43 police forces in England and Wales and in March 1995 there were 127,222 police officers. (Home Office, 1995g: p92). Until 31 March 1995 each force had an authorised establishment, that is, a maximum number of officers which it was allowed to employ. Establishments varied from 798 in the City of London to 28,240 in the Metropolitan Police District. In most forces there was generally a small gap between the numbers of officers actually in post (force 'strength') and its establishment. The size of this shortfall fell from 27 per cent of the overall establishment in 1966 to less than 1 per cent in 1992. Strength rose by 22 per cent between 1974 and 1990. This was largely the result of existing posts being filled, rather than establishments being increased. Increased interest in joining, or remaining in, the police service may partly be due to a substantial pay increase in 1978 (followed by annual index linked rises until 1992) and to the general high level of unemployment. Another change worthy of note is that the proportion of officers who are female changed from 4.4 per cent in 1974 to 13.9 per cent in 1995 (Home Office 1995 p93). From 1 April 1995 each force has a cash limited budget, and the chief officer has discretion as to the number of officers who will be employed.

Obviously, the overall strength of any force is comprised of officers at a variety of ranks. In a provincial force, the 'batting order' runs as follows: Chief Constable, Assistant Chief Constable, Superintendent, Chief Inspector, Inspector, Sergeant, Constable. The two London forces are each headed by a Commissioner and the ranks between them and Superintendent differ from those of their provincial counterparts.

In order to make proper management of resources feasible, each force obviously has to be broken up into a number of parts. Following the amalgamations which created the existing forces in 1974, the usual practice was to divide the force into territorial divisions, each with a Chief Superintendent at its head (the rank of Chief Superintendent ceased to exist on 31 March 1995). A division was further divided into sub-divisions, managed by a Superintendent or Chief Inspector. In recent years there had been a trend towards developing 'jumbo' divisions which might have four or more sub-divisions. The idea behind this was to provide Sub-Divisional Commanders with a greater responsibility for the operational management of their areas, and to free Divisional Commanders to consider policy issues. This development has now been overtaken. In a series of papers examining different aspects of policing, the Audit Commission has caused police forces to examine their structures and methods and to consider seriously the implementation of change in order to maximise efficiency and effectiveness. Paper number 9 is entitled *Reviewing the Organisation of Provincial Police Forces* (Audit Commission 1991). It questions the validity of the divisional tier of management, and suggests that removal of this intermediate tier between a force's headquarters and operational units will produce several benefits. Examples include a reduction in management on-costs, releasing more officers from administrative functions and a shortening of lines of command.

The Audit Commission recommends that operational policing should be carried out by territorial sub-units known as 'basic command units'. These units should have enough resources to be self-sufficient in all normal circumstances. Their managers would be more directly responsible and accountable for the day-to-day policing of an area and for providing quality of service. These recommendations have the support of Her Majesty's Chief Inspector of Constabulary and across the country more and more forces are being re-structured on the basis of two tiers of management, that is, the force headquarters and basic command units.

Routine operational duties are still generally carried out by shifts of officers who are responsible for policing within a command unit area during their tour of duty. A shift is usually made up of an Inspector, two or three sergeants, and a number of constables. Numbers vary according to the size and workload of an operational unit. In smaller urban areas and rural sections, it is unlikely that there will always be an Inspector, or even a sergeant, providing constant supervision. Even in large urban areas, some forces have pioneered a style of policing in which teams of officers are made responsible for policing defined geographical areas. Giving officers longer term responsibility for a piece of territory, rather than making them accountable only for the way they police a larger area for a given span of time each working day, is considered to encourage ownership of policing problems on the appropriate patch and to be more conducive to the development of community policing. Command units will also have officers on specialist duties such as criminal investigation, crime prevention and juvenile liaison. Certain specialist functions such as drug squads, management research sections and serious crime teams will usually be controlled from force headquarters.

At present the responsibility for policy matters and for the proper management of a force lies with the Chief Constable or Commissioner. Each chief officer has a considerable degree of autonomy as to the way in which he discharges his functions. However, this autonomy is subject to a number of limitations. Police accountability is a subject which has aroused controversy for many years, and will be explored in the section which follows.

14.2 Police accountability

With effect from 1 April 1995, the Police and Magistrates' Courts Act 1994 made significant changes to the arrangements by which the police are made accountable. Still further changes may come as the Home Secretary announced in July 1996 that new disciplinary proceedings would be introduced in 1997. The standard of proof is to be changed and in exceptional circumstances such proceedings could take place before criminal proceedings. However, this section will include discussion of the superseded legislation and procedures because of their influence on the topic of police accountability. This subject has often given rise to controversy. This is not surprising, for there is no common agreement on what accountability is. In most dictionaries 'accountable' means 'answerable'. Chief Constables have such a definition in mind when they make claims like this one by Barry Pain, then Chief Constable of Kent:

> 'We are already not only accountable to our authorities, but also to the Home Secretary for the efficient running of our forces ... and, more importantly, we are accountable to the courts' (*Sunday Times Supplement*, 26 September 1982:48).

Some supporters of greater police accountability argue for a more liberal interpretation. For example, two unsuccessful Private Member's Bills introduced by Labour MP Jack Straw, and aimed at increasing police accountability, would have reduced the independence of Chief Constables by allowing Police Authorities to decide on matters of policing policy (Savage, 1984). There is an obvious distinction between the police having to answer for what they do, and their being subject to control.

As there is no general agreement about what accountability is, it is not surprising that the parties cannot agree about how accountable the police actually are, or about how accountable they should be. The law in this area is vague, and partly to blame for the confusion. The legislators chose to compromise, when often the main actors will not.

It will be argued that many of the difficulties concerning police accountability stem from the way in which the major participants interpret the arrangements for the organisation and control of policing, and from the quality of the contributions they make.

Before moving on to discuss the various sources of police accountability and their effectiveness, it is proposed to stress why external accountability is essential. To say that the police possess enormous power is not being melodramatic. The actions of individual officers affect people's lives. Their collective behaviour, and the policies implemented by chief officers can, ultimately, influence the quality of life of whole communities.

In exercising their powers, the police are allowed considerable discretion. This 'lies at the heart of the policing function' (Scarman 1981:4.58). The authority to exercise discretion exists at all levels. Leaving aside external restraints, internal restrictions generally require each officer below the rank of Chief Constable to consider policy from above when he makes decisions. A logical conclusion would be that the constable is more constrained than any other rank. The reality is different.

A police constable's power to act derives not from delegated authority but from 'an original authority' (*Fisher v Oldham Corporation* [1930] KB 364). This confers not only an entitlement to use his legal powers, but also discretion as to how to use them, within the law. Furthermore, the nature of police duties obliges the patrol officer to exercise discretion. Most of his decisions must be made without the benefit of supervision, often instantaneously, and sometimes on matters of life and death (Bittner, 1970). His role often precludes him from policing 'by the book' (Waudhuber, 1979). Manning outlines the paradox in this way:

> 'The complex command structure and hierarchy ... tend to mystify the basic fact that the control of police work lies in the hands of the lowest functionaries' (1979:65).

The purpose of highlighting the broad distribution of power within the police structure is to show that any discussion of police accountability is incomplete if it touches only on those sources of accountability which affect chief officers.

As well as noting the extent of police power, it is essential to recognise its nature. When they decide whether or not to enforce laws, the police are legislating, an activity which is essentially political. According to Hahn:

> '... the practices of police officers ... seem to reflect an even more fundamental form of political action ... at the base of the broader legislative and judicial process that is responsible for defining the standards of acceptable social conduct' (1971:14).

Simey suggests that 'it is accountability alone which justifies the exercise of power in a democracy' (1985:3), and the discussion so far indicates that the nature and scope of police power demands that they be accountable. The relevant responsibilities of Chief Constables, Police Authorities and the Home Secretary were set out in the Police Act 1964, as amended by the Police and Magistrates' Courts Act 1994 and consolidated by the Police Act 1996. The report of the Royal Commission on the Police, which preceded the 1964 Act in its original form, referred to the need to:

> '... put an end to the anomaly that a Police Authority appears to have responsibilities for efficient policing of its area, yet has no technical competence in the matter' (Home Office, 1962a:158).

The Act did not have that effect. Its ambiguous drafting left the relationship between Chief Constables and Police Authorities unclear. The Act was itself a source of much of the confusion.

The Police Act 1964 did not give the Police Authority any power to instruct the Chief Constable on policing policy for the area. The recent amendments do not change this in any direct way. Indeed, s10(1) of the 1996 Act provides that a police force 'shall be under the direction and control of the Chief Constable'. Under s6 the Police Authority shall secure:

> '... the maintenance of an efficient and effective police force for its area.'

The Authority's powers include the appointment of the Chief Constable, and the right to require him to retire on the grounds that he is inefficient. In each case the approval of the Home Secretary is required.

The Authority also determines the budget of the force, and the scale of provision and maintenance of buildings, vehicles and equipment.

The relationship between the Authority, the Chief Constable and the Home Secretary has been radically altered by new powers and obligations introduced by the Police and Magistrates' Courts Act 1994. Before the beginning of each financial year, each Police Authority is required to determine objectives for the policing of its area. These have to be consistent with key objectives established by the Home Secretary, but may also relate to other matters (the Home Secretary's power to set key objectives is discussed later in this section). Before determining its objectives, the Authority has to consult the Chief Constable and must consider any views obtained through consultative groups established under s106 of the Police and Criminal Evidence Act 1984.

In carrying out its functions, the Authority is required to have regard to: the key objectives; its own local objectives; the performance targets which it has established; and its local policing plan.

Each Police Authority is required to publish a plan setting out the proposed arrangements for the policing of its area during the next financial year. This must state the Authority's priorities for the year, describe the proposed allocation of financial resources, and include the key and local objectives, together with any performance targets which the Authority has set.

The Authority will issue the local policing plan after considering a draft which the Chief Constable is required to submit to it. the Authority must consult the Chief Constable before issuing a plan which differs from the draft.

Home Office Circular 27/1994 describes the main purposes of the local policing plan as being:

1. To act as an agreement between the Chief Constable and the Authority about policing priorities during the year.
2. To inform the public of the policing services and standards they can expect.
3. To aid performance monitoring by the Chief Constable, the Authority, Her Majesty's Inspectorate and the Home Office.

There is no statutory requirement for the Chief Constable and the Police Authority to reach agreement about the contents of the plan, but the expectation in the circular that they will do so is reinforced in guidance produced by the Audit Commission under the title *Cheques and Balances: a Management Handbook on Police Planning and Financial Delegation*. This proposes that the two parties should develop protocols for resolving differences of opinion.

The Chief Constable's autonomy will clearly be constrained by the requirement to have regard to the Authority's local policing plan. Although the circular makes it clear that a Chief Constable may deviate from the plan if his operational judgment guides him to do so, he would be expected to explain the reason for his departure to the Police Authority.

If the Police Authority is to discharge its functions under the 1996 Act, it must have sufficient information. The Chief Constable is required to submit an Annual Report to the Authority (s22). The style of presentation varies, but in most cases the content is basic and well edited, and provides insufficient detail for outsiders to challenge policing practices. Home Office guidance suggests that the report should include details of performance against key indicators, but leaves Chief Constables with discretion in respect or other information to be included.

Section 22 also empowers the Authority to call on the Chief Constable to provide *ad hoc* reports on matters connected with the area's policing. However, if the Chief Constable believes the report would contain information which, in the public interest, ought not to be disclosed, or which is not needed by the Authority for the discharge of its functions, he can refuse, and ask the authority to refer its request to the Home Secretary, who has the final say. In a sense, the proviso in s22 grants the chief officer a power of censorship over what the Authority (arguably) needs to know to perform its functions. As Marshall comments:

> '... it is a little odd that committees are entitled to ask questions on any matter relating to the policing of an area ... but that some matters are implicitly held not to be the business of the Police Committee' (1973:53).

To put this oddity into perspective, there will surely be occasions when the withholding of information is justified. A familiar example is that of Captain Popkess, then Chief Constable of Nottingham City Police. He refused to supply his Watch Committee with a report on an investigation into alleged corruption by City Councillors, and they suspended him. His reinstatement was ordered by the Home Secretary. The potential jeopardy to the investigation, had the information been released, is obvious. (Marshall, 1965, 10–14).

Given the importance of adequate data as a basis for fulfilling their functions, it is surprising that when it comes to seeking information, many Police Authorities show 'a tentativeness which in some cases amounts almost to passivity' (Regan, 1983:6).

One area in which the Chief Constable was fully accountable to the Police Authority, even before. the 1964 Act was amended by the 1994 Act, was that of finance. The local authority provides 49 per cent of a force's budget, with the remainder coming from the Treasury. All expenditure is liable to scrutiny by the District Auditor. The Chief Constable must be able to satisfy the Authority that all spending is essential. In addition, each Police Authority sets a standing limit, expenditure above which requires prior authorisation from the Authority. Thus, before embarking on some projects, a Chief Constable is obliged to seek the approval of his Police Authority.

Control over a force's purse strings is vital to enable a Police Authority to fulfil its duty of maintaining an efficient and effective force. However, the power granted can be manipulated to influence operational policy. According to Simey:

> 'It is by the exercise of authority over expenditure that political control can properly be exerted ... the heart of the matter lies here and not in meddling in the direct operation of services' (1985:31).

In the past, by blocking funds, some authorities have forced the withdrawal of officers from regional crime squads, frozen recruitment, and vetoed the purchasing of riot equipment (*The Times*, 3 September 1984 and 14 December 1984).

However, there are signs that the courts are prepared to restrict such financial manipulation. In 1984, during the Miners' Strike, the South Yorkshire Police Authority resolved not to finance the policing of picket lines. The Attorney-General immediately sought an interlocutory injunction, and in the High Court Lord Justice Watkins said:

> 'I want to make sure that the Chief Constable is free to take whatever steps he believes are necessary to maintain law and order' (*The Times*, 14 December 1984).

The authority withdrew its resolution.

Although Police Authorities' powers to issue a policing plan and to exert financial leverage do provide them with a certain amount of influence, this does not alter the legal reality of direction and control lying in the hands of Chief Constables. An assertion by Clayton and Tomlinson (1984) that the constitutional autonomy of chief officers has no legal basis, and that there is nothing in law to prevent Police Authorities from giving operational orders to Chief Constables appears to be at odds with reality, and has not yet been borne out in practice.

It has already been said that immense power is available to the police. Just as there is a need to prevent misuse resulting from internal bias or abuse, it is essential to exclude improper interference from outside.

Until March 1995 Police Authorities were comprised of two-thirds elected representatives, and one-third Justices of the Peace. The presence of magistrates did not alter the fact that the controlling political party was frequently able to ensure decisions were in line with party policy. The possible dangers if operational control of the police was vested in a body dominated by one political party are plain. There are numerous examples from both sides of the Atlantic of politically motivated abuses of police operations (Lea and Young, 1984:234–7; Jefferson and Grimshaw, 1984:36–45). Miller (1977) suggests that external political control which conflicts with internal ideologies creates a backlash effect, leading to greater politicisation of the police.

From 1 April 1995 each Police Authority is a body corporate. Generally it will have 17 members, of whom nine will be local councillors and three will be magistrates. Using a shortlist prepared by the Home Secretary, five independent members are selected by a local panel including council members. The Chairman is appointed by the Authority. In earlier drafts of the Bill, it had been proposed that the Chairman be selected by the Home Secretary. It could be suggested that the reduction in party political influence is healthy. However, it is also arguable that the addition of independent members to Police Authorities could weaken democratic accountability by reducing the part played by locally elected representatives.

Having examined the uncertain relationship between Chief Constables and Police Authorities, what does the Police Act 1996 have to say about the role of the Home Secretary? Section 36 requires him to:

'... exercise his powers in such a manner and to such an extent as appears to him best calculated to promote the efficiency and effectiveness of the police.'

The Home Secretary has a power under s37 of the Police Act 1996, to determine objectives for the policing of all force areas. These are referred to as 'key objectives'. Consultation is to take place with representatives of Police Authorities and of Chief Constables before the order determining the key objectives is made. The Home Secretary will also be able to direct Police Authorities to establish performance targets for each of these objectives and will have the power to impose conditions with which those targets are to conform.

Key objectives will be contained in a statutory instrument and are likely to be published in the October preceding the financial year during which they will apply. The key objectives for 1995/96 were:

1. To maintain and if possible increase the number of detections for violent crimes.
2. To increase the number of detections for burglaries of people's homes.
3. To target and prevent crimes which are a particular local problem, including drug-related criminality, in partnership with the public and local agencies.
4. To provide high visibility policing so as to reassure the public.
5. To respond promptly to emergency calls from the public.

The Home Secretary has been given further new powers which will enable him to influence the performance of Police Authorities. These include the power to issue codes of practice concerning the discharge of Police Authorities' functions and the ability to direct an authority to adopt specific remedial measures if Her Majesty's Inspectorate submits an adverse report about a force's efficiency or effectiveness.

The 1996 Act provides other powers which enable the Home Secretary to oversee the activities of chief officers and of Police Authorities. He collects information through the Inspectors of Constabulary (s54), he receives the Police Authority's Annual Report, and he can call for additional reports (s43). Section 49 enables the Home Secretary to order the holding of an inquiry into matters concerning the policing of an area. Lord Scarman's inquiry into the Brixton disorders of 1981 is a prominent example (Cmnd. 8427/1981) of such an inquiry.

The Home Secretary can call on the Police Authority to require the Chief Constable to retire on the grounds that he is inefficient (s42). If the Police Authority is not discharging its duty, s41 empowers the Home Secretary to withhold the exchequer grant of 51 per cent of the police budget. As with the Police Authority, the powers conferred by the Act on the Home Secretary are designed to promote police efficiency, and not to grant operational control.

The Home Secretary issues advice to chief officers, often by Home Office Circular. Examples of such circulars are 114/83 (effectiveness and efficiency in the police service); 105/88 (civilianisation); and 27/94 (production of policing plans). Matters such as these are of operational significance, and as chief officers comply with them, their autonomy is obviously restricted. Morgan has described the way in which the current government makes chief officers accountable through the use of such devices as 'transparent stewardship' (1985:7). In contrast with more direct forms of control, this type of stewardship allows the government to continue to support the operational independence of the police. From time to time there are allegations that a Home Secretary has given operational instructions to Chief Constables, particularly during major industrial disputes. These have not been proved, and former Labour Party leader Neil Kinnock even described the then Home Secretary, Douglas Hurd, as 'doing his best to move away from politicising the police' (*Police Review*, 25 April 1986:889).

Mention was made earlier of central service. The majority of officers seconded to central service appointments are engaged in training other police officers. In England

and Wales, recruits to the service receive 15 weeks of their 31 weeks of foundation training at one of six regional training centres. Each centre serves a number of forces. The foundation course is carried out in a 'sandwich' style with the operational modules being conducted in the officer's own force. Sergeants and Inspectors undergo courses at a number of regional training centres. The curricula for each of these courses are set by the Home Office Central Planning and Training Unit, which is also staffed by officers on central service. The same establishment trains the trainers who work at the regional centres. The Metropolitan Police force has separate but similar arrangements. Training for officers of the rank of Chief Inspector and above is provided at the Police Staff College. Changes in training policy have to be agreed by the Police Training Council whose members include representatives from the Home Office, local authorities and the police staff associations. Although different bodies have their say, ultimately there is one voice, and therefore a considerable amount of uniformity is introduced via the training process. This also impinges on the autonomy of chief officers.

The law is claimed to be the most important source of police accountability (Scarman, 1981:4.60). Close examination shows that even this area of accountability is qualified. The courts recognise the need for Chief Constables to exercise discretion in choosing between conflicting priorities. They have said that this discretion is not absolute (*R* v *Commissioner of the Metropolis, ex parte Blackburn* [1968] 2 QB 118), but it appears the courts will not interfere if they consider the Chief Constable to be performing his duty in enforcing the law. They might act if they consider he is not discharging his duty (*R* v *Commissioner of Police of the Metropolis, ex parte Blackburn (No 3)* [1973] 2 QB 241). However, it is clear that the courts would not issue directions to a Chief Constable save in very exceptional circumstances (*R* v *Chief Constable of Devon and Cornwall, ex parte Central Electricity Generating Board* [1981] 3 All ER 826). In a case concerning an alleged 'no-go' policy in Toxteth, the Court of Appeal said it was not for the courts to review a Chief Constable's choice of methods provided he had not exceeded the limits of his discretion (*R* v *Oxford, ex parte Levey* (1986) The Times 1 November).

The individual police officer is subject to general laws when dealing with the public. If he breaks the law, he renders himself liable to civil or criminal action, but how effective is this restriction? Many persons aggrieved by police conduct would be unlikely to invoke civil remedies because of the expense involved, and the difficulty of providing proof. Similarly, an officer who breaks the law risks prosecution, but a former Director of Public Prosecutions admitted that before agreeing that a police officer should be prosecuted, he looked for a higher degree of proof than in other cases, because of a tendency by juries to believe evidence given by police defendants (*The Guardian*, 7 February 1981). During 1992, the highly publicised Rodney King case, in which Los Angeles police officers were acquitted of assaulting a prisoner in spite of apparently damning video evidence, made it appear that the reluctance of juries to convict officers is an international phenomenon.

Another way in which the law is claimed to keep the police in check is the possible sanction of evidence being excluded on the grounds that it has been obtained by the police exceeding their powers. In view of the widespread publicity given to alleged police malpractice in the cases of the Guildford Four, the Birmingham Six and other defendants, that claim is likely to be questioned by many observers. It should be remembered that the allegations concern events which happened in the 1970s and it seems reasonable to suggest that the law in this area has been tightened considerably by the Police and Criminal Evidence Act 1984, in particular by ss76 and 78. Furthermore, after since the convictions of the people concerned were overturned, a Royal Commission was set up to examine the criminal justice system. Among the changes which it has initiated is the establishment of an independent body which will investigate alleged miscarriages of justice. The Criminal Appeal Act 1995 provided for this and a Criminal Cases Review Comission commenced work during 1996. It will take over the role from the Home Secretary in relation to cases that have been through the appeal process and yet are still viewed as being potential miscarriages of justice.

Manning (1980) describes the law as being a limited constraint upon police work and, at least in the United States, as having a legitimising rather than a controlling function. It has been alleged that police practice takes advantage of the limited controls of procedural law, especially in relation to weak minorities (Box, 1981:169).

Plainly, the various sources of police accountability which existed prior to April 1995 were affected by qualifications and areas of uncertainty. Given their inadequacy, there was a need to examine modifications or alternatives which recognised the demand for proper accountability, together with the requirement of preserving police independence.

Time will tell whether the changes made by the Police and Magistrates Courts' Act 1994 will exert a positive influence on police accountability. It could be argued that the new arrangements will have that effect. Police Authorities will have to consult communities before deciding on priorities for policing their areas and will publish details of their objectives and performance targets in a plan. Chief Constables will need to have regard to the plan when directing the force.

Every Police Authority will be obliged to issue a report at the end of each financial year. This will include an assessment of the extent to which the annual policing plan has been carried out. In addition to publishing both the plan and the annual report, the Authority has to submit copies to the Home Secretary.

Owing to an increased responsibility on the part of the Authority to monitor performance and publish results, it is probable that members of the public will have more information about their local force and will therefore be in a better position to judge its effectiveness. However, as the Home Secretary's key objectives need to be included in a local policing plan and will account for a significant proportion of a force's resources, the opportunity for Police Authorities and forces to pay attention to local needs may be limited. It is not surprising that while this legislation was being proposed, John Newing, Chief Constable of Derbyshire, called police accountability one of 'the issues of the moment' (1992:26).

14.3 Policing by consent: myth or reality?

If one accepts that there are limitations in the different methods of achieving police accountability, one also has to recognise that any alternatives must be able to preserve a proper amount of police independence. One possible approach is shown in attempts to introduce effective consultation procedures. Lord Scarman describes the necessity of effective consultation in this way:

> 'A police force, the Chief Officer of which does not discuss ... matters of policing openly and responsively with the community, is certain in the long run to find its efficiency undermined by loss of community support' (1981: para 5.64).

The notion that to be effective the police need the support of the community has been expressed by orthodox and revisionist commentators on the police (eg Reith, 1948; Brogden 1982), and by chief officers.

In a sense, it should be unnecessary for the police to have to consult the public or to make special efforts to secure its support, since one of the central claims of orthodox accounts is that British society is 'policed by consent'. Within that perspective, police officers are merely citizens in uniform who are given a mandate by the community to police its members on its behalf. Reiner suggests that from an orthodox viewpoint, the police are reputed to 'exercise the crystallised power of the people' (1985:17). This rosy image has previously been reflected in claims by spokespersons for the police that they 'discharge the communal will' (Mark, 1977) and have views on crime 'close to the general wishes of the community' (Evidence of the Police Federation to the Royal Commission on Criminal Procedure, Cmnd 8092/1981).

Such claims, even when they were made, were at variance with findings that the police felt themselves to be isolated from the public (Clark, 1965; Box, 1981:171–8).

Nowadays, very few commentators would boldly voice the rhetoric of policing by consent without adding qualifications. Even without looking for sinister connotations, the possibility of policing by consent is challenged by the fact that the police have no clear understanding of what the community wants from them. A report on the Metropolitan Police by Wolff Olins included this comment:

> 'The organisation is uncertain of its role ... Is it crime detection or crime prevention, or are police officers social workers in uniform?' (Cited in Hirst, 1991:5).

The gap between the expectations of the police and those of the public was also illustrated by research conducted on behalf of the Joint Consultative Committee of the three police staff associations. In 1989 the Committee commissioned a major research programme, largely provoked by the view that traditional styles of policing were being eroded by pressures towards economy, efficiency and effectiveness. Among the research methods adopted were separate surveys involving members of the public, members of Police Consultative Committees, and police officers at a variety of ranks. The first two surveys were conducted independently of the police, but the final report, published as the *Operational Policing Review*, is put forward as 'unashamedly the work of the police service' (Joint Consultative Committee, 1990: Preface). The Review makes no attempt to hide the fact that police officers' views are at variance with those of the public on a number of important points. Respondents in both groups were asked to identify five offences, from a given list of 15, on which they thought the police should expend most time and energy. The following offences achieved the positions shown:

Table 5: *Examples of ranking of offences on which police should expend most time and energy, from perspectives of police and public*

Ranking out of 15 offences

Offence	Public survey	Police survey
Sexual assaults on women	1	3
Residential burglary	2	1
Drunk driving	3	8
Fighting/rowdyism in the streets	9	6
Parking/traffic offences	12	12
Litter	10	14

(Source: Joint Consultative Committee, 1990.)

Rankings were close for residential burglary and identical for parking and general traffic offences, but otherwise there were marked variations. The Review gave more examples of differences of opinion. The public wanted to see more officers patrolling on foot, whereas the police thought the existing balance was right. In relation to the investigation of crimes, 68 per cent of officers felt the police should concentrate on those crimes which they had a better chance of solving. Thirty per cent of officers believed all crimes should be investigated equally, whatever the likely outcome. The responses from the members of the public were almost a mirror image. Seventy-three per cent said all crime should be investigated equally, whereas 23 per cent thought the police should concentrate on offences which they were more likely to solve. In most forces, reported crimes are now 'screened', and only those with a reasonable chance of being solved are allocated to an officer for investigation. Very serious crimes are always investigated. With reference to the use of discretion, 76 per cent of the public felt the police should use discretion when enforcing the law, compared with 94 per cent of police officers. These findings confirm that if the police are to receive the support of the community, they must obtain a representative range of views, rather than relying on their own assumptions.

Following the Scarman Report, s106 of the Police and Criminal Evidence Act 1984 imposed a duty on Police Authorities, in consultation with Chief Constables, to make arrangements to obtain the views of people in the area on policing and to obtain public co-operation in crime prevention. This statutory intervention was preceded by Home Office circulars which advocated voluntary interim arrangements. The exhortations of the Home Office have not been fully successful in achieving the development of truly representative Police Consultative Committees (PCCs). In the early days of the legislation, some local authorities failed to establish any consultative arrangements and others ignored the spirit of the Act by making arrangements which excluded the police (Police Review, 19th December, 1986; Home Office, 1986a). The latest guidelines were issued in Home Office Circular 62/1989, which emphasises openness of meetings, flexibility of arrangements and a need for members to be as representative of the community as possible. However, it is still questionable how far the meetings of PCCs represent the views of local people. Of the PCC members in the survey conducted for the *Operational Policing Review*, 90 per cent were affiliated to some other group. This is not to say such members cannot be representative of the general community, but 10 per cent seems a very small proportion of people, with no affiliations, who are simply interested in the way their area is policed. In the same survey, 17 per cent of respondents indicated that the meetings of their PCCs were never open to the public. Only 53 per cent replied that all meetings were open. The authors of the survey suggest that members who said their meetings were not open to the public may have been mistaken. A more accurate picture might have been that the public simply never attended. It is possible that many people are simply not interested enough in the way their community is policed to turn out for meetings. Another possibility is that the existing structure is too formal.

Whatever the explanation might be, it seems clear that something more than periodic consultation is required if the police and the community are to agree on a strategy for policing.

The preceding paragraphs suggest that policing by consent may be a false concept simply because of shortcomings in the way the police view community needs. Certain commentators have different reasons for regarding policing by consent as an illusion.

It is sometimes assumed that consent and public support were features of traditional policing but that they have broken down or been withdrawn in recent decades. Evidence of a crisis of consent is said to be provided by the inner city disorders of 1981 and 1985 and by opinion polls which show declining satisfaction with police performance. Changes in policing styles are blamed for the alleged breakdown. Reiner claims that in the 1950s policing by consent was at the highest level that could be reached, since that decade represented the 'high point of police legitimation' (1985:61).

Significant changes in policing began to occur in the 1960s. For example, 'unit beat policing' was introduced across Britain. Although this system included features such as home beat officers, which ought to have enabled the police and the community to identify with each other, it also introduced the panda car. Members of the 'put more bobbies on the beat' lobby identify the panda car as the scourge of traditional policing. Personal radios came into use during the same period. Increased mobility and the capacity for instant communication between an officer and his station allowed the police to respond instantly to calls from the public. In the years since then, access to telephones has become much more widespread, making it easier for people to contact the police about a range of matters which might have been unreported had it been necessary to walk to a police station or telephone kiosk. 'Fire brigade' policing, that is, responding to calls from the public, has now become the norm, with preventative patrol becoming a method which is only adopted when sufficient manpower is available. Being insulated by moving cocoons of metal and glass, it was inevitable that police officers would come to have less routine contact with the public.

Another argument used to support the notion that consent has withered away is that Britain has become a more pluralistic society. It is assumed that until recently Britain was a much more homogeneous society characterised by the kind of consensus which was essential for policing by consent to exist.

Those who claim that support for the police has only recently begun to decline are obviously assuming that the picture used to be different. Orthodox writers on the history of the police acknowledge that when modern police forces were introduced, they were met by hostility and opposition. However, they go on to suggest that within a short period, the animosity was replaced by support and approval. Writing about the Metropolitan Police, Critchley claims:

'Their imperturbability, courage, good humour and sense of fair play won first the admiration of Londoners and then their affection ... cautiously feeling their way against a hostile public, [they] brought peace and security to London in place of the turmoil and lawlessness of centuries' (1978:55).

Compare that description with the view of one resident of Islington during the 1930s:

'[T]he police were most generally characterised as the enemy, avoided where possible, never to be trusted, feared and hated in equal doses' (White, 1983).

In contrast to their orthodox counterparts, revisionist commentators take the view that the police have never been accepted, at least by the working class. Writers from both perspectives also differ in their accounts of the sources of opposition to the police.

For traditional writers, early opposition to the new police came from all social classes. The landed gentry saw the police as a further extension of the state into local affairs, and as another way of undermining their own powers. The middle classes objected to the cost of a regular police force, as well as the potential for interference in civil liberties. The working class feared political use of the police, both to intervene in labour disputes and to assist in the criminalisation of social activities, such as gambling. However, as all classes came to recognise the benefits provided by policing, this initial suspicion and animosity is said to have subsided, with the police receiving widespread support by the end of the nineteenth century.

Brogden (1982) suggests the traditional writers fall into two camps. One approach is characterised by Reith (1948, 1952, 1956) who portrays the British police officer as an impartial exemplar of good moral standards who symbolised national unity and thereby gained public support. The second camp is occupied by the institutionalist approach which holds that the police were targets for hostility aroused by a range of other new institutions developing at the same time because of state-sponsored changes in working practices, education and electoral reform. Gradually, hostility towards these institutions (and thus towards the police as scapegoats) began to recede.

In revisionist descriptions, the extent to which opposition to the police was reduced was affected by the social class of the onlooker. In the 1830s the middle and upper classes became more disposed to recognise the benefits of policing as the settlement of the reform crisis united them 'in support of the social order' (Miller, 1977:106). However, throughout the nineteenth century, conflict between the police and the working class was said to be 'chronic and endemic' in many poor communities (Storch, 1976). Assaults on officers were common and riots with the police as targets took place in northern industrial towns.

Dixon tells us that a traditional feature of working class culture was to regard the law as being class orientated (1984:64). Not unnaturally, the same label was applied to policing (Reynolds *et al*, 1911; Roberts, 1971).

Industrial disputes and large scale public demonstrations are obvious examples of occasions when police/working class conflict may be brought into sharp focus. Instances of violent confrontation can be found at various times from the inception of the modern police force through to the present day. The General Strike (1926), Grosvenor Square (1968), and the Miners' Strike (1984–5) are just a few notable examples. The police are frequently seen as strike breakers and as instruments of employers or the state (Bowden, 1978; Weinberger, 1987). Nevertheless, clashes on picket lines are only one source of evidence for the claim that the police serve class interests. As most contact occurs during routine interactions in the community, that is equally or more likely to be the setting in which the quality of relationships is decided (Macdonald, 1973).

Interference by the police in the daily lives of the working class is alleged to have been a major cause of resentment. According to Storch, during the nineteenth century, middle class elites were trying 'to mould a labouring class amenable to new disciplines of work and leisure' (1976:481). Traditional working class recreational activities, such as gambling, drinking and cock fighting, were outlawed or subjected to legal control. The police, although not making the laws, were responsible for enforcing them and were therefore the objects of aggression (Cohen, 1979; Dixon, 1984). People gathering in the street to socialise would be moved on by the police, and pubs, fairs and other gathering places would receive visits to ensure regulations were being followed. Although it is likely that such supervision would be sporadic and not continuous, it seems that the impression created for the working class was one of being under constant police supervision (Reynolds *et al*, 1911; Storch, 1976).

From a revisionist viewpoint, the police are seen as maintaining the *status quo*, to the benefit of those with property and power, at the cost of the working class. They are the iron fist in the velvet glove for, Reiner suggests, 'under the guise of impartial law enforcement and order maintenance' ... (the police) prevent specific struggles from succeeding' (1978:70).

It is not necessary to accuse the police of complicity in this apparently deliberate attempt to keep the working classes in their place. They could equally well be unwitting agents, fulfilling a role allotted to them as a 'buffer between governing elites and the masses' (Bowden, 1978:22). Both Miller (1977) and Bowden (1978) describe the genius behind the idea of a police force as being its capacity to shift criticism from political rulers to a mediating institution. The police are peculiarly well suited to perform the role of scapegoat because although most police officers are drawn from the working and lower middle classes, the nature of their occupation thrusts them into a no-man's land in which they do not readily belong to any class (Reiner, 1985; Smith and Gray, 1985).

Ironically, it is feasible that no matter what the police do to gain public support, they will be hampered by the fact that they divert hostility away from political elites because of their perceived role as guardians of the *status quo*. According to Whitaker, 'People who feel society is unfair are not likely to help the police' (1979:15).

An obsessive and paranoic concentration on the capacity of police action to serve class interests could lead to a failure to recognise the real benefits which have accrued to the working class from policing. Since disadvantaged sections of society suffer the effects of crime, it is not surprising that some revisionists accept that the poor and the working class have made considerable use of the services of the police (Davis, 1984; Dixon, 1984; Ignatieff, 1979; White, 1983). Furthermore, although the lower classes felt resentment and disgruntlement towards the police (and may continue to do so) it would be a mistake to equate those feelings with a 'rejection of the legitimacy of the police' (Reiner, 1985:41).

If one does recognise that an effective police service can and does have benefits for all sections of society, it should be possible to resist the pessimistic suggestions in much of the discussion above that public consent and support for policing has all but disappeared, if it ever existed. One of the strongest critics of modern policing argues that, owing to limited public awareness of legal practices and to secrecy about many aspects of the criminal justice system, 'popular myths about justice, fairness and impartiality persist' (Scraton, 1985:19). Although Scraton suggests those beliefs about very positive aspects of policing and the criminal justice system have been falsely induced in the minds of an ignorant public, he nevertheless concedes that such beliefs are held. Whatever their origins, surely such beliefs are likely to engender public approval of and support for policing? Recent opinion polls still tend to show a high level of satisfaction with police performance. For example, in a public survey conducted for the *Operational Policing Review*, 59 per cent of the sample thought the police in their area were doing a fairly good job and 18 per cent that they were doing a very good job; 19 per cent thought their local police were doing a rather poor or very poor job (Joint Consultative Committee, Public Survey:

Table 2.3a). As was said earlier, the same survey showed noticeable variations between the priorities which the public would set for the police and those which the police tend to set for themselves.

It has not been established that British policing is affected by a major crisis of consent. Nevertheless, surveys have shown a reduction in public satisfaction during recent years. That in itself could indicate declining support. One of the obstacles to achieving universal public support was alluded to earlier, that is, the pluralistic nature of modern society. In the discussion above, society was divided into simplistic categories of upper, middle and working class. Such a naïve classification is misleading. Lea and Young (1984) in calling for the introduction of effective and accountable community policing recognise the divergence of views within a working class community and the necessity for broad debate in order to establish community needs. Scraton, however, doubts the feasibility of establishing social cohesion even within working class communities. Given the varying demands likely to be made on the police from within a community, it is difficult to see how the police could please enough of the people for enough of the time to begin to attain true policing by consent.

The difficulty of maintaining public approval is exacerbated by the breadth of the police role. Brogden (1982) suggests that activities concerned with the service role of the police attract more public support than those relating to the detection of crime. The police retain a very broad range of responsibilities including the prevention and detection of crime and the maintenance of order. There are times when the police have to cast off the velvet glove and use the iron fist. Chesshyre comments:

> 'When all the wheels have come off ... cars burned, streets barricaded, the police have only one role. They become a civilian army charged with re-establishing the *status quo*' (1990:184).

There is little support for the creation of a separate force to maintain public order, so police officers will continue to have to fulfil a multitude of roles including helper, crime recorder, detective, harbinger of bad news and queller of disorder. So far as building public confidence and support is concerned, the only progress possible is likely to be in terms of three steps forward, two steps back, or even vice versa. Public consent is not something which can be gained and kept in perpetuity. Nor is it naturally occurring. Consent and approval have to be constructed and the relationship between the police and the public has to be continually re-negotiated, because it is 'fragile, tenuous and incomplete' (Dixon, 1984:70; see also Brogden, 1982:205 and Shaw and Williamson, 1972). In some areas, consent will never be linked to active approval. Instead, it will be more akin to a grudging acceptance of the police.

14.4 Introducing change into policing

Senior police officers have recognised the need to change 'the ethos of policing, its values and standards, from regulation and enforcement to service and protection' (Hirst, 1991:8).

In 1990, the Association of Chief Police Officers (ACPO) announced its Strategic Policy on Quality of Service Delivery. Writing about this policy, Michael Hirst, who was then the Chief Constable of Leicestershire, explained that instead of assessing its effectiveness by in-house criteria, the police service had agreed to attempt to appreciate and meet the public's expectations. Furthermore, chief officers had committed themselves to ensuring that police officers and the community share the same expectation of service delivery.

In view of the disappointing performance of PCCs and the undeniable fact that community expectations must vary widely, the task that ACPO has set itself is far from easy. Hirst admitted as much, and said that if the service's commitment to meet community expectations were seen as cosmetic or as peripheral to mainstream policing, it would fail (1991:9). There are hints in Hirst's own article that the seeds of failure have already been sown. For example, having established the community's policing priorities, the police will 'balance them against our professional judgment and agree a new level of expectation' (Hirst, 1991:12). The question must be asked: will community priorities and police judgment have equal weight in the bargaining scales or will the police maintain the right of veto? If the latter is true, doesn't consultation become a cosmetic exercise?

Hirst also referred to another objective which could be every bit as difficult as gauging public needs: 'The challenge now is to translate our intentions into measurable action at street level' (1991:8).

Police discretion is discussed under '14.2 Police accountability' (above) and under '14.5 The decision to prosecute' (below). Notwithstanding the fact that the police service is a hierarchical organisation with a well-defined rank structure and a comprehensive discipline code, the lower ranks retain considerable discretion. These ranks carry out most of their duties without the presence of supervisors and in low visibility situations. It is a long way from one end of the police chain of command to the other, and policy decisions made by chief officers can be very much diluted by the time they reach street level. Police officers are creative choice makers and have the ability to modify official policy (Skolnick, 1966; Manning, 1980; Fielding, 1988). For example, in the early 1980s considerable efforts were made to establish community policing. Although these efforts were strongly endorsed at senior level their success was limited. This was partly due to lack of support by lower ranking officers (Brown and Iles, 1985:30).

A chief officer may announce that crime detection and the processing of offenders are to receive less attention in order to enhance the service role of the police, but if constables and their immediate supervisors believe such activities constitute the central feature of real policing, they are likely to carry on in much the same way as they did before. Ironically, Hirst argues that one of the reasons for the police not providing as good a service as they could is that junior officers are given too little scope. He also blamed poor leadership and the absence of a shared mission (1991:13).

In order to address the absence of a shared mission, the following statement of common purpose has been agreed by the three police staff associations, Her

Majesty's Inspectors of Constabulary, unions representing civilian employees, and the Home Office:

> 'The purpose of the police is to uphold the law fairly and firmly; to prevent crime; to pursue and bring to justice those who break the law; to keep the Queen's peace; to protect, help and reassure the community; and to be seen to do all this with integrity, common sense and sound judgment.
>
> We must be compassionate, courteous and patient, acting without fear or favour or prejudice to the rights of others. We need to be professional, calm and restrained in the face of violence and apply only that force which is necessary to accomplish our lawful duty.
>
> We must strive to reduce the fears of the public and, so far as we can, to reflect their priorities in the action we take. We must respond to well-founded criticism with a willingness to change.'

It is encouraging that the *raison d'être* of the service has been set out in black and white, but although the wording is different, the statement says much the same as the first commissioners for the Metropolitan Police did in 1829 when they described the purpose of the new force. One should not be too surprised if police officers (who after all are paid to be suspicious) study the statement and ask 'What's new?'. The last decade has seen significant changes in the training of recruits and supervisors as well as the introduction of the Police and Criminal Evidence Act. The media, politicians and sections of the public have subjected the police to allegations of racism, brutality and fabrication of evidence. Certainly, there is evidence that these kinds of behaviour have gone on, but it has not been established that they are institutionalised features of policing. For most police officers such accusations will be undeserved and offensive. If the rank and file of the police service believe the quality of service message to be another example of implied criticism and imposed change, they will adapt to it, but they will probably not accept it.

An unwanted effect of foisting change on junior officers may be to cause them to close ranks and to seek protection within an occupational culture which reinforces and supports existing working practices. During training a police recruit learns the benefits of peer reference groups. Colleagues can provide guidance and support; interpret ambiguous messages about the police role; and reduce feelings of isolation and low esteem produced by unfavourable encounters with the public (Harris, 1973). The recruit is also amenable to the suggestions of trainers, but once he joins the operational environment, he enters a culture in which common sense and experience are regarded as superior to the theoretical notions expressed in the classroom (Fielding, 1988, 1988a). Subcultural values are developed as a means of adapting to police work and because they help to make sense of experiences (Reiner, 1985).

The points made here are very basic and are not intended to imply the existence of a single police culture with ideas and beliefs which are adhered to by all police officers. The intention is to show that police subcultures can operate as a means for police officers to exclude outsiders, a term which might include senior officers, politicians, or indeed anyone else.

If the Strategic Policy on Quality of Service Delivery is to succeed, it cannot simply be imposed on the rank and file of the police service. Just as the police service has to obtain public support, so too must ACPO sell its policy to the rest of the service. Officers must have ownership of the policy before they will commit themselves to it fully.

Notwithstanding these efforts to introduce self-initiated change, during his spell as Home Secretary, Kenneth Clarke showed the government's determination to make substantial alterations to the structure and organisation of policing. In May 1992, Mr Clarke set up an inquiry into police responsibilities and rewards, under the chairmanship of Sir Patrick Sheehy. This inquiry was only the tip of an iceberg.

In a statement to Parliament on 23 March 1993, Mr Clarke announced 'the biggest reorganisation of the police service for more than 30 years' (*The Times*, 24 March 1993). Although Michael Howard brought a slightly different approach to these reforms when he took over as Home Secretary, the central ideas survived and many of the proposals were described in a Police Reform White Paper published in June 1993.

This document claimed that the main changes would: allow the government to set key objectives for policing; alter the composition and some of the functions of police authorities and give them greater strength; provide Chief Constables with more freedom to manage their budgets in order to respond more effectively to local needs; streamline police management; replace the current complicated method of funding with cash limited budgets; allow Chief Constables and police authorities to decide on the right mixture of manpower without seeking approval from the centre; strengthen Her Majesty's Inspectorate; simplify the procedures for amalgamating police forces; and amend the police rank structure, pay and conditions of service to facilitate the recruitment and retention of high quality officers and reflect wide differences in the responsibilities of individual officers. These changes were presented in such a way as to emphasise their positive aspects. As was seen at section 14.2 when discussing the legislation which has implemented some of these reforms, they have also had the effect of increasing the government's ability to influence policing.

The proposals for altering the police rank structure, pay and conditions of service were obviously linked to the Sheehy inquiry. The Sheehy Report was published within days of the White Paper and contained 272 recommendations. Many of these were highly contentious and provoked a strong reaction from the police staff associations. On 26 October 1993, following consultation with interested parties, the Home Secretary announced his response to the Report. Some of the more radical proposals were rejected, but others were accepted, including a suggestion that certain middle management ranks should be scrapped. Several of the recommendations were passed on for the attention of the Police Negotiating Board.

Proposals contained in the White Paper and some of those accepted from the Sheehy Report have been incorporated into the Police and Magistrates' Courts Act 1994. Although the Act does not seek to make an immediate reduction in the number of police forces in England and Wales, it amends s32 of the Police Act

1996, enabling the Home Secretary to alter police areas by order. Notice has to be given and time allowed for objections to be made, but the procedure for bringing about amalgamations will be much less troublesome for a Home Secretary than the process which formerly had to be followed.

In the White Paper and in ministerial pronouncements, the rationale behind these changes to the organisation of policing is described in terms of the improvements which will result in the service given to the public. However, it is apparent from the earlier discussion at section 14.2 that the capacity of central government to influence policing activity has been substantially increased. The use to which this enhanced influence will be put remains to be seen.

14.5 The decision to prosecute

A number of studies have emphasised that a large part (probably the majority) of a police officer's time is spent in a helping or service role (Punch, 1979; Punch and Naylor, 1973). This might involve him in such tasks as finding lost children, helping people who have locked themselves out of houses, or giving crime prevention advice. Nevertheless, one of the primary functions of the police (and the one of most relevance to this book) is enforcing the law. For present purposes we are not concerned with what happens when an offender appears before a court. In this section we will examine the process by which the decision is made as to whether or not to prosecute an offender, concentrating in particular on three aspects:

1. The role of the police.
2. The arguments in favour of separating investigation from prosecution.
3. The role of the Crown Prosecution Service.

Cautioning of offenders, as an alternative to prosecution, will be dealt with in the next section.

The role of the police

In the discussion of police accountability, above, it was shown that the exercise of discretion is an important and legitimate feature of police work. A police officer can become aware that an offence has been committed in a variety of ways. In some cases he will witness the offence himself, so that he becomes aware of the offender at the same time. At other times the offence will be reported by a victim or witness, who might also identify the person responsible. Sometimes the officer will discover the offender by investigating the offence. No matter how the offence comes to his notice, the officer has an immediate choice to make, that is, what to do about it. If he witnesses an offence, the officer might decide to turn a blind eye. If he is investigating an offence reported by someone else, he might decide not to waste too much energy in pursuing his inquiries. In either case, the officer is not exercising his discretion – it is more reasonable to regard him as neglecting his duty. If the crime which he does nothing about is serious, he could face disciplinary proceedings, or even prosecution. A police motorcyclist was convicted of neglecting his duty as a public official, at common law, when he rode off after seeing a man receive a severe beating which ultimately proved to be fatal (*R* v *Dytham* [1979] 3 All ER 641).

Mention has already been made of a number of cases which illustrate how reluctant the courts are to force chief officers to enforce particular laws. The case of *R* v *Coxhead* [1986] Crim LR 251, tells us a little about the attitude of the courts to the exercise of discretion by individual officers. In this case the appellant was a police sergeant who was in charge at a police station when a motorist was brought in for the purposes of undergoing the breathalyser procedure. The sergeant recognised him as the son of a police inspector who was suffering from a heart condition. In order to avoid further distress to the motorist's father, the sergeant allowed him to go, without following the breath test procedure. The sergeant was prosecuted for perverting the course of justice. His defence was that his decision was within the proper scope of discretion which a police officer could exercise. The trial judge ruled that the extent of such discretion depended on the facts and was a matter for determination by the jury. The jury convicted. The Court of Appeal dismissed the sergeant's appeal, saying that in minor cases the police had very wide discretion, but that in major cases they had virtually no discretion at all. They agreed that a jury should decide where a particular case lay. The comment in the *Criminal Law Review* suggests, not surprisingly, that it seems unusual to leave such an issue to be decided by a jury. The law does not provide any clear guidelines as to the boundaries of police discretion, and internal guidelines will undoubtedly vary between police forces.

We are more concerned with those occasions where a police officer who discovers an offender makes a legitimate choice about what to do. Thus an officer who catches someone committing a minor traffic offence can choose one of several options. He might give the motorist a verbal warning there and then. In appropriate cases, he could use the vehicle defect rectification scheme. This involves giving the motorist a form specifying the defect found. If the motorist has the defect repaired, then reports to a police station within a specified period and produces the form duly endorsed by the repairer, he will not be prosecuted. Alternatively, the offender might be given a fixed penalty notice. If he pays the fee within 28 days of issue, he will not be prosecuted. The officer's final option is to report the offender, in order for prosecution to be considered.

For minor offences not related to motoring, and which would normally be dealt with by way of summons rather than arrest, for example, depositing litter, there are fewer options. Generally speaking, the officer could choose between warning the offender or reporting him.

In relation to offences where there is a power of arrest, the options become broader, but in view of the range of offences that might be involved, the situation is complicated. An officer might come across a group of people who are drunk in the street and behaving in a disorderly manner. His first choice of action will often be to try to calm the people down and send them on their way. If this fails they could be arrested.

In another example, the officer might be called to deal with an alleged shoplifter. Having listened to the accounts of those concerned, he must consider the evidence available. It might appear to him that no offence has occurred, in which case it would be likely that he would advise the complainant accordingly, and no further police action would be taken. If there is sufficient evidence that an offence has occurred, the officer might arrest the alleged offender. Alternatively, he might interview the alleged shoplifter without making an arrest, and report him for the offence.

The exercise of discretion by the police officer who first becomes aware of an offence is obviously of major significance, since his choice can determine whether or not the matter goes any further. Once an alleged offender has been reported or arrested, the exercise of discretion by supervisory officers becomes important.

On those occasions when an offender has been reported, the reporting officer submits a file to his supervisors. Recommendations may be made by his sub-divisional supervisors, but most forces have prosecutions departments, which consider such files and decide what course of action to take. The main options are: to take no further action; to issue a warning (verbal or written, depending on the circumstances); or to prosecute. As we will see later, if a decision is made to prosecute, proceedings are taken over by the Crown Prosecution Service (CPS).

When an alleged offender is arrested and taken to a police station, the custody officer is responsible for determining whether there is sufficient evidence to charge him with that offence. If the custody officer decides there is sufficient evidence, the person must be charged or released without charge, with or without bail (s37(1), (7) Police and Criminal Evidence Act 1984). The custody officer will be a sergeant. In cases where the custody officer authorises a person to be charged, a file will be submitted to the CPS. In some cases where there would be sufficient evidence to charge an offender, but certain conditions apply, it is possible that he will receive an immediate caution. In most such cases, however, a file will be submitted via the arresting officer's supervisors. They could decide to take no further action or to issue a caution. The police can decide to charge the offender, but after they have done so, the file will then be sent to the CPS. Alternatively, when the police favour prosecution they might submit the file to the CPS for advice before reaching a definite decision. This could happen where the weight of the evidence is questionable.

As is the case with the first officer to deal with an offence, the exercise of discretion by supervisory officers is of fundamental importance in determining the outcome of a particular case. The CPS enter the equation once a decision is made to prosecute, but the police are able to prevent that stage from being reached by choosing from a variety of different options.

The arguments in favour of separating investigation from prosecution

Until 1986, the police were responsible both for investigating offences and for continuing a prosecution once an offender had been charged or summonsed to appear before a court. England and Wales was one of the few countries where such a situation existed. In most jurisdictions prosecutions were carried out by a service which was separate from the police. The system we had, where the functions of investigation and prosecution were performed by a single body, was criticised on several grounds. A number of criticisms were set out in a report by JUSTICE, published in 1970. In paraphrased form, these included the following:

1. Even an honest officer may be so committed to 'winning' a case that he continues a prosecution even if the evidence is weak.
2. The police are not properly placed to evaluate the public policy aspects of decisions to prosecute.
3. The dominant position of the police might tempt them to bargain with suspects in relation to charges, evidence and the plea.
4. The police may exercise pressure on prosecuting council to pursue a hard line, contrary to his better judgement.

And more importantly:

5. The vigorous investigation of crime, and the careful assessment of evidence in order to decide whether to prosecute were two distinct functions which the existing system confused.
6. The existing system concentrated on winning or losing. This was contrary to the principle that a prosecution must be seen to be independent, impartial and fair.

JUSTICE proposed the introduction of a system similar to that in Scotland, where the decision to prosecute is taken by a Procurator Fiscal, except for minor offences. The situation was considered by the Royal Commission on Criminal Procedure. Police organisations opposed the idea of removing their power to commence and continue prosecutions. The Director of Public Prosecutions (DPP) was not strongly critical of the existing system and was not in favour of any substantial change. The Royal Commission considered that a prosecution system should meet three criteria, namely fairness; openness and accountability; and efficiency. Its major criticisms of the existing system were in relation to accountability and efficiency. The system's failure to meet both of these criteria was in part due to a marked variation between forces and their access to prosecuting solicitors. Some forces had prosecuting solicitor's departments, others did not and would engage the services of solicitors on an *ad hoc* basis to prosecute in more complicated cases. Where there were such departments, some were accountable to the police authority and others to the county council. Some departments advised the police before prosecutions were commenced, and some did not. There was no central co-ordination by the DPP. These variations meant that accountability and efficiency were difficult if not impossible to achieve. The Royal

Commission recommended the introduction of a new system in which each police area would have a separate agency, headed by a Crown Prosecutor who was answerable to the police authority. This agency would decide whether to continue a prosecution after the police had decided to charge a suspect. The recommendations in this part of the Commission's report, published in 1981, were not fully accepted by the government. The government established a Working Party on Prosecution arrangements and published its report in 1983 as part of the White Paper *An Independent Prosecution Service for England and Wales.*

The role of the Crown Prosecution Service

The government's proposals were subsequently incorporated into the Prosecution of Offences Act 1985. The Act established the CPS, a national prosecution service for England and Wales, under the direction of the DPP. Each CPS area is led by a Chief Crown Prosecutor who is responsible to the DPP.

The CPS takes over the prosecution of all criminal cases which are commenced by the police. However, if the involvement of the police is limited to the custody officer charging a suspect brought to the police station by another agency, such as the Customs and Excise, that other agency will be able to continue the proceedings, and will not have to hand over the case to the CPS. That conclusion was reached by the Queen's Bench Divisional Court in *R* v *Stafford Magistrates Court, ex parte Commissioners of Customs and Excise (*1990) The Times 5 April. The court held that the case of *R* v *Ealing Magistrates, ex parte Dixon* [1989] Crim LR 656 (in which the opposite conclusion had been reached) was wrongly decided.

The Act also reduces the discretion of chief officers to some extent. A chief officer of police is obliged to inform the DPP of a serious offence which is alleged to have occurred in his area if there is a prima facie for prosecution (s8).

If the police have charged an offender, the CPS is empowered either to not start proceedings, or to discontinue them (s23). To do this the CPS must give notice to the court, with reasons, before any evidence has been heard. At a later stage, the CPS can withdraw the charges or offer no evidence. The CPS can also vary the charges.

The CPS commenced operation in 1986, and the DPP issued a Code for Crown Prosecutors consisting of a set of guidelines to assist them in exercising their discretion whether or not to prosecute, or to continue proceedings (*Law Society Gazette*, 23 July 1986:2308). A revised version was issued in June 1994. The most important criteria are concerned with sufficiency of evidence and with the public interest:

Criteria relating to sufficiency of evidence
The code describes the sufficiency of evidence as the first question to be determined when considering whether to institute or continue criminal proceedings. Before deciding in favour of either of those courses of action, a Crown Prosecutor must be satisfied that there is admissible, substantial and reliable evidence that an identifiable

person has committed a criminal offence. It is not enough for there to be a prima facie case, there must be a realistic prospect of obtaining a conviction.

Criteria relating to the public interest

Before he can institute or continue proceedings, the Crown Prosecutor has to be satisfied that the public interest requires a prosecution. He has to consider the likely effect of a prosecution, successful or unsuccessful, on public morale and order. Broadly speaking, the more serious an offence, the more likely it would be that the public interest would require a prosecution to follow. The Crown Prosecutor should consider Home Office guidelines on the cautioning of offenders. Having considered such factors, if the Crown Prosecutor is still in doubt he should also take account of the attitude of the local community and information about the prevalence of the offence in that area or nationally. If doubt still remains, he should usually decide in favour of prosecution, so that a court can make the ultimate decision.

The code for prosecutors emphasises the high visibility and importance of a decision to discontinue proceedings. It emphasises the point that the CPS does not exist to rubber stamp police decisions to prosecute. Prosecutors are required to continually review the propriety of proceedings after they have commenced. The Code also has something to say about prosecutors accepting pleas to less serious offences rather than proceeding to a full trial on the original charge. The overriding consideration is said to be that this can only be done if the court will still be able to pass a sentence which is consistent with the seriousness of the defendant's actions. If that requirement is met, the resource advantages of accepting a quick guilty plea are an important consideration, although the administrative benefits must not outweigh the interests of justice.

Since its inception the CPS has been dogged by problems, mostly connected with lack of resources and in particular shortages of staff. From the beginning, workloads were excessive, and morale was low (*The Times*, 8 April 1987). There have been numerous stories about files being lost, cases being dismissed because of errors, and of poor relations between police and the CPS. Some commentators suggested these difficulties would disappear in time, but others who believed they were endemic to the system, like Zander (1988), seem to have predicted developments more accurately. As recently as November 1993, the Chairman of the Metropolitan Police Federation was calling for the resignation of the DPP, Barbara Mills, claiming that the CPS was more interested with satisfying its own bureaucracy than with furthering justice. However, the Metropolitan Police Commissioner acknowledged that the police service contributes to the level of cases which are not pursued by the CPS, by submitting files of poor quality. The DPP made a similar point when appearing before the House of Commons Select Committee on Home Affairs in February 1994. In presenting the results of a survey carried out in November 1993, Mrs Mills indicated that 43 per cent of the 10,000 cases which were discontinued during that month were dropped because of insufficient evidence. In the year to September 1993, 1.5 million cases were submitted to the CPS and 185,000 were discontinued. The DPP rejected suggestions that standards were being set too high and argued that the police needed to gain a better understanding of evidential requirements (*Police Review*, 5 November 1993 and 4 February 1994). It is disappointing, especially for victims, that after ten years, these two important agencies in the criminal justice system have still not fully got their acts together and that energy should be expended in what amounts to mutual mud flinging.

14.6 Cautioning policy

Introduction

For some years, the police have followed a policy of cautioning some juveniles as an alternative to prosecuting them. The philosophy supporting such a procedure was that in the case of certain juveniles, usually first offenders, the public interest would be better served by issuing a formal caution rather than by taking the juvenile to court. Cautioning of adults has been promoted more vigorously in recent years. An obvious additional advantage of removing people from the criminal justice process at an early stage is that it saves time and money.

Cautioning practice has tended to vary considerably between police forces. For example, in 1988 the cautioning rate for juveniles ranged between 54 per cent and 86 per cent in relation to males, and between 70 per cent and 91 per cent for females. Cautioning rates for all persons, for indictable offences in 1995 varied between 27 per cent in Merseyside and 54 per cent in Surrey (Home Office, 1996a p89). These rates indicate the proportion of persons cautioned out of the total number of people found guilty or cautioned for indictable offences. Ditchfield (1976) suggests that variations between forces can partly be explained by differences in patterns of crime. However, Wilkinson and Evans (1990) argue that variations in cautioning rates are more fully accounted for by differences in police practice. A study by Gelsthorpe and Giller (1990) also discovered variations in practice within police forces.

Guidance to police forces

In 1985, the Home Office issued Circular 14/1985 to Chief Constables. This contained new guidelines on cautioning both juveniles and adults, and was intended to promote effectiveness and consistency in cautioning practice. As the cautioning rates cited above are for 1988, it seems reasonable to conclude that those aims were not achieved. In July 1990, the Home Office cancelled the circular and replaced it with Circular 59/1990. That circular set out national standards for cautioning and took into account the findings of the work by Wilkinson and Evans, and of separate research by the Association of Chief Police Officers into methods of diverting young offenders.

Guidance on the cautioning of offenders is now contained in Home Office Circular 18/1994, which is intended to:

1. Discourage the use of cautions in inappropriate cases, eg offences which are triable on indictment only.
2. Seek greater consistency between police force areas.
3. Promote the better recording or cautions.

In most respects, the guidance in the latest circular and in the revised national standards for cautioning which accompany it are similar to those contained in Circular 59/1990 which it supersedes.

The police are described in the Home Office Annual Report for 1995 (Cm 2808) presented to Parliament in March 1995 as having 'discretion whether to charge an offender or formally to caution him or her'. It goes on to say that cautioning, properly used, is an effective deterrent to those who have committed minor offences or who have offended for the first time. However, it states that 'multiple cautioning can lead to an offender becoming an habitual criminal before even coming to court' suggesting that those who abuse the chance offered by a caution should generally be prosecuted.

In March 1995, new guidance was issued to the police aimed at curbing the inappropriate use of cautioning. The use of cautioning is now ruled out for 'the most serious offences' and strongly discouraged repeat cautioning. There was a noticeable impact, with 19,000 or 6 per cent fewer cautions in the 12 months ending in September 1994. The most recent 'Criminal Statistics 1995' show that the number cautioned has declined further with only 291,000 cautions in 1995 (Home Office 1996a p94).

However, more than half the criminals arrested for serious offences such as rape, child abuse and burglary were allowed to go free with a caution, according to *The Sunday Times* 18 February 1996. Statistics revealed that Surrey, Wiltshire, Essex, Gloucestershire and Hertfordshire were amongst the most lenient forces, whilst South Wales and Durham cautioned about a quarter of serious offenders. Victim Support said it was alarmed by the variations between different police forces and responded to the figures by suggesting 'if you are burgled in Surrey, you want to know that crime will be treated as seriously as it would be in Durham, and you also want to know that the likelihood of your burglar being prosecuted does not depend on the whim of a local police officer'.

The purpose of a formal caution
A formal caution is intended to:

1. deal quickly and simply with less serious offenders;
2. divert such offenders from the criminal courts;
3. reduce the chances of their re-offending.

The circular emphasises that a formal caution is not the only alternative to prosecution. For example, in certain cases it will be appropriate for the police to give an offender an informal warning, or for them to take no further action. A caution is not a sentence – it cannot be tied to a requirement to make reparation or to compensate the victim.

The criteria to be met before cautioning

Several conditions must be met before a caution can be given:

1. The evidence must be sufficient to give a realistic prospect of conviction. If the evidence is insufficient, cautioning is ruled out.
2. The offender must admit the offence. The admission must be clear and reliable. If the offender's mental health or intellectual capacity were in doubt, a caution would not be appropriate but prosecution would not be inevitable in such a case – the police might take no further action or consider referral to another agency which could help the offender.
3. The offender (or in the case of a juvenile his parent or guardian) must consent to a caution being issued. Consent should not be sought until a decision has been made that a caution is the appropriate course of action – in other words it is not possible to offer a caution as an inducement to admit the offence. When consent is sought, the offender (or parent/guardian) must have the significance of the procedure explained to him:

   a) a record of the caution will be kept;
   b) if the person offends again, the caution may influence the decision whether to prosecute for the new offence;
   c) if the person is convicted of another offence in the future, the caution may be cited in court.

The public interest

If the first two of the above conditions are met, consideration should be given to whether a caution is in the public interest. The factors which should be taken into account are:

1. The nature of the offence. Cautions must never be given for the most serious indictable-only offences. Their use for other indictable-only offences will only be appropriate in exceptional circumstances. A caution will not be appropriate when the victim has suffered significant harm or loss. The term 'significant' is to be construed with reference to the circumstances of the victim. In cases of doubt, the assistance of the CPS should be sought.
2. The likely penalty if the offender were to be convicted by a court. The circular refers to the Code for Crown Prosecutors which suggests that prosecution may not be appropriate where the offence is not particularly serious and the probable sentence would be an absolute or conditional discharge. The likelihood of a more substantive penalty being imposed does not mean that a caution could not be given.
3. The offender's age and state of health. The circular retains a presumption in favour of not prosecuting the elderly or infirm and people suffering from a

mental illness or a severe physical illness. It goes on to state that the presumption against prosecution should be extended to other groups of adults where the criteria for cautioning are met.

4. The offender's previous criminal history. An offender's previous record is important but is not decisive on its own. The existence of a previous caution or conviction does not rule out a further caution if other factors exist which suggest that a caution would be appropriate. For example, there might have been an appreciable lapse of time since the last offence, the previous and most recent offences might be different in character and seriousness, or a previous caution might have had a noticeable effect on the pattern of offending. However, the circular suggests that a caution should not be given when there can be no reasonable expectation that it will curb the recipient's offending.

5. The offender's attitude to the offence. Two factors are to be considered. The first is the wilfulness with which the offence was committed. The second is the offender's subsequent attitude. A demonstration of regret, such as apologising to the victim or an offer to put matters right, are features which might support the use of a caution.

The views of the victim

The circular suggests that before a caution can be given the victim should normally be contacted to assess such factors as:

1. His view of the offence.
2. The extent of any damage or loss. The significance of the loss or damage should be considered in relation to the victim. The effect of the caution should be explained to the victim.
3. Whether there is any continuing threat from the offender. Although cautioning might otherwise be appropriate, in some cases a prosecution may be necessary in order to protect the victim from the future attentions of the offender.
4. Whether the offender has paid any compensation or made any form of reparation. The police must not become involved in negotiating over the making of reparation or the provision of compensation.

The consent of the victim to a caution is desirable but not essential.

The manner in which a caution is administered

For most offenders, the circular suggests that the caution must be given in formal circumstances, at a police station, by a uniformed police officer. The officer should normally be of the rank of Inspector or above, but a community constable or community liaison officer might be considered to be more appropriate in some cases. A juvenile must always be cautioned in the presence of a parent, guardian or other appropriate adult. Persons who are vulnerable for some other reason should also be cautioned in the presence of an appropriate adult. The manner in which a caution is given will obviously vary in practice, according to the personal styles of different officers.

Recording cautions

The circular states that all formal cautions should be recorded and provides for the Home Secretary to give directions as to how records will be kept. It suggests that cautioning should be monitored on a force-wide basis.

Comments about the Home Office guidelines

It has already been pointed out that Circular 14/1985 failed to achieve consistency in cautioning practice, because there continued to be marked variations between forces even after its introduction. Starting in 1985, the Avon and Somerset Constabulary embarked on a study of the cautioning of adults within its force area (Westwood, 1990). One finding was that the proportion of young adults who were being cautioned was considerably smaller than the equivalent proportion of adults aged 21 or over. This seemed to be contrary to the intentions of Circular 14/1985. The study also suggested that because someone with several previous convictions was less likely to be cautioned, the guidelines led to a lower cautioning rate for people living in areas with the worst social conditions. For various reasons, a person from such an area stood a greater chance of receiving a first conviction. Within a system which required previous convictions to be taken into account when deciding whether to caution an offender, every decision was being influenced by decisions made in the past. The force drew up new guidelines and ran a trial in which previous convictions, except for the most recent one, were disregarded at the stage of deciding whether or not to prosecute an offender. The seriousness of the offence was made paramount. Safeguards were built in to avoid the risk of petty persistent offenders escaping prosecution indefinitely. Apart from these differences, the guidelines were very similar to the 1985 circular. During the trial period, cautioning rates rose to approximately twice the national average for both adults and young adults. The guidelines were subsequently adopted across the whole force area.

In a study of the effects of Circular 14/1985 on cautioning of juveniles, Wilkinson and Evans (1990) found that cautioning rates increased after it was issued. They also discovered that although consistency of practice had not been achieved, variations in rates between forces had narrowed a little.

In *Criminal Statistics for England and Wales 1993*, it is suggested that the circulation of a draft of the new circular, during late 1993, was followed by a marked reduction in the number of people receiving cautions (Home Office, 1994:92). Reference is made to research carried out for the Home Office which indicates that cautioning is an effective method for preventing further offending by less serious offenders, but that its effectiveness diminishes after the first caution. During 1993, there continued to be marked variations in cautioning rates between different police forces. These have continued with the 1995 statistics revealing that Merseyside cautions in only 27 per cent of cases whilst the rate for Surrey is 54 per cent (Home Office 1995a p105).

The role of the Crown Prosecution Service in relation to cautioning

If the police decide to caution an offender, the CPS cannot reverse that decision, and substitute prosecution. Indeed, they will not be involved at all. When the police submit a file to the CPS and the Crown Prosecutor takes the view that a caution will be more suitable than a prosecution, the police should be informed accordingly.

Other alternatives to prosecution

A formal caution is not the only alternative to prosecution. Home Office Circular 18/1994 indicates that sometimes it will be appropriate to give an offender an informal warning or to ensure that he obtains help from another agency. There are some instances where it would be reasonable to take no further action at all. The circular suggests that a caution has a deterrent effect and that it denotes society's disapproval of the offender's actions. Occasions when such an effect is not considered necessary seem to be suited to one of these different alternatives to prosecution.

Bibliography

Abbott, E (1936) *The Tenements of Chicago, 1908–1938*, Chicago: University of Chicago Press.

Aichhorn, A (1925) *Wayward Youth*, New York: Meridian Books.

Ainsworth, MD, Andry, RG, Harlow, RG, Lebovici, S, Mead, M, Pugh, DG and Wootton, B (1962) *Deprivation of Maternal Care: A Reassessment of its Effects*, World Health Organisation.

Akers, RL (1967) 'Problems in the sociology of deviance: social definitions and behavior', *Social Forces* 46: 455–65.

Alderson, J (1979) *Policing Freedom*, Plymouth: McDonald and Evans.

Allatt, P (1984) 'Residential security: containment and displacement of burglary', *Howard Journal*, 23: 99–116.

Allsopp, JF and Feldman, MP (1975) 'Extraversion, neuroticism and psychoticism and anti-social behaviour in school girls', *Social Behaviour and Personality*, 2: 184.

Allsopp, JF and Feldman, MP (1976) 'Personality and anti-social behaviour in school boys', *British Journal of Criminology*, 16: 337–51.

American Psychiatric Association (1968) *Diagnostic and Statistical Manual of Mental Disorders*, Washington, DC: American Psychiatric Association.

Andry, RG (1957) 'Faulty paternal and maternal child relationships, affection and delinquency', *British Journal of Delinquency*, VIII: 34–48.

Andry, RG (1962) 'Paternal and maternal roles and delinquency', in MD Ainsworth *et al* (1962), *Deprivation of Maternal Care: A Reassessment of its Effects*, World Health Organisation.

Aronfreed, J (1961) 'The nature, variety and social patterning of moral responses to transgression', *Journal of Abnormal and Social Psychology*, 63: 223.

Arthur, J, Cookson, P, Cross, J, Pandeli, M, Wigzell, J and Wills, D (1979) *Six Quakers Look at Crime and Punishment*, London: Quaker Social Responsibility and Education.

Aubert, W (1952) 'White collar crime and social structure', *American Journal of Sociology*, 58: 263–71.

Audit Commission (1991) *Reviewing the Organisation of Provincial Police Forces*, London: HMSO.

Bagley, C (1965) 'Juvenile delinquency in Exeter: an ecological and comparative study', *Urban Studies*, 2: 33–50.

Baldwin, J (1975) 'British areal studies of crime: an assessment', *British Journal of Criminology*, 15: 211–27.

Baldwin, J and Bottomley, AK (eds) (1978) *Criminal Justice: Selected Readings*, Oxford: Martin Robertson.

Baldwin, J and Bottoms, AF (1976) *The Urban Criminal*, London: Tavistock.

Bandura, A (1973) *Aggression: a Social Learning Analysis*, Englewood Cliffs: Prentice Hall.

Bandura, A and Walters, RH (1959) *Adolescent Aggression*, New York: Ronald Press.

Baumhart, RC (1961) 'How ethical are businessmen?' *Harvard Business Review*, 39: 6–19, 156–76.

Baxter, R and Nuttall, C (1975), 'Severe sentences: no deterrent to crime', *New Society* 31: 11.

Beccaria, C (1764) *Dei delitti e delle pene*, translated as *On Crimes and Punishments*, by Paolucci, H (1963) Indianapolis: Bobbs-Merrill.

Becker, GS (1968) 'Crime and Punishment: an economic approach', *Journal of Political Economy*, 76(2): 169–217.

Becker, HS (1963) *Outsiders: Studies in the Sociology of Deviance*, New York: Free Press.

Becker, HS (ed) (1964) *The Other Side*, New York: Free Press.

Becker, HS (1974) 'Labelling theory reconsidered', in P Rock and M McIntosh (eds) *Deviance and Social Control*.

241

Bennett, T (1986) 'Situational crime prevention from the offender's perspective', in K Heal and G Laycock (eds) *Situational Crime Prevention: From Theory into Practice*, London: HMSO.

Bennett, T (1987) *An Evaluation of Two Neighbourhood Watch Schemes in London*, executive summary of final report to the Home Office Research and Planning Unit, Cambridge: University of Cambridge.

Bennett, T and Wright, R (1984) *Burglars on Burglary: Prevention and the Offender*, Aldershot: Gower.

Bentham, J (1780) *An Introduction to the Principles of Morals and Legislation* (amended version edited by JH Burns and HLA Hart (1982), London: Methuen).

Berman, L (1938) *New Creations in Human Beings*, New York: Doubleday.

Beyleveld, D (1978) *The Effectiveness of General Deterrents Against Crime: An Annotated Bibliography of Evaluative Research*, Cambridge: Cambridge Institute of Criminology.

Beyleveld, D (1979) 'Deterrence research as a basis for deterrence policies', *Howard Journal*, 18: 135.

Beyleveld, D, Bottoms, A and Wiles, P (1979) 'Is there any evidence that hanging deters killers?' *New Society* 48: 759–61.

Bittner, E (1970) *The Functions of the Police in Modern Society*, Washington, DC: US Government Printing Office.

Black, DJ (1970) 'Production of crime rates', *American Sociological Review*, 35: 733.

Blackburn, R and Maybury, C (1985) 'Identifying the psychopath: the relation of Cleckley's criteria to the interpersonal domain', *Personality and Individual Differences*, 6: 375–86.

Blumberg, AS (1967) *Criminal Justice*, Chicago: Quadrangle Books.

Blumberg, M (1989) 'Issues and controversies with respect to the management of AIDS in corrections', *The Prison Journal*, LXXIX: 1–13.

Blundell, WE (1978) 'Equity funding: "I did it for the jollies"', in JM Johnson and DJ Douglas (eds) *Crime at the Top*, New York: Lippincott.

Bonger, W (1916) *Criminality and Economic Conditions*, Boston: Little, Brown.

Bonger, (1936) *Introduction to Criminology*, London: Methuen.

Bonger, W (1943) *Race and Crime*, New York: University Of Columbia Press.

Bonger, W (1969) *Criminality and Economic Conditions*, Bloomington: Indiana University Press.

Bottomley, AK (1979) *Criminology in Focus: Past Trends and Future Prospects*, Oxford: Martin Robertson.

Bottomley, AK (1986) 'Blue-prints for criminal justice: reflections on a policy plan for the Netherlands', *Howard Journal*, 25: 199–215.

Bottomley, AK and Coleman, C (1981) *Understanding Crime Rates*, Farnborough: Gower.

Bottoms, AE (1981) 'The suspended sentence in England 1967–1978', *British Journal of Criminology*, 21: 2–3.

Bottoms, AE and McClean, JD (1976) *Defendants in the Criminal Process*, London: Routledge.

Bottoms, AE and McClintock, FH (1973) *Criminals Coming Of Age*, London: Heinemann.

Bowden, T (1978) *Beyond the Limits of the Law*, London: Penguin.

Bowker, LH (1978) *Women, Crime and the Criminal Justice System*, Lexington, Mass: Heath.

Bowlby, J (1944) 'Forty-four juvenile thieves', *International Journal of Psychoanalysis*, 25: 1–57.

Bowlby, J (1952) *Maternal Care and Mental Health* (2nd edn), World Health Organisation.

Bowlby, J (1979) *The Making and Breaking of Affectional Bonds*, London: Tavistock.

Bowlby, J and Salter-Ainsworth, MD (1965) *Child Care and the Growth of Love*, Harmondsworth: Penguin.

Bowley, AL (1915) *The Effect of the War on the External Trade of the United Kingdom*, London: Cambridge University Press.

Bowley, AL (1928) *Official Statistics: What they Contain and How to Use Them*, London: Oxford University Press.

Box, S (1981) *Deviance, Reality and Society*, London: Holt, Rinehart and Winston.

Box, S (1983) *Power, Crime and Mystification*, London: Tavistock.

Braithwaite, J (1984) *Corporate Crime in the Pharmaceutical Industry*, London: Routledge and Kegan Paul.

Brantingham, PL (1986) 'Trends in Canadian crime prevention', in K Heal and G Laycock (eds) *Situational Crime Prevention: From Theory into Practice*, London: HMSO.

Brantingham, PJ and Brantingham, PL (eds) (1981) *Environmental Criminology*, Beverly Hills: Sage.

Brantingham, PL and Brantingham, PJ (1984) 'Burglar mobility and crime prevention planning', in R Clarke and T Hope (eds) *Coping with Burglary*, Boston: Kluwer-Nijhoff.

Brantingham, PJ and Jeffery, CR (1981) 'Afterword: crime, space and criminological theory', in PJ Brantingham and PL Brantingham (eds) *Environmental Criminology*.

Bright, JA (1969) *The Beat Patrol Experiment*, Home Office Police Research and Development Branch (unpublished).

Brogden, M (1982) *The Police: Autonomy and Consent*, London: Academic Press.

Brown, B (1986) 'Women and crime – the dark figure of criminology', *Economy and Society*, 15: 355–402

Brody, S and Tarling, R (1980) *Taking Offenders Out Of Circulation*, Home Office Research Study No 64, London: HMSO.

Brody, S (1976) *The Effectiveness of Sentencing: a Review of the Literature*, Home Office Research Study No 35, London: HMSO.

Brown, D and Iles, S (1985) *Community Constables: A Study of a Policing Initiative*, Research and Planning Unit Paper No 30, London: HMSO.

Bulmer, M (1982) *Social Research Ethics: an Examination of the Merits of Covert Participant Observation*, London: Macmillan.

Burgess, RL and Akers, RL (1968) 'A differential association-reinforcement theory of criminal behavior', *Social Problems*, 14: 128–47.

Burrows, J (1980) 'Natural surveillance and vandalism to telephone kiosks', in RVG Clarke and P Mayhew (eds) *Designing Out Crime*, London: HMSO.

Burrows, J (1986) *Investigating Burglary: The Measurement of Police Performance*, Home Office Research Study No 88, London: HMSO.

Burt, C (1945) *The Young Delinquent*, London: University of London Press.

Burton, RV, Maccoby, E, and Allinsmith, W (1961) 'Antecedents of resistance to temptation in four-year-old children', *Child Development*, 32: 689.

Calvert, ER (1936) *Capital Punishment in the Twentieth Century*, London: Putnam.

Carlen, P (1985) *Criminal Women: Some Autobiographical Accounts*, Cambridge: Blackwell.

Carson, WG (1980) 'White-collar crime and the institutionalization of ambiguity: the case of the early Factory Acts', in G Geis and E Stotland (eds) *White Collar Crime: Theory and Research*, Beverly Hills: Sage.

Casey, M (1966) 'Sex chromosomal abnormalities in two state hospitals for patients requiring special security', *Nature*, 5 February: 641–3.

Chambliss, W (1975) 'Toward a political economy of crime', *Theory and Society*, 2: 152–3.

Chambliss, WJ and Seidman, RB (1971) *Law, Order and Power*, Reading: Addison-Wesley.

Chatterton, MR (1976) 'Police in social control', in JFS King (ed) *Control Without Custody?* Cambridge: Cambridge Institute of Criminology.

Chesno, FA and Kilmann, PR (1975) 'Effects of stimulation intensity on sociopathic avoidance learning', *Journal of Abnormal Psychology*, 84: 144–50.

Chesshyre, R (1989) *Inside the Force*, London: Sidgwick and Jackson.

Christiansen, KO (1968) 'Threshold of tolerance in various population groups illustrated by results from the Danish criminologic twin study', in AVS de Reuck and R Porter (eds) *The Mentally Abnormal Offender*, Boston: Little, Brown.

Christiansen, KO (1974) 'Seriousness of criminality and concordance among Danish twins', in R Hood (ed) *Crime, Criminology and Public Policy*, New York: Free Press.

Cirel, P, Evans, P, McGillis, D and Whitcomb, D (1977) *Community Crime Prevention Program, Seattle: An Exemplary Project*, Washington, DC: US Government Printing Office.

Clark, JP (1965) 'Isolation of the police:a comparison of British and American situations', *Journal of Criminal Law, Criminology and Police Science*, 56: 307–19.

Clarke, RVG (1980) 'Situational crime prevention: theory and practice', *British Journal of Criminology*, 20: 136–47.

Clarke, RVG (1987) 'Rational choice theory and prison psychology', in BJ McGurk *et al* (eds) *Applying Psychology to Imprisonment: Theory and Practice*, London: HMSO.

Clarke, R and Hope, T (eds) (1984) *Coping with Burglary*, Boston: Kluwer-Nijhoff.

Clarke, RVG and Hough, M (1984) *Crime and Police Effectiveness*, Home Office Research Study No 79, London: HMSO.

Clarke, RVG and Mayhew, P (eds) (1980) *Designing Out Crime*, London: HMSO.

Clarke, RVG and Mayhew, P (1989) 'Crime as opportunity: a note on domestic gas suicide in Britain and the Netherlands', *British Journal of Criminology*, 29: 35–46.

Cleckley, H (1964) *The Mask of Sanity*, St. Louis, Missouri: CV Mosby. (2nd edn published 1976).

Clinard, MB (1952) *The Black Market: A Study of White Collar Crime*, New York: Holt, Rinehart and Winston.

Clinard, MB (1964) 'The theoretical implications of anomie and deviant behaviour', in MB Clinard (ed) *Anomie and Deviant Behaviour*, New York: Free Press.

Clinard, MB (ed) (1964) *Anomie and Deviant Behaviour*, New York: Free Press.

Clinard, MB and Quinney, R (1973) *Criminal Behavior Systems: A Typology*, New York: Holt, Rinehart and Winston.

Clinard, MB and Yeager, PC (1980) *Corporate Crime*, New York: Free Press.

Cloward, RA and Ohlin, LE (1960) *Delinquency and Opportunity: a Theory of Delinquent Gangs*, New York: Free Press.

Cohen, AK (1955) *Delinquent Boys: The Culture of the Gang*, New York: Free Press.

Cohen, AK (1965) 'The sociology of the deviant act: anomie theory and beyond', *American Sociological Review*, 30: 5–14.

Cohen, AK and Short, JF (1958) 'Research on delinquent subcultures', *Journal of Social Issues*, 14: 20–37.

Cohen, LE and Stark, R (1974) 'Discriminatory labelling and the five-finger discount', *Journal of Research into Crime and Delinquency*, 11: 25–39.

Cohen, P (1979) 'Policing the working-class city', in B Fine (ed) *Capitalism and the Rule of Law*, London: Hutchinson.

Cohen, S (ed) (1971) *Images of Deviance*, Harmondsworth: Penguin.

Cohen, S (1980) *Folk Devils and Moral Panics*, Oxford: Martin Robertson.

Cohen, S and Taylor, L (1972) *Psychological Survival*, Harmondsworth: Penguin.

Coleman, CA and Bottomley, AK (1976) 'Police conceptions of crime and "no crime"', *Criminal Law Review*, 344–60.

Conklin, JE (1977) *Illegal But Not Criminal*, New Jersey: Spectrum.

Conklin, JE (1981) *Criminology*, New York: Macmillan.

Cooley, CH (1956) *Social Organisation* and *Human Nature and the Social Order*, published in one volume, Glencoe: Free Press (first published in 1902 by Charles Scribner's Sons)

Cornish, DB and Clarke, RVG (1986) 'Situational prevention, displacement of crime and rational choice theory', in K Heal and G Laycock (eds) *Situational Crime Prevention: From Theory into Practice*, London: HMSO.

Cornish, DB and Clarke, RVG (eds) (1986a) *The Reasoning Criminal: Rational Choice Perspectives on Offending*, New York: Springer-Verlag.

Cornish, DB and Clarke, RVG (1987) 'Understanding crime displacement: an application of rational choice theory', *Criminology*, 25: 901–16.

Cortes, JB and Gatti, FM (1972) *Delinquency and Crime: A Biopsychosocial Approach*, New York: Seminar Press.

Cressey, D and Ward, D (eds) (1969) *Delinquency, Crime and Social Process*, New York: Harper and Row.

Critchley, TA (1978) *A History of the British Police in England and Wales*, London: Constable.

Croft, J (1980) foreword in RVG Clarke and P Mayhew (eds) *Designing Out Crime*, London: HMSO.

Cross, Sir Rupert (1975) *The English Sentencing System*, London: Butterworths.

Crowe, RR (1972) 'The adopted offspring of women criminal offenders', *Archives of General Psychiatry*, 27(5): 600–3.

Cullen, FT, Link, BG and Polanzi, CW (1982) 'The seriousness of crime revisited', *Criminology*, 20: 83–102.

Curtis, LA (1975) *Violence, Race, and Culture*, Lexington, Massachusetts: Heath.

Dalgard, SO and Kringlen, E (1976) 'A Norwegian twin study of criminality', *British Journal of Criminology*, 16: 213–32.

Davidson, RN (1981) *Crime and Environment*, Beckenham: Croom Helm.

Davies, J (1971) *Phrenology, Fad and Science: a 19th Century American Crusade*, Hamden: Archon Books.

Davies, W and Feldman, P (1981) 'The diagnosis of psychopathy by forensic specialists', *British Journal of Psychiatry*, 138: 329–31.

Davis, J (1984) 'A poor man's system of justice', *The Historical Journal*, 27:2.

Davis, NJ (1972) 'Labeling theory in deviance research: a critique and re-consideration', *Sociological Quarterly*, 13: 453.

Davis, NJ (1975) *Sociological Constructions of Deviance*, Dubuque, Iowa: Brown.

Dell, S (1971) *Silent in Court*, London: Bell.

Dentler, RA and Monroe, LJ (1961) 'Social correlates of early adolescent theft', *American Sociological Review*, 26: 733–43.

Dentler, RA, Monroe, LJ, Zamoff, B and Zamoff, R (1966) *Five Scales of Juvenile Misconduct*, Columbia University.

Denzin, NK (1977) 'Notes on the criminological hypothesis: a case study of the American liquor industry', *American Sociological Review*, 42: 905–20.

Ditchfield, JA (1976) *Police Cautioning in England and Wales*, London: HMSO.

Ditchfield, JA (1989) 'Offending on parole', in Home Office Research Bulletin No 26, London: HMSO.

Dixon, D (1984) *Illegal Gambling and Histories of Policing in Britain*, University of Hull, unpublished.

Douglas, JD (1971) *American Social Order: Social Rules in a Pluralistic Society*, New York: Free Press.

Dowie, M (1979) 'The corporate crime of the century', *Mother Jones*, November: 23–49.

Downes, D (1966) *The Delinquent Solution*, London: Routledge and Kegan Paul.

Downes, D (1979) 'Praxis makes perfect: a critique of critical criminology', in D Downes and P Rock (eds) *Deviant Interpretations*, Oxford: Martin Robertson.

Downes, D and Rock, P (1979) *Deviant Interpretations*, Oxford: Martin Robertson.

Driver, ED (1960) 'Charles Buckman Goring', in H Mannheim (ed) *Pioneers in Criminology*, London: Stevens.

Durkheim, E (1951) *Suicide*, New York: Free Press.

Durkheim, E (1965) *The Division of Labor in Society*, New York: The Free Press.

Edelhertz, H (1970) *The Nature, Impact and Prosecution of White-Collar Crime*, US Department of Justice.

Ehrlich, I (1975) 'The deterrent effect of capital punishment: a question of life or death', *American Economic Review*, 65: 397.

Elliott, D and Mayhew, P (1988) 'Trends in residential burglary in England and Wales 1972–1985', in J Mott (ed) *Home Office Research and Planning Unit Bulletin No 25*, London: HMSO.

Erickson, ML and Empey, LM (1963) 'Court records, undetected delinquency and decision-making', *Journal of Criminal Law, Criminology and Police Science*, 54: 456–69.

Erikson, K (1962) 'Notes on the sociology of deviance', *American Journal of Sociology*, 68: 171.

Etzioni, A (1961) *A Comparative Analysis of Complex Organisations*, Glencoe: Free Press.

Eysenck, HJ (1959) *Manual of the Maudsley Personality Inventory*, London: University of London Press.

Eysenck, HJ (1963) 'On the dual nature of extraversion', *British Journal of Social Clinical Psychology*, 2: 46.

Eysenck, HJ (1970) *Crime and Personality*, London: Granada.

Eysenck, HJ (1977) *Crime and Personality*, (3rd edn) London: Routledge and Kegan Paul.

Eysenck, HJ and Eysenck, SBG (1968) 'A factorial study of psychoticism as a dimension of personality', *Multivariate Behavioural Research* (special issue).

Eysenck, HJ and Eysenck, SBG (1970) 'Crime and personality: an empirical study of the three-factor theory', *British Journal of Criminology*, 10: 225.

Eysenck, SBG, Rust, J and Eysenck, HJ (1977) 'Personality and the classification of adult offenders', *British Journal of Criminology*, 17: 169–79.

Farberman, HA (1975) 'A criminogenic market structure: the automobile industry', *Sociological Quarterly*, 16: 438–57.

Farrington, DP and Dowds, EA (1985) 'Disentangling criminal behaviour and police reaction', in DP Farrington and J Gunn (eds) *Reaction to Crime: the Public, the Police, Courts and Prisons*, Chichester: John Wiley and Sons.

Feldman, MP (1977) *Criminal Behaviour: A Psychological Analysis*, Bath: The Pitman Press.

Ferguson, T (1952) *The Young Delinquent in his Social Setting*, Oxford: Oxford University Press.

Ferrero, GL (1911) *Criminal Man According to the Classification of Cesare Lombroso*, New York: Putnam.

Ferri, E (1917) *Criminal Sociology*, Boston: Little, Brown.

Fielding, NG (1988) *Joining Forces: Police Training, Socialization and Occupational Competence*, London: Routledge.

Fielding, NG (1988a) 'Socialization of recruits into the police role', in P Southgate (ed) *New Directions in Police Training*, London: HMSO.

Fitzgerald, M and Sim, J (1982) *British Prisons*, Oxford: Blackwell.

Fitzgerald, M, McLennan, G and Pawson, J (1981) *Crime and Society: Readings in History and Theory*, London: Routledge and Kegan Paul.

Forde, RA (1978) 'Twin studies, inheritance and criminality', *British Journal of Criminology*, 18(1): 71–4.

Forrester, D, Chatterton, M and Pease, K (1988) *The Kirkholt Burglary Prevention Project, Rochdale*, Crime Prevention Unit Paper 13, London: Home Office.

Fowler, FJ, McCalla, ME, and Mangione, TW (1979) *Reducing Residential Crime and Fear: The Hartford Neighborhood Crime Prevention Program*, Washington, DC: US Government Printing Office.

Fowler, FJ and Mangione, TW (1982) *Neighborhood Crime, Fear and Social Control: A Second Look at the Hartford Program*, Washington, DC: US Government Printing Office.

French, P (1979) 'The corporation as a moral person', *American Philosophical Quarterly*, 16: 207–15.

Freud, S (1935) *A General Introduction to Psycho-Analysis*, translated by Joan Riviere, New York: Liveright.

Galbraith, J (1967) *The New Industrial State*, London: Hamish Hamilton.

Gall, FG and Spurzheim, G (1809) *Recherches sur le Systeme Nerveux*.

Garfinkel, H (1956) 'Conditions of successful degradation ceremonies', *American Journal of Sociology*, 6: 420–4.

Garofalo, R (1914) *Criminology*, Boston: Little, Brown.

Garofalo, J (1978) *The Police and Public Opinion: An Analysis of Victimization and Attitude Data From 13 American Cities*, Washington, DC: US Government Printing Office.

Geis, G (1967) 'The heavy electrical equipment antitrust cases of 1961', in MB Clinard and R Quinney (eds) *Criminal Behavior Systems*, New York: Holt, Rinehart and Winston.

Geis, G (1968) *White-Collar Criminal: The Offender in Business and the Professions*, New York: Atherton.

Geis, G and Meier, RF (1977) *White-Collar Crime*, New York: Free Press.

Gelsthorpe, L (1987) 'Gender and justice: current issues in feminism and criminology', paper presented to the British Criminology Conference, July 1987.

Gelsthorpe, L and Giller, H (1990) 'More justice for juveniles: does more mean better?' *Criminal Law Review*, 153–64.

Gibbens, TCN (1963) *Psychiatric Studies of Borstal Lads*, Oxford: Oxford University Press.

Gibbons, DC (1970) *Delinquent Behavior*, Englewood Cliffs: Prentice Hall.

Gibbons, DC and Garrity, DL (1962) 'Definitional analysis of certain criminal types' *Journal of Criminal Law, Criminology and Police Science*, 53: 27–35.

Gibbons, DC (1975) 'Offender typologies-two decades later', *British Journal of Criminology*, 15: 140–56.

Gibbons, DC (1979) *The Criminological Enterprise: Theories and Perspectives*, Englewood Cliffs: Prentice Hall.

Gibbs, JP (1966) 'Conceptions of deviant behaviour: the old and the new', *Pacific Sociological Review*, 9: 9–14.

Gibbs, JP (1975) *Crime, Punishment and Deterrence*, New York: Elsevier.

Gibson, HB (1967) 'Teachers' ratings of schoolboys' behaviour related to patterns of scores on the new Junior Maudsley Inventory', *British Journal of Educational Psychology*, 37: 347.

Glaser, D (1956) 'Criminality theories and behavioral images', *American Journal of Sociology*, 61: 433–44.

Glaser, D (1974) *Handbook of Criminology*, New York: Rand McNally.

Glaser, D (1978) *Crime in Our Changing Society*, New York: Holt, Rinehart and Winston.

Glueck, S and Glueck, E (1950) *Unravelling Juvenile Delinquency*, London: Oxford University Press.

Glueck, S and Glueck, E (1956) *Physique and Delinquency*, New York: Harper.

Goddard, HH (1914) *Feeblemindedness: Its Causes and Consequences*, New York: Macmillan.

Goddard, HH (1928) 'Feeblemindedness: a question of definition', *Journal of Psycho-Asthenics*, 33: 225.

Goffman, E (1961) *Asylums*, New York: Doubleday.

Goffman, E (1963) *Stigma: Notes on the Management of Spoiled Identity*, Englewood Cliffs: Prentice-Hall.

Gold, M (1966) 'Undetected delinquent behaviour', *Journal of Research in Crime and Delinquency*, 3: 27–46.

Gomme, A (1992) 'The management of HIV disease in the correctional setting', *Prison Service Journal*, 87: 54–73.

Gordon, DM (1971) 'Class and the economics of crime', *Review of Radical Political Economics*, 3: 51–75.

Gordon, DM (1973) 'Capitalism, class, and crime in America', *Crime and Delinquency*, 19: 163–86.

Goring, C (1913) *The English Convict: A Statistical Study*, London: HMSO.

Gostin, L and Staunton, M (1985) 'The case for prison standards: conditions of confinement, segregation and medical treatment', in M Maguire, J Vagg and R Morgan (eds) *Accountability and Prisons*, London: Tavistock.

Greenberg, DF (ed) (1981) *Crime and Capitalism: Readings in Marxist Criminology*, Palo Alto: Mayfield.

Greenwood, P (1981) 'The myth of female crime', in A Morris and L Gelsthorpe (eds) *Women and Crime*, Cambridge: Cropwood Conference Series.

Gregory, J (1986) 'Sex, class and crime:towards a non-sexist criminology', in R Matthews and J Young (eds), *Confronting Crime*, London: Sage.

Griffiths, J (1970) 'Ideology in criminal procedure *or* a third 'model' of the criminal process', *Yale Law Journal*, 79: 359.

Griffiths, JAG (1985) *The Politics of the Judiciary*, London: Fontana.

Gross, E (1978) 'Organizational sources of crime: a theoretical perspective', in NK Denzin (ed), *Studies in Symbolic Interaction*, Greenwich: JAI Press.

Grygier, T (1969) 'Parental deprivation: a study of delinquent children', *British Journal of Criminology*, 9: 209.

Guerry, AM (1833) *Essai sur la Statistique Morale de la France*, Paris: Crochard.

Hahn, H (1971) *Police in Urban Society*, Beverly Hills: Sage.

Hall, S, Critcher, C, Jefferson, A, Clarke, J and Roberts, B (1978) *Policing the Crisis: Mugging, the State and Law and Order*, London: Macmillan.

Hall, S and Jefferson, T *Resistance Through Rituals*, London: Hutchinson.

Hall Williams, JE (1982) *Criminology and Criminal Justice*, London: Butterworths.

Halsey, AH (ed) (1972) *Trends in British Society Since 1900*, London: Macmillan.

Hammett, TM (1988) *AIDS in Correctional Facilities: Issues and Options*, (2nd edn) Washington, DC: National Institute of Justice.

Hann, RG (1976) *Deterrence and the Death Penalty: a Critical Review of the Research of Isaac Ehrlich*, Ottawa: Research Division of the Solicitor General of Canada.

Harding, C, Hines, B, Ireland, R and Rawlings, P *Imprisonment in England and Wales, A Concise History*, London: Croom Helm.

Harding, C and Koffman, L (1988) *Sentencing and the Penal System: Text and Materials*, London: Sweet and Maxwell.

Harding, C and Koffman, L (2 edn 1995) *Sentencing and the Penal System: Text and Materials*, London: Sweet and Maxwell.

Hare, DR (1970) *Psychopathy: Theory and Research*, New York: Wiley.

Hare, DR (1980) 'A research scale for the assessment of psychopathy in criminal populations', *Personality and Individual Differences*, 1: 111–19.

Hare, DR and Jutari, JW 'Twenty years of experience with the Cleckley Psychopath', in WH Reid, D Dorr, JI Walker, and JW Bonner (eds), *Unmasking the Psychopath: Antisocial Personality and Related Syndromes*, New York: Norton.

Harris, R (1973) *The Police Academy: an Inside View*, New York: Wiley.

Hassall, C and Trethowan, WM (1972) 'Suicide in Birmingham', *British Medical Journal*, 18th March, 717–18.

Hay, D (1977) 'Property, authority and criminal law', in *Albion's Fatal Tree: Crime and Society in Eighteenth Century England*, London: Allen Lane.

Heal, K and Laycock, G (eds) (1986) *Situational Crime Prevention: From Theory into Practice*, London: HMSO.

Healy, W and Bronner, AF (1936) *New Light on Delinquency and its Treatment*, New Haven: Yale University Press.

Heidensohn, F (1968) 'The deviance of women – a critique and an enquiry', *British Journal of Sociology*, 19: 2.

Heidensohn, F (1987) 'Women and crime-questions for criminology', in P Carlen and A Worrall (eds) *Gender, Crime and Justice*, Milton Keynes: Open University Press.

Heidensohn, F (1989) *Crime and Society*, Basingstoke: Macmillan.

Hillier, B (1973) 'In defence of space', *RIBA Journal*, November, 539–44.

Hindelang, MJ (1979) 'Sex differences in criminality', *Social Problems*, 27: 143–56.

Hindelang, MJ and Weis, JG (1972) 'Personality and self-reported delinquency: an application of cluster analysis', *Criminology*, 10: 268–94.

Hippchen, LJ (1977) 'Contributions of biochemical research to criminological theory', in RF Meier (ed) *Theory in Criminology: Contemporary Views*, London: Sage.

Hirschi, T (1969) *Causes of Delinquency*, Los Angeles: University of California Press.

Hirschi, T and Hindelang, MJ (1977) 'Intelligence and delinquency: a revisionist review', *American Sociological Review*, 42: 572–87.

Hirst, M (1991) 'The way ahead', *Policing*, 7:4.

Hoffman, ML and Saltzstein, HD (1967) 'Parent discipline and the child's moral development', *Journal of Personality and Social Psychology*, 5: 45.

Hoghughi, MS and Forrest, AR (1970) 'Eysenck's theory of criminality: an examination with approved school boys', *British Journal of Criminology*, 10: 240.

Hollin, CR (1989) *Psychology and Crime: An Introduction to Criminological Psychology*, London: Routledge.

Home Office (1959) *Penal Practice in a Changing Society: Aspects of Future Development (England and Wales)*, London: HMSO.

Home Office (1962) *Report of the Departmental Committee on the Probation Service*, London: HMSO.

Home Office (1962a) *Report of the Royal Commission on the Police*, London: HMSO.

Home Office (1965) *The Adult Offender*, London: HMSO.

Home Office (1966) *Report of the Inquiry into Prison Escapes and Security*, London: HMSO. (The Mountbatten Report)

Home Office (1968) *The Regime For Long-Term Prisoners in Conditions of Maximum Security*, Report of the Advisory Council on the Penal System, London: HMSO. (The Radzinowicz Report)

Home Office (1969) *People in Prison*, London: HMSO.

Home Office (1970) *Non-Custodial and Semi-Custodial Penalties*, Report of the Advisory Council on the Penal System, London: HMSO. (The Wootton Report)

Home Office (1975) *Report of the Committee on Mentally Abnormal Offenders*, London: HMSO. (Report of the Butler Committee)

Home Office (1979) *The Sentence of the Court, a Handbook for Courts on the Treatment of Offenders*, London: HMSO.

Home Office (1979a) *Report of the Committee of Inquiry into the United Kingdom Prison Services*, London: HMSO.

Home Office (1981) *Review of Parole in England and Wales*, London: HMSO.

Home Office (1981a) *Royal Commission on Criminal Procedure*, London: HMSO.

Home Office (1983) *An Independent Prosecution Service for England and Wales*, London: HMSO.

Home Office (1984) *Managing the Long-Term Prison System*, Report of the Control Review Committee.

Home Office (1985) *Report of Her Majesty's Chief Inspector of Prisons 1984*, London: HMSO.

Home Office (1986) *Home Office Standing Conference on Crime Prevention: Report of the Working Group on Residential Burglary*, London: Home Office.

Home Office (1986a) *The Sentence of the Court, a Handbook for Courts on the Treatment of Offenders* (4th edn), London: HMSO.

Home Office (1986b) *Racial Attacks and Harassment*, London: HMSO.

Home Office (1987) *Prison Statistics, England and Wales, 1986*. London: HMSO.

Home Office (1988) *Criminal Statistics, England and Wales, 1987*, London: HMSO.

Home Office (1988a) *The Parole System in England and Wales*, Report of the Review Committee, London: HMSO. (The Carlisle Report)

Home Office (1989) *Criminal Statistics, England and Wales, 1988*, London: HMSO.

Home Office (1989a) *Report of Her Majesty's Chief Inspector of Prisons, 1988*, London: HMSO.

Home Office (1989b) *Prison Statistics, England and Wales, 1988*, London: HMSO.

Home Office (1989c) *Report of the Parole Board for 1988*, London: HMSO.

Home Office (1989d) *Statistics of Offences Against Prison Discipline and Punishments England and Wales 1988*, London: HMSO.

Home Office (1989e) *The 1988 British Crime Survey*, London: HMSO.

Home Office (1990) *Crime, Justice and Protecting the Public*, London: HMSO.

Home Office (1990a) News release to accompany *Crime, Justice and Protecting the Public*, London: Home Office.

Home Office (1990b) *Prison Statistics, England and Wales*, 1988, London: HMSO.

Home Office (1991) *Safer Communities: the local delivery of crime prevention through the partnership approach*, London: Home Office.

Home Office (1991a) *Prison Disturbances 1990*, Report of an Inquiry by the Rt Hon Lord Justice Woolf and His Honour Judge Stephen Tumin, Cm. 1456.

Home Office (1991b) *Custody, Care and Justice: the way ahead for the Prison Service in England and Wales*, London: HMSO.

Home Office (1991c) *Report of Her Majesty's Chief Inspector of Prisons, January 1990 to March 1991*, London: HMSO.

Home Office (1991d) *A Digest of Information on the Criminal Justice System*, London: HMSO.

Home Office (1992a) *Report on the Work of the Prison Service, April 1991 to March 1992*, London: HMSO.

Home Office (1993) *Criminal Statistics, England and Wales 1992*, London: HMSO.

Home Office (1993a) *Prison Service Annual Report and Accounts, April 1992–March 1993, Volume 1*, London: HMSO.

Home Office (1993b) *Prison Statistics, England and Wales 1992*, London: HMSO.

Home Office (1993c) *The 1992 British Crime Survey: Home Office Research Study 132*, London: HMSO.

Home Office (1993d) *Report of Her Majesty's Chief Inspector of Constabulary for the Year 1992*, London: HMSO.

Home Office (1994) *Criminal Statistics, England and Wales 1993*, London: HMSO.

Home Office (1994a) *Report of Her Majesty's Chief Inspector of Constabulary for the Year 1993*, London: HMSO.

Home Office Annual Report (1995) (Cm 2808).

Home Office (1996a) Criminal Statistics, England and Wales 1995, London, HMSO.
Home Office (1996b) The 1995 British Crime Survey, London, HMSO.
Hoem Office (1996c) Protecting the Public, London, HMSO.
Home Office (1996d) Prison Statistics, England and Wales 1994, London, HMSO.
Home Office (1996e) Prison Service Annual Report 1994–1995, London, HMSO.
Home Office (1996f) The Prison Population in 1995, London, HMSO.
Home Office (1996g) Her Majesty's Chief Inspector of Constabulary, Annual Report 1994–1995, London, HMSO.
Hood, R (1974) 'Criminology and penal change', in R Hood (ed) *Crime, Criminology and Public Policy*, London: Heinemann.
Hooton, EA (1939) *The American Criminal: An Anthropological Study*, Cambridge, Mass: Harvard University Press.
Hough, M, Clarke, RVG and Mayhew, P (1980), 'Introduction', in RVG Clarke and P Mayhew (eds), *Designing Out Crime*, London: HMSO.
Hough, M and Mayhew, P (1985) *Taking Account of Crime: Key Findings From the Second British Crime Survey*, Home Office Research Study No 85, London: HMSO.
Howarth, E (1986) 'What does Eysenck's psychoticism scale really measure?' *British Journal of Psychology*, 77: 223–7.
Hunter, H (1966) 'YY chromosomes and Klinefelter's syndrome', *The Lancet*, 1: 984.
Husain, S (1988) *Neighbourhood Watch in England and Wales: a Locational Analysis*, Crime Prevention Unit Paper 12, London: Home Office.
Hutchings, B and Mednick, SA (1977) 'Criminality in adoptees and their adoptive and biological parents: a pilot study', in S Mednick and KO Christiansen (eds), *Biosocial Bases of Criminal Behavior*, New York: Gardner Press.

Ignatieff, M (1979) 'Police and people: the birth of Mr Peel's blue locusts', *New Society*, 30 August.

Jacobs, J (1962) *The Death and Life of Great American Cities*, New York: Jonathan Cape.
Jacobs, PA, Brunton, M and Melville, MM (1965) 'Aggressive behaviour, mental subnormality and the XYY male', *Nature*, 208: 1351–2.
Jefferson, T and Grimshaw, R (1984) *Controlling the Constable*, London: Muller.
Jeffery, CR (1971) *Crime Prevention Through Environmental Design*, Beverly Hills: Sage.
Jephcott, P and Carter, MP (1954) 'The social background of delinquency', an unpublished manuscript of the University of Nottingham, cited in T Morris, *The Criminal Area: a Study in Social Ecology*, London: Routledge and Kegan Paul.
Joint Consultative Committee of the Police Staff Associations of England and Wales (1990) *Operational Policing Review*, Surbiton, Joint Consultative Committee.
Jones, D (1976) *The Health Risks of Imprisonment*, Lexington: Lexington Books.
Jones, H (1958) 'Approaches to an ecological study', *British Journal of Delinquency*, 8: 277–93.
Justice (1970) *The Prosecution Process in England and Wales*, London: Justice Educational Research Trust.
Jutari, JW and Hare, RD (1983) 'Psychopathy and selective attention during performance of a complex perceptual-motor task', *Psychophysiology*, 20: 146–51.

Kelling, G, Pate, T, Dieckman, D and Brown, C (1974) *The Kansas City Preventive Patrol Experiment*, Washington, DC: Police Foundation.
King, M (1981)*The Framework of Criminal Justice*, London: Croom Helm.
King, R and Morgan, R (1980) *The Future of the Prison System*, Farnborough: Gower.
Kitsuse, JI (1962) 'Societal reaction to deviant behavior: problems of theory and method', *Social Problems*, 9: 247–56.
Kitsuse, JI and Dietrick, DC (1959) 'Delinquent boys: a critique', *American Sociological Review*, 24: 208–15.
Kitsuse, JI and Cicourel, AV (1963) 'A note on the uses of official statistics', *Social Problems*, 11: 131.

Kramer, RC (1984) 'Corporate criminality: the development of an idea', in E Hochstedler, *Corporations as Criminals*, Beverly Hills: Sage.

Kranz, H (1936) *Lebenschicksale Krimineller Zwillinge*, Berlin: Springer-Verlag.

Kress, J (1979) 'Bourgeois morality and the administration of criminal justice', *Crime and Social Justice*, 12: 44–50.

Kretschmer, E (1921) *Korperbau und Charakter*, Berlin: Springer, English translation as *Physique and Character*, by WJH Sprott (1964), New York: Cooper Square.

Lander, B (1954) *Towards an Understanding of Juvenile Delinquency*, New York: Columbia University Press.

Lange, J (1930) *Crime as Destiny*, London: Allen and Unwin.

Lawrence, G (1989) *A Handbook of Preventive Policing Skills*, Stafford: Home Office Crime Prevention Centre (limited circulation).

Laycock, G (1985) *Property Marking: a Deterrent to Domestic Burglary?* Crime Prevention Unit 3, London: Home Office.

Lea, J and Young, J (1984) *What Is To Be Done About Law and Order?* Harmondsworth: Penguin.

Lee, B (1983) 'On standing up and being counted', *The Lancet*, 4 June: 268.

Lemert, E (1964) 'Social structure, social control, and deviation' in MB Clinard (ed) *Anomie and Deviant Behaviour*, New York: Free Press.

Lemert, E (1967) *Human Deviance, Social Problems and Social Control*, Englewood Cliffs: Prentice Hall.

Lemert, E (1976) 'Response to critics: feedback and choice' in LA Coser and ON Larsen (eds), *The Uses of Controversy in Sociology*, New York: Free Press.

Leonard, EB (1982) *Women, Crime and Society*, New York: Longman.

Liazos, A (1972) 'The poverty of the sociology of deviance: nuts, sluts and "preverts" ', *Social Problems* 20: 103–20.

Lindesmith, AR and Levin, Y (1937) 'The Lombrosian myth in criminology', *American Journal of Sociology*, 42: 653–71.

Little, A (1963) 'Professor Eysenck's theory of crime: an empirical test on adolescent offenders', *British Journal of Criminology*, 4: 152.

Little, A (1965) 'Parental deprivation, separation and crime: a test on adolescent recidivists', *British Journal of Criminology*, 5: 419.

Lloyd, C, Mair, G and Hough, M (1994) *Explaining Reconviction Rates: a Critical Analysis*, Home Office Research Study No 136, London: HMSO.

Lombroso, C (1876) *L'uomo delinquente* (*The Criminal Man*), Milan: Hoepli.

Lombroso, C and Ferri, E (1895) *The Female offender*, London: Fisher Unwin.

Longford, Earl (1964) *Crime – A Challenge To Us All*, London: Transport House.

Lykken, DT (1955) 'A study of anxiety in the sociopathic personality', Doctoral dissertation, University of Minnesota, cited in MP Feldman, *Criminal Behaviour: a Psychological Analysis*, Bath: The Pitman Press.

Macdonald, I (1973) 'The creation of the British police', *Race Today*, Vol 5.

McBarnet, D (1981) *Conviction: Law, the State and the Construction of Justice*, London: Macmillan.

McConville, M and Bridges (1994) *Criminal Justice in Crisis: Law in a Social Setting*, Cheltenham: Elgar Publications.

McCord, W, McCord, J and Zola, IK (1959) *Origins of Crime: A New Evaluation of the Cambridge-Somerville Youth Study*, New York: Columbia University Press.

McCord, W and McCord, J (1964) *The Psychopath: An Essay on the Criminal Mind*, New York: Van Nostrand Reinhold.

McDonald, L (1982) 'Theory and evidence of rising crime in the nineteenth century', *British Journal of Sociology*, 33: 404–20.

McEwan, AW (1983) 'Eysenck's theory of criminality and the personality types and offences of young delinquents', *Personality and Individual Differences*, 4: 201–4.

McEwan, AW and Knowles, C (1984) 'Delinquent personality types and the situational contexts of their crimes', *Personality and Individual Differences*, 5: 339–44.

McGurk, BJ and McDougall, C (1981) 'A new approach to Eysenck's theory of criminality', *Personality and Individual Differences*, 2: 338–40.

Maguire, M, Vagg, J and Morgan, R (eds) (1985) *Accountability and Prisons*, London: Tavistock.

Mankoff, M (1971) 'Societal reaction and career deviance: a critical analysis', *Sociological Quarterly*, 12 : 204–18.

Mannheim, H (1948) *Juvenile delinquency in an English Middletown*, London: Kegan Paul, Turner, Trubner and Co Ltd.

Mannheim, H (1955) *Group Problems in Crime and Punishment*, London: Routledge and Kegan Paul.

Mannheim, H (1960) *Pioneers in Criminology*, London: Stevens.

Mannheim, H (1965) *Comparative Criminology*, Vol 1, London: Routledge and Kegan Paul.

Mannheim, H and Wilkins, LT (1955) *Prediction Methods in Relation to Borstal Training*, London: HMSO.

Manning, PK (1979) The social control of police work', in S Holdaway (ed), *The British Police*, London: Edward Arnold.

Manning, PK (1980) *The Narcs Game*, Boston: MIT.

Mark, R (1977) *Policing a Perplexed Society*, London: George Allen and Unwin.

Marshall, G (1965) *Police and Government*, London: Methuen.

Marshall, G (1973) 'The government of the police since 1964', in JC Anderson and PJ Stead (eds) *The Police We Deserve*, London: Wolfe.

Marshall, T and Walpole, M (1985) *Bringing People Together: Mediation and Reparation Projects in Great Britain*, Research and Planning Unit Paper No 33, London: HMSO.

Martin, JP and Webster, D (1971) *The Social Consequences of Conviction*, London: Heinemann.

Martinson, R (1974) 'What works? – questions and answers about prison reform', *The Public Interest*, 35: 22–54.

Marx, K (1904) *Contribution to a Critique of Political Economy*, Chicago: Charles H Kerr.

Marx, K and Engels, F (1965) *The German Ideology*, London: Lawrence and Wishart.

Marx, K and Engels, F (1969) *Selected Works*, (Vol 3) Moscow: Progress Publishers.

Matthews, R and Young, J (1986) *Confronting Crime*, London: Sage.

Matza, DM (1964) *Delinquency and Drift*, New York: Wiley.

Matza, DM (1969) *Becoming Deviant*, Englewood Cliffs: Prentice-Hall.

Mawby, I (1977) 'Defensible space: a theoretical and empirical appraisal', *Urban Studies*, 14: 169–79.

Mawby, RI (1977a) 'Kiosk vandalism: a Sheffield Study', *British Journal of Criminology*, 17: 30–46.

Mawby, RI (1979) *Policing the City*, Farnborough: Saxon House.

Mayhew, H (1968) *London Labour and the London Poor, Vol IV: Those That Will Not Work, Comprising Prostitutes, Thieves, Swindlers and Beggars*, New York: Dover Publications.

Mayhew, P (1979) 'Defensible space: the current status of a crime prevention theory', *Howard Journal* 18: 150–9.

Mayhew, P (1981) 'Crime in public view: surveillance and crime prevention', in PJ Brantingham and PL Brantingham (eds) *Environmental Criminology*, Beverly Hills: Sage.

Mayhew, P (1984) 'Target-hardening: how much of an answer?' in R Clarke and T Hope (eds) *Coping with Burglary*, Boston: Kluwer-Nijhoff.

Mayhew, P, Clarke, RVG, Sturman, A and Hough, JM (1976) *Crime as Opportunity*, Home Office Research Study No 34, London: HMSO.

Mayhew, P, Clarke, RVG and Hough, JM (1980) 'Steering column locks and car theft', in RVG Clarke and P Mayhew (eds) *Designing Out Crime*, London: HMSO.

Mead, GH (1918) 'The psychology of punitive justice', *American Journal of Sociology*, 23: 577–602.

Meier, RF (1977) *Theory in Criminology: Contemporary Views*, London: Sage.

Mercer, J (1972) 'IQ: the lethal label', *Psychology Today*, September: 44.

Merton, RK (1938) 'Social structure and anomie', *American Sociological Review*, 3: 672–82.

Merton, RK (1956) 'The social-cultural environment and anomie', in HL Witmer and R Kotinsky (eds) *New Perspectives for Research on Juvenile Delinquency*, Washington, DC: US Department of Health, Education and Welfare.

Merton, RK (1968) *Social Theory and Social Structure*, Glencoe: Free Press.

Michael, J and Adler, M (1933) *Crime, Law and Social Science*, London: Kegan Paul.

Michalowski, RJ and Bohlander, EW (1976) 'Repression and criminal justice in capitalist America', *Sociological Inquiry*, 46(2): 99.

Miller, WB (1958) 'Lower class culture as a generating milieu of gang delinquency', *Journal of Social Issues*, 14: 5, reprinted in ME Wolfgang, L Savitz and N Johnston (eds) (1970) *The Sociology of Crime and Delinquency*, New York: John Wiley and Sons.

Miller, WR (1977) *Cops and Bobbies: Police Authority in New York and London, 1830–1870*, Chicago: University of Chicago Press.

Molitch, M (1937) 'Endocrine disturbance in behavior problems', *American Journal of Psychiatry*, March: 1179.

Morgan, D (1981) 'Men, masculinity and the process of sociological enquiry', in H Roberts (ed) *Doing Feminist Research*, London: Routledge and Kegan Paul.

Morgan, P (1975) *Child Care: Sense and Fable*, London: Temple Smith.

Morgan, R (1985) 'Police accountability: current developments and future prospects', paper presented to the Police Foundation Conference, Harrogate, 1985.

Morris, N (1974) *The Future of Imprisonment*, Chicago: University of Chicago Press.

Morris, P and Beverly, F (1975) *On Licence: a Study of Parole*, London: John Wiley and Sons.

Morris, T (1957) *The Criminal Area: A Study in Social Ecology*, London: Routledge and Kegan Paul.

Morris, T and Blom-Cooper, L (1979) *Murder in England and Wales Since 1957*, The Observer.

Mungham, G and Pearson, G (eds) (1976) *Working Class Youth Culture*, London: Routledge and Kegan Paul.

Naess, S (1959) 'Mother-child separation and delinquency', *British Journal of Delinquency*, 10: 22.

Naess, S (1962) 'Mother-child separation and delinquency: further evidence', *British Journal of Criminology*, 2: 361.

National Crime Prevention Institute (1986) *Understanding Crime Prevention*, Boston: Butterworths.

Nee, C and Taylor, M (1988) 'Residential burglary in the Republic of Ireland', *Howard Journal*, 27: 105–16.

Newing, J (1992) 'Police accountability', *Policing*, 8: 262–78.

Newman, DJ (1957) 'Public attitudes toward a form of white-collar crime', *Social Problems*, 4: 228–32.

Newman, DJ (1958) 'White collar crime: an overview and analysis', *Law and Contemporary Problems*, 23: 735–53.

Newman, DJ (1966) *Conviction*, Boston: Little, Brown.

Newman, O (1972) *Defensible Space: Crime Prevention Through Urban Design*, New York: Macmillan.

Newman, O (1976) *Defensible Space: People and Design in the Violent City*, London: The Architectural Press.

Newman, O (1980) *Community of Interest*, New York: Anchor Press.

Nielsen, J (1968) 'XYY syndrome in a mental hospital', *British Journal of Criminology*, 8: 186–202.

Northam, G (1988) *Shooting in the Dark: Riot Police in Britain*, London: Faber and Faber.

Nuttall, CP, with Bernard, EE, Fowles, AJ, Frost, A, Hammond, WH, Mayhew, P, Pease, K, Tarling, R, and Weatheritt, MJ (1977) *Parole in England and Wales*, Home Office Research Study No 38, London: HMSO.

Nye, FI (1958) *Family Relationships and Delinquent Behavior*, New York: Wiley.

Oatham, E and Simon, F (1972) 'Are suspended sentences working?' *New Society*, 3 August: 233.

Packer, HL (1969) *The Limits of the Criminal Sanction*, Stanford: Stanford University Press.

Palmer, T (1975) 'Martinson revisited', *Journal of Research in Crime and Delinquency*, 12(2): 133–52.

Park, RE Burgess, EW and McKenzie, RD (1925) *The City*, Chicago: University of Chicago Press.

Park, RE (1952) *Human Communities*, Glencoe: The Free Press.

Parker, H (1974) *View From the Boys*, Newton Abbot: David and Charles.

Parsons, T (1951) *The Social System*, New York: Free Press.

Pauling, L (1968) 'Orthomolecular psychiatry', *Science*, 160: 265–71.

Pearson, G (1976) '"Paki-bashing" in a north east Lancashire cotton town: a case study and its history', in G Mungham and G Pearson (eds) *Working Class Youth Culture*, London: Routledge and Kegan Paul.

Pearson, G (1976a) 'In defence of hooliganism: social theory and violence', in N Tutt (ed) *Violence*, London: HMSO.

Pease, K (1981) *Community Service Orders – A First Decade of Promise*, London: Howard League.

Platt, T (1974) 'Prospects for a radical criminology in the United States', *Crime and Social Justice*, 1: 2–10.

Plint, T (1851) *Crime in England*, London: Charles Gilpin.

Plummer, K (1979) 'Misunderstanding labelling perspectives', in D Downes and P Rock (eds) *Deviant Interpretations*, Oxford: Martin Robertson.

Pollak, O (1950) *The Criminality of Women*, Connecticut: Greenwood.

Pollak, O (1961) *The Criminality of Women*, New York: AS Barnes.

Pope, CE (1977) *Crime-Specific Analysis: The Characteristics of Burglary Incidents*, Washington, DC: US Department of Justice.

Porterfield, A (1946) *Youth in Trouble*, Austin, Texas: Lee Potishman Foundation.

Poyner, B (1983) *Design Against Crime: Beyond Defensible Space*, London: Butterworths.

President's Commission on Law Enforcement and Administration of Justice (1967) *Task Force Report: Crime and its Impact – An Assessment*, Washington, DC: US Government Printing Office.

Price, WH and Whatmore, PB, 'Behaviour disorders and pattern of crime among XYY males identified at a maximum security hospital', *British Medical Journal* 1: 533.

Prins, H (1982) *Criminal Behaviour: An Introduction to Criminology and The Penal System*, London: Tavistock.

Pryce, K (1979) *Endless Pressure: a Study of West Indian Life-styles in Bristol*, Harmondsworth: Penguin.

Punch, M (1979) 'The secret social service', in S Holdaway (ed) *The British Police*, London: Edward Arnold.

Punch, M and Naylor, T (1973) 'The police-a social service', *New Society*, 24: 358–61.

Quay, HC (1965) 'Personality and delinquency', in HC Quay (ed) *Juvenile Delinquency*, Princeton: Van Nostrand.

Quetelet, MA (1842) *A Treatise on Man*, Edinburgh: William and Robert Chambers.

Quinney, R (1970) *The Social Reality of Crime*, Boston: Little, Brown.

Quinney, R (1974) *Critique of Legal Order*, Boston: Little, Brown.

Quinney, R (ed) (1974a) *Criminal Justice in America*, Boston: Little, Brown.

Quinney, R (1975) *Criminology*, Boston: Little, Brown.

Quinney, R (1977) *Class, State and Crime*, London: Longman.

Quinney, R and Wildeman, J (1977) *The Problem of Crime: A Critical Introduction to Criminology*, New York: Harper and Row.

Radzinowicz, L (1966) *Ideology and Crime: A Study of Crime in its Social and Historical Context*, London: Heinemann.

Radzinowicz, L and Hood, R (1986) *A History of English Criminal Law, Volume 5: The Emergence of Penal Policy*, London: Stevens.

Radzinowicz, L and King, JFS (1979) *The Growth of Crime*, London: Penguin.

Redl, F and Wineman, D (1951) *Children Who Hate*, New York: Free Press.

Regan, DE (1983) *Are The Police Under Control?* A Social Affairs Research Paper.

Reiner, R (1978) 'The police, class and politics', *Marxism Today*, March.

Reiner, R (1985) *The Politics of the Police*, Brighton: Wheatsheaf Books.

Reiser, M and Klyver, N (1982) *Needed: A Modern Police Training Model*, Los Angeles Police Department.

Reiss, AJ 'Delinquency as the failure of personal and social controls', *American Sociological Review*, 16: 196–207.

Reith, C (1948) *A Short History of the Police*, Oxford: Oxford University Press.

Reith, C (1952) *The Blind Eye of History*, London: Faber.

Reith, C (1956) *A New Study of Police History*, London: Oliver and Boyd.

Reppetto, TA (1974) *Residential Crime*, Cambridge, Massachusetts: Ballinger.

Reppetto, TA (1976) 'Crime prevention and the displacement phenomenon', *Crime and Delinquency*, 22: 166–77.

Reynolds, S *et al* (1911) *Seems So!*, London: Macmillan.

Rhodes, WM and Conly, C (1981) 'Crime and mobility: an empirical study', in PJ Brantingham and PL Brantingham (eds) *Environmental Criminology*, Beverly Hills: Sage.

Roberts, R (1971) *The Classic Slum*, Manchester: Manchester University Press.

Robins, D and Cohen, P (1978) *Knuckle Sandwich: Growing Up in the Working Class City*, Harmondsworth: Penguin.

Robins, LN (1966) *Deviant Children Grown Up*, Baltimore: Williams and Wilkins.

Robison, SM (1936) *Can Delinquency Be Measured??* New York: Columbia University Press.

Rock, P (1979) 'The sociology of crime, symbolic interactionism and some problematic qualities of radical criminology', in D Downes and P Rock (eds) *Deviant Interpretations*, Oxford: Martin Robertson.

Romig, D (1978) *Justice For Our Children: An Examination of Juvenile Delinquent Rehabilitation Programs*, Lexington: DC Heath.

Rose, D (1996) *In the Name of the Law*, London: Jonathan Cape.

Rosenbaum, DP (1986) *Community Crime Prevention: Does It Work?* Beverly Hills: Sage.

'Runciman Report' (1993) *Report of Royal Commission on Criminal Justice* Cm 2263 (HMSO).

Rutter, M (1981) *Maternal Deprivation Reassessed*, Harmondsworth: Penguin.

Rutter, M and Giller, H (1983) *Juvenile Delinquency: Trends and Perspectives*, Harmondsworth: Penguin.

Sanders, WB (1977) *Detective Work: A Study of Criminal Investigations*, New York: Free Press.

Sapsford, RJ (1978) 'Life sentence prisoners: psychological changes during sentence', *British Journal of Criminology*, 18: 128.

Sarbin, T and Miller, J (1970) 'Demonism revisited: the XYY chromosomal anomaly', *Issues in Criminology*, 5: 195–207.

Savitz, L, Turner, SH and Dickman, T (1977) 'The origin of scientific criminology: Franz Joseph Gall as the first criminologist', in RF Meier, *Theory in Criminology: Contemporary Views*.

Scarman, LG (1981) *The Scarman Report: the Brixton Disorders*, Harmondsworth: Penguin.

Scarr, HA (1973) *Patterns of Burglary*, Washington, DC: US Government Printing Office.

Schauss, A (1981) *Diet, Crime and Delinquency*, Berkeley, California: Parker House.

Schmauk, FJ (1970) 'Punishment, arousal, and avoidance learning in sociopaths', *Journal of Abnormal Psychology*, 76: 325–35.

Schrager, LS and Short, JF (1978) 'Toward a sociology of organizational crime', *Social Problems*, 25: 407–19.

Schrager, LS and Short, JF (1980) 'How serious a crime? Perceptions of organizational and common crimes', in G Geis and E Stotland (eds), *White Collar Crime: Theory and Research*, New York: Sage.

Schur, EM (1969) 'Reactions to deviance: a critical assessment', *American Journal of Sociology*, 75: 318.

Schur, EM (1971) *Labeling Deviant Behavior*, New York: Harper and Row.

Schwartz, RD and Skolnick, JH (1962) 'Two studies of legal stigma', *Social Problems*, 10: 132.

Schwendinger, H and Schwendinger, J (1970) 'Defenders of order or guardians of human rights', *Issues in Criminology*, 7: 72–81, also in I Taylor, P Walton and J Young (eds) (1975) *Critical Criminology*, London: Routledge and Kegan Paul.

Schwendinger, H and Schwendinger, J (1973) *Sociologists of the Chair*, New York: Basic Books.

Schwendinger, H and Schwendinger, J (1977) 'Social class and the definition of crime', *Crime and Social Justice*, 7: 4–13.

Schwitzgebel, RK (1974) 'The right to effective treatment', *California Law Review*, 62: 936–956.

Scott, JE and Al-Thakeb, F (1977) 'The public's perceptions of crime: a co-operative analysis of Scandinavia, Western Europe, the Middle East and the United States', in CR Huff (ed), *Contemporary Corrections: Social Control and Conflict*, Beverly Hills: Sage.

Scraton, P (1985) *The State of the Police*, London: Pluto Press.

Scura, WC and Eisenman, R (1971) 'Punishment learning in psychopaths with social and nonsocial reinforcers', *Corrective Psychiatry and Journal of Social Therapy*, 17: 58.

Sellin, T (1938) *Culture Conflict and Crime*, New York: Social Science Research Council.

Sellin, T (1950) *General Report on the Sociological Aspects of Criminology*, paper submitted to the Second International Congress on Criminology, Paris, 1950.

Sellin, T and Wolfgang, ME (1964) *The Measurement of Delinquency*, New York: Wiley.

Shah, SA and Roth, LH (1974) 'Biological and psychophysiological factors in criminality', in D Glaser (ed) *Handbook of Criminology*, New York: Rand McNally.

Shaw, B (1922) Preface in S Webb and B Webb, *English Prisons Under Local Government* (printed privately).

Shaw, CR (1929) *Delinquency Areas: A Study of the Geographic Distribution of School Truants, Juvenile Delinquents and Adult Offenders in Chicago*, Chicago: University of Chicago Press.

Shaw, CR (1931) *The Natural History of a Delinquent Career*, Chicago: University of Chicago Press.

Shaw, CR and McKay, HD (1969) *Juvenile Delinquency and Urban Areas*, Chicago: University of Chicago Press.

Shaw, M and Williamson, W (1972) 'Public attitudes to the police', *The Criminologist*, Autumn.

Sheldon, WH (1940) *Varieties of Human Physique*, London: Harper.

Sheldon, WH (1949) *Varieties of Delinquent Youth*, London: Harper.

Sheldon, WH (1954) *Atlas of Man*, London: Harper.

Short, JF and Strodtbeck, FL (1965) *Group Process and Gang Delinquency*, Chicago: University of Chicago Press.

Silverman, M (1977) 'The epidemiology of drug promotion', *International Journal of Health Services*, 7: 157–66.

Simey, M (1985) *Government by Consent: the Principle and Practice of Accountability*, London: Bedford Square Press.

Simon, FH (1971) *Prediction Methods in Criminology*, Home Office Research Study No 7, *London*: HMSO.

Simon, RJ (1975) *The Contemporary Woman and Crime*, Washington, DC: US Government Printing Office.

Simons, RL (1978) 'The meaning of the IQ delinquency relationship', *American Sociological Review*, 43: 268–70.

Sinden, PG (1980) 'Perceptions of crime in capitalistic America: the question of consciousness manipulation', *Sociological Focus*, 13: 75–85.

Skogan, WG (ed) (1976) *Sample Surveys of the Victims of Crime*, Cambridge, Massachusetts: Ballinger

Skolnick, J (1966) *Justice Without Trial*, New York: Wiley.

Slapper, G (1996) 'Criminal Statistics and White Lies', *New Law Journal*, 19 April: 570.

Smart, C (1976) *Women, Crime and Criminology*, London: Routledge.

Smart, C (1981) 'Response to Greenwood', in A Morris and L Gelsthorpe (eds) *Women and Crime*, Cambridge: Cropwood Conference Series.

Smith, D (1988) 'Crime prevention and the causes of crime', *Social Studies Review*, 3: 196–9.

Smith, DA and Visher, AC (1980) 'Sex and involvement in crime: a quantitative review of the empirical literature', *American Sociological Review*, 45, 691–701.

Smith, DE and Smith, DD (1977) 'Eysenck's psychoticism scale and reconviction', *British Journal of Criminology*, 17: 387.

Smith, DJ and Gray, J (1985) *Police and People in London*, (The PSI Report), Aldershot: Gower.

Soothill, K (1972) 'The suspended sentence for ex-prisoners', *Criminal Law Review*: 535.

Soothill, K (1981) 'The suspended sentence for ex-prisoners revisited', *Criminal Law Review*: 821.

Sparks, R (1971) 'The use of the suspended sentence', *Criminal Law Review*: 384.

Sparks, RF, Genn, H and Dodd, DJ (1977) *Surveying Victims*, London: Wiley.

Spitzer, S (1975) 'Toward a Marxian theory of deviance', *Social Problems*, 22: 638–51.

Stanley, L and Wise, S (1983) *Breaking Out, Feminist Consciousness and Feminist Research*, London: Routledge and Kegan Paul.

Staw, BM and Szwajkowski, E (1975) 'The scarcity-munificence component of organizational environments and the commission of illegal acts', *Administrative Science Quarterly*, 20: 345–54.

Steadman, HJ (1972) 'The psychiatrist as a conservative agent of social control', *Social Problems*, 20(2): 263–71.

Steer, D (1970) *Police Cautions, a Study in The Exercise of Police Discretion*, Oxford: Blackwell.

Stern, V (1986) *Bricks of Shame: Britain's Prisons*, Harmondsworth: Penguin.

Storch, RD (1976) 'The policeman as domestic missionary: urban discipline and popular culture in Northern England 1850–1880', *Journal of Social History*, Summer.

Stumpfl, F (1936) *Die Ursprunge des Verbrechens om Lebenshauf Von Zwillingen*, Leipzig: Verlag.

Sturman, A (1980) 'Damage on buses: the effects of supervision', in RVG Clarke and P Mayhew (eds) *Designing Out Crime*, London: HMSO.

Sullivan, RF (1973) 'The economics of crime: an introduction to the literature', *Crime and Delinquency*, 19: 138–49.

Sutherland, E (1940) 'White-collar criminality', *American Sociological Review*, 5: 1–12.

Sutherland, E (1945) 'Is "white-collar crime" crime? *American Sociological Review*, 10: 132–9.

Sutherland, E (1949) *White Collar Crime*, New York: Dryden Press.

Sutherland, EW and Cressey, DR (1955, 1960, 1978) *Criminology*, Philadelphia: Lippincott. (various editions referred to–the latest is the 10th, published in 1978).

Swartz, J (1975) 'Silent killers at work', *Crime and Social Justice*, 3: 15–20, also in MD Ermann and RJ Lundman (eds) (1978) *Corporate and Governmental Deviance*, Oxford: Oxford University Press.

Sykes, GM and Matza, D (1957) 'Techniques of neutralization: a theory of delinquency, *American Sociological Review*, 22: 664–70.

Syndulko, K (1978) 'Electrocortical investigations of sociopathy', in RD Hare and D Schalling (eds) *Psychopathic Behaviour: Approaches to Research*, Chichester: Wiley.

Taft, DR and England, RW (1964) *Criminology*, New York: Macmillan.

Tappan, PW (1947) 'Who is the criminal?' *American Sociological Review*, 12: 96–102.

Tappan, PW (1949) *Juvenile Delinquency*, New York: McGraw Hill.

Tappan, PW (1960) *Crime, Justice and Correction*, New York: McGraw Hill.

Taylor, I (1971) 'Football mad: a speculative sociology of soccer hooliganism', in E Dunning (ed) *The Sociology of Sport*, London: Frank Cass and Company Limited.

Taylor, I (1976) 'Spectator violence around football: the rise and fall of the "Working Class Weekend" ', *Research Papers in Education*, 3(2): 4–9.

Taylor, I, Walton, P and Young, J (1973) *The New Criminology*, London: Routledge and Kegan Paul.

Taylor, I, Walton, P and Young, J (eds) (1975) *Critical Criminology*, London: Routledge and Kegan Paul.

Tennent, G and Gath, D (1975) 'Bright delinquents', *British Journal of Criminology*, 15: 386.

Thomas, D (1982) 'Out of court', The *Guardian*, 8 March.

Thomas, WI and Znaniecki, F (1927) *The Polish Peasant in Europe and America*, New York: Alfred A Knopf

Thrasher, F (1947) *The Gang*, Chicago: University of Chicago Press.

Titus, R (1984) 'Residential burglary and the community response', in R Clarke and T Hope (eds) *Coping With Burglary*, Boston: Kluwer-Nijhoff.

Toby, J (1957) 'Social disorganization and stake in conformity: complementary factors in the predatory behavior of hoodlums', *Journal of Criminal Law, Criminology and Police Science*, 48: 12–17.

Toby, J (1961) 'Delinquency and opportunity', *British Journal of Sociology*, 12(3): 282–9.

Toby, J (1969) 'Affluence and adolescent crime', in DR Cressey and DA Ward (eds) *Delinquency, Crime and Social Process*, New York: Harper and Row.

Trace, M (1990) 'HIV and drugs in British prisons', *Druglink*, January/February: 12–15.

Trasler, G (1962, 1967) *The Explanation of Criminality*, London: Routledge and Kegan Paul.

Trasler, G (1986) 'Situational crime control and rational choice: a critique', in K Heal and G Laycock (eds) *Situational Crime Prevention: From Theory into Practice*, London: HMSO.

Turk, AT (1969) *Criminality and Legal Order*, Chicago: Rand McNally.

Uglow, S (1995) Criminal Justice, London, Sweet and Maxwell.

Vold, GB (1958) *Theoretical Criminology*, New York: Oxford University Press.
Vold, GB and Bernard, TJ (1986) *Theoretical Criminology*, (3rd edn), New York: Oxford University Press.

Waldo, GP and Chiricos, TG (1972) 'Perceived penal sanction and self-reported criminality; a neglected approach to deterrence research', *Social Problems*, 19: 522–40.
Walker, N (1971) *Crimes, Courts and Figures: an Introduction to Criminal Statistics*, Harmondsworth: Penguin.
Walker, N (1980) *Punishment, Danger and Stigma: the Morality of Criminal Justice*, Oxford: Basil Blackwell.
Walker, N (1985) *Sentencing: Theory, Law and Practice*, London: Butterworths.
Waller, I and Okihiro, N (1978) *Burglary: The Victim and the Public*, Toronto: University of Toronto Press.
Wallis, CP and Maliphant, R (1967) 'Delinquency areas in the county of London', *British Journal of Criminology*, 7: 250–84.
Ward, C (ed) *Vandalism*, London: The Architectural Press.
Waudhuber, RM (1979) 'Police discretionary authority: a model for police training', *The Police Chief*, October: 91–2.
Weinberger, B (1987) 'Police Perceptions of Labour', in F Snyder and D Hay (eds) *Labour, Law and Crime*, London: Tavistock.
West, DJ (1969) *Present Conduct and Future Delinquency*, London: Heinemann.
West, DJ and Farrington, DP (1973) *Who Becomes Delinquent?* London: Heinemann.
West, DJ and Farrington, DP (1977) *The Delinquent Way of Life*, London: Heinemann.
Westwood, D (1990) 'Adult cautioning', *Policing*, 6: 383–98.
Wheeler, S (1967) 'Criminal statistics: a reformulation of the problem', *Journal of Criminal Law, Criminology and Police Science*, 58(3): 317–24.
Wheeler, S (1976) 'Trends and problems in the sociological study of crime', *Social Problems*, 23: 525–33.
Whitaker, B (1979) *The Police in Society*, London: Eyre Methuen.
White, J (1983) 'Police and people in London in the 1930's', 11 Oral Histories.
Whyte, WF (1943) *Street Corner Society: the Social Structure of the Italian Slum*, Chicago: University of Chicago Press.
Wilkins, LT (1964) *Social Deviance: Social Policy, Action and Research*, London: Tavistock.
Wilkins, LT (1965) 'New thinking in criminal statistics', *Journal of Criminal law, Criminology and Police Science*, 56: 277.
Wilkinson, P (1977) *Terrorism and the Liberal State*, London: Macmillan.
Wilkinson, C and Evans, R (1990) 'Police cautioning of juveniles: the impact of Home Office Circular 14/1985', *Criminal Law Review*, 165–76.
Willis, A (1977) 'Community service as an alternative to imprisonment', *Probation Journal*, 24: 120–2.
Wilson, JQ (1975) *Thinking About Crime*, New York: Basic Books.
Wilson, S (1980) 'Vandalism and "defensible space" on London housing estates', in RVG Clarke and P Mayhew (eds) *Designing Out Crime*, London: HMSO.
Winchester, S and Jackson, H (1982) *Residential Burglary: The Limits of Prevention*, Home Office Research Study No 74, London: HMSO.
Witkin, HA (1977) 'XYY and XXY men: criminality and aggression', in S Mednick and KO Christiansen (eds) *Biosocial Bases of Criminal Behavior*, New York: Gardner Press.
Wolfgang, ME, Figlio, RM and Thornberry, T (1975) *Criminology Index 1945–1972*, New York: Elsevier.
Wolfgang, ME and Ferracuti, F (1981) *The Subculture of Violence*, Beverly Hills: Sage.
Woodward, M (1955) *Low Intelligence and Delinquency*, Institute for the Study and Treatment of Delinquency.

Wootton, B (1959) *Social Science and Social Pathology*, London: Allen and Unwin.
Wootton, B (1962) 'A social scientist's approach to maternal deprivation', in MD Ainsworth (*et al*) *Deprivation of Maternal Care: A Reassessment of its Effects*, World Health Organisation.
Wright, R and Logie, RH (1988) 'How young house burglars choose targets', *Howard Journal*, 27: 92–104.
Wright, M (1982) *Making Good: Prisons, Punishment and Beyond*, London: Burnett Books.

Yablonsky, L (1962) *The Violent Gang*, New York: Macmillan.
Yerkes, RM (ed) (1921) 'Psychological examining in the United States Army', *Memoirs of the National Academy of Sciences*, 15: 791, Washington, DC: US Government Printing Office.
Young, J (1971) *The Drug Takers: The Social Meaning of Drugtaking*, London: Paladin.
Young, J (1975) 'Working-class criminology', in I Taylor, P Walton and J Young (eds) *Critical Criminology*, London: Routledge and Kegan Paul.
Young, J (1981) 'Thinking seriously about crime', in M Fitzgerald, G McLennan and J Pawson (eds) *Crime and Society: Readings in History and Theory*, London: Routledge and Kegan Paul.
Young, J (1986) 'The failure of criminology: the need for a radical realism', in R Matthews and J Young *Confronting Crime*, London: Sage.
Young, J (1988) 'Radical criminology in Britain: the emergence of a competing paradigm', in P Rock (ed) *A History of British Criminology*, Oxford: Clarendon Press.
Young, W (1979) *Community Service Orders*, London: Heinemann.

Zander, M (1988) *Cases and Materials on the English Legal System*, London: Weidenfeld and Nicolson.
Zehr, H (1981) 'The modernization of crime in Germany and France, 1830 to 1913', in I Shelley (ed) *Readings in Comparative Criminology*, Carbondale: Southern Illinois University Press.
Zimbardo, PG (1973) 'A field experiment in auto-shaping', in C Ward (ed) *Vandalism*, London: The Architectural Press.
Zorbaugh, H (1925) 'Natural areas of the city', in EW Burgess (ed) *The Urban Community*, Chicago: University of Chicago Press.

Index

Law Update 1997

Law Update 1998 edition – due March 1998

An annual review of the most recent developments in specific legal subject areas, useful for law students at degree and professional levels, others with law elements in their courses and also practitioners seeking a quick update.

Published around March every year, the Law Update summarises the major legal developments during the course of the previous year. In conjunction with Old Bailey Press textbooks it gives the student a significant advantage when revising for examinations.

Contents

Administrative Law • Civil and Criminal Procedure • Commercial Law • Company Law • Conflict of Laws • Constitutional Law • Contract Law • Conveyancing • Criminal Law • Criminology • English Legal System • Equity and Trusts • European Union Law • Evidence • Family Law • Jurisprudence • Land Law • Law of International Trade • Public International Law • Revenue Law • Succession • Tort

For further information on contents, please contact:

Mail Order
Old Bailey Press
200 Greyhound Road
London
W14 9RY
United Kingdom

Telephone No: 00 44 (0) 171 385 3377
Fax No: 00 44 (0) 171 381 3377

ISBN 0 7510 0782 X
Soft cover 234 x 156 mm
396 pages   £6.95
Published March 1997

Methods of Research in Law

by Dr Charles Chatterjee

When conducting research in law, a thorough knowledge of the subject area is not enough. The research must also follow a method and apply techniques for analysing facts and data.

Methods of Research in Law is a guide to the techniques of carrying out research and developing ideas. The work deals with:

Ethics in Research
Certain Important Terms and Concepts
Tools of Research
Research Planning and Research Design
Sources of Information
Techniques of Interpretation of Documents
Layout of Thesis, Footnoting and Bibliography

It is an essential handbook for those students whose degrees demand an element of legal research, or those who are carrying out research for a postgraduate degree. Within the broad area of social sciences, there are a number of common elements of research which will also make this book of interest to those studying economics, business studies and international relations.

Professor Chatterjee has many years of experience in supervising postgraduate students in law, and as well as having completed a number of pieces of original research.

ISBN 1 85836 070 6
Published January 1997
Price £9.95
336 pages

To order your copy, please contact:

Claudine Pryce
Old Bailey Press
200 Greyhound Road
London
W14 9RY

Telephone No: 00 44 (0) 171 385 3377
Fax No: 00 44 (0) 171 381 3377
E-Mail Address: hlt@holborncollege.ac.uk

Methods of Research in Law

by Dr Charles Sampford

Using the Net for Research in Business, Law and Related Subjects

by Kevin McGuinness, Steele Raymond, Professor of Business Law
and Tom Short, Principal Lecturer and Researcher,
both at Bournemouth University

Using the Net is an essential guide for all lawyers and business people using the Internet worldwide. Starting with a general introduction to gaining access to the Internet, the book goes on to provide analysis of sites of interest under a series of subject headings. These include:

Advertising Law

Banking

Bankruptcy and Insolvency

Civil Procedure

Contract, Consumer and Commercial Law

Corporate Law and Securities

Expert Witnesses

Finance

Insurance

International Law and Relations

Law Practice Management

Negotiation and ADR

Newspapers

Patents and IP

For ease of use, a disk is included with the book giving direct access to 2,000 primary sites linking to 100,000s of specific sources of information.

This book assimilates a vast body of invaluable information for lawyers, business people, accountants and financiers and particularly for those conducting research in any of these fields.

For further information on contents, please contact:

Claudine Pryce
Old Bailey Press
200 Greyhound Road
London
W14 9RY
United Kingdom

Telephone No: 00 44 (0) 171 385 3377
Fax No: 00 44 (0) 171 381 3377

Published February 1997
ISBN 1 85836 072 2
Price £19.95   298 pages approx
E-Mail Address: hlt@holborncollege.ac.uk

2nd edition publishing January 1998

Old Bailey Press

The Old Bailey Press integrated student library is planned and written to help you at every stage of your studies. Each of our range of Textbooks, Casebooks, Revision WorkBooks and Statutes are all designed to work together and are regularly revised and updated.

We are also able to offer you Suggested Solutions which provide you with past examination questions and solutions for most of the subject areas listed below.

You can buy Old Bailey Press books from your University Bookshop or your local Bookshop, or in case of difficulty, order direct using this form.

Here is the selection of modules covered by our series:

Administrative Law; Commercial Law; Company Law; Conflict of Laws (no Suggested Solutions Pack); Constitutional Law: The Machinery of Government; Obligations: Contract Law; Conveyancing (no Revision Workbook); Criminology (no Casebook or Revision WorkBook); Criminal Law; English Legal System; Equity and Trusts; Law of The European Union; Evidence; Family Law; Jurisprudence: The Philosophy of Law (Sourcebook in place of a Casebook); Land: The Law of Real Property; Law of International Trade; Legal Skills and System; Public International Law; Revenue Law (no Casebook); Succession: The Law of Wills and Estates; Obligations: The Law of Tort.

Mail order prices:

Textbook £10

Casebook £10

Revision WorkBook £7

Statutes £8

Suggested Solutions Pack (1991–1995) £7

Single Paper 1996 £3

Single Paper 1997 £3.

To complete your order, please fill in the form below: ✂

Module	Books required	Quantity	Price	Cost
		Postage		
		TOTAL		

For UK, add 10% postage and packing (£10 maximum).
For Europe, add 15% postage and packing (£20 maximum).
For the rest of the world, add 40% for airmail.

ORDERING

By telephone to Mail Order at 0171 385 3377, with your credit card to hand

By fax to 0171 381 3377 (giving your credit card details).

By post to:

Old Bailey Press, 200 Greyhound Road, London W14 9RY.

When ordering by post, please enclose full payment by cheque or banker's draft, or complete the credit card details below.

We aim to despatch your books within 3 working days of receiving your order.

Name

Address

Postcode   Telephone

Total value of order, including postage: £

I enclose a cheque/banker's draft for the above sum, or

charge my ☐ Access/Mastercard ☐ Visa ☐ American Express
Card number

☐☐☐☐ ☐☐☐☐ ☐☐☐☐ ☐☐☐☐

Expiry date ☐☐☐☐

Signature: ....Date: ....